Kate Field

SELECTED LETTERS

Kate Field
Selected Letters

EDITED AND WITH
AN INTRODUCTION BY

Carolyn J. Moss

SOUTHERN ILLINOIS UNIVERSITY PRESS

Carbondale and Edwardsville

Copyright © 1996 by the Board of Trustees,
Southern Illinois University
All rights reserved
Printed in the United States of America
99 98 97 96   4 3 2 1

Library of Congress Cataloging-in-Publication Data

Field, Kate, 1838–1896.
  [Correspondence. Selections]
  Kate Field : selected letters / edited with an introduction by
Carolyn J. Moss.
     p.   cm.
  Includes bibliographical references (p.) and index.
  1. Field, Kate, 1838–1896—Correspondence.   2. Women authors,
American—19th century—Correspondence.   3. Women journalists—
United States—Correspondence.   I. Moss, Carolyn J.   II. Title.
PS1669.F2Z48   1996
818'.409—dc20
[B]   96-10190
ISBN 0-8093-2078-9 (cl : alk. paper)   CIP

The paper used in this publication meets the minimum requirements
of American National Standard for Information Sciences—Permanence
of Paper for Printed Library Materials, ANSI Z39.48-1984.

Frontispiece: Kate Field. Courtesy of the West Virginia State Archives, Boyd B. Stutler Collection.

To Sidney,
mon ami de coeur

Contents

	List of Illustrations	ix
	Preface	xi
	List of Abbreviations	xiii
	Acknowledgments	xv
	Introduction	xvii
	Chronology	xxxi
Part One 1843–1859	St. Louis Childhood Boston Schoolgirl Trip to Europe	1
Part Two 1859–1861	Florentine Days The Brownings, the Trollopes, Isa Blagden, and Literary Visitors	15
Part Three 1862–1871	Returns to America Achieves Fame as Journalist, Lecturer, and Author	31
Part Four 1871–1873	Voyage to England Death of Mother Grief and Readjustment	77
Part Five 1874–1879	Becomes Playwright and Actress Promotes Bell's Telephone Helps Establish Shakespeare Memorial Theatre	109

CONTENTS

Part Six 1879–1883	Founder of Ladies' Co-operative Dress Association	155
Part Seven 1883–1886	Campaign Against the Church of Jesus Christ of Latter-Day Saints	173
Part Eight 1887–1889	Crosses America to Lecture Against Prohibition Promotes Alaska	195
Part Nine 1889–1894	Owner-Editor of *Kate Field's Washington*	205
Part Ten 1895–1896	En Route to San Francisco and Hawaii Final Days	227
	Appendix A Calendar of Additional Kate Field Letters	237
	Appendix B Selected Works of Kate Field	247
	Index	249

Illustrations

Kate Field	*frontispiece*
Kate Field's father, Joseph Matthew Field	2
Kate Field's mother, Eliza Riddle Field	3
Kate Field as journalist	32
Whitelaw Reid	46
Sample of a Kate Field letter	55
Laurence Hutton	67
Edmund Clarence Stedman	111
Kate Field on stage	113
The Shakespeare Memorial Theatre	142
Gaiety Theatre playbill	143
Lilian Whiting	168
Kate Field as publisher-editor	208
Nameplate of the first issue of *Kate Field's Washington*	209
Brevet for the *Palmes académique* conferred on Kate Field by the French	223

Preface

AS THE YEAR 1996 is the centennial of Kate Field's death, it is fitting that a memorial mark the occasion; fitting, too, that this memorial be composed of her own letters, which, given their autobiographical impulse, show her as a living woman rather than as a biographer's re-created image.

That her contemporaries attached much importance to her correspondence is attested by the fact that her letters were preserved and found their way into more than thirty archives. Though the comparison is no doubt arbitrary, Poe's letters (apart from those owned by private individuals) exist in only twenty-one institutions and Emily Dickinson's (again apart from private ownership) in only fourteen. Less arbitrarily, the number of the preserved holograph letters of Field, Poe, and Dickinson might have been compared, had not Lilian Whiting, Field's biographer and friend, destroyed a great number of the Field letters she collected.

Kate Field's achievements as journalist, author, lecturer, actress, and owner-editor of *Kate Field's Washington* are impressive indeed, but the dauntless spirit of this voteless, unmarried, and at times destitute woman in a man's world is more impressive still. For like Thoreau and Whitman, she answered Emerson's call for an American Scholar, despite the fact that the great Transcendentalist, though he tried to see the world as pictured in the mind of God, seems not to have had a woman in mind. For unthinkingly he declared that "The scholar is . . . Man Thinking"; that "Whoso would be a man, must be a nonconformist"; that "Society everywhere is in conspiracy against the manhood of every one of its members"; and that "The main enterprise of the world for splendor, for extent, is the upbuilding of a man." Nor, apparently, did it occur to the Sage of Concord to write so much as an essay on Representative Women. As "Woman Thinking," Kate Field's mission, by her own precept and example, to say nothing of her own powerful urge for self-fulfillment, was to encourage women to enter the Emersonian world, where (to adapt Emerson's lovely phrase) they could find gifts after their will.

Editorial Procedures

In the preparation of this one-volume edition of Kate Field's letters, all of her known manuscript letters were collected, chronologized, and annotated. When such manuscripts no longer existed, published versions were used. Those versions, relatively few and almost all in fragmentary form, have been published in only two places—in Charles Warren Stoddard's memoir "Kate Field, Cosmopolite" (*National Magazine,* January 1906) and in Lilian Whiting's biography *Kate Field: A Record* (1899). (Other scholars, of course—Trollopians especially—have drawn on the published and manuscript letters for their own special purposes.)

In the final phase of the editing, only the more substantive letters were retained, and, at times, passages in these letters were deleted when they were trivial or when they duplicated information already conveyed. When deletions occur in letters drawn from Whiting and Stoddard, the ellipsis marks are generally theirs; all others are the editor's.

To save space, the complimentary closings—all of an innocuous nature (e.g., "Yours sincerely, Kate Field" or "Ever yours, K. F.")—were dropped in almost all instances. The few exceptions were made when the complimentary close was part of the letter, in which case diagonals were used to indicate separate lines (e.g., "I am sure she was as much pleased as / Yours sincerely, / Kate Field"). Also dropped were such final obligatory remarks as "With good wishes" and "Love to the Family."

The chief object in editing these letters was clarity. Misspellings and grammatical errors, surprisingly few, were silently corrected. Likewise, to ease readers over otherwise obscure passages, commas (in the use of which Kate Field was profligate) were sometimes deleted or on occasion added. Also, for the same purpose, editorial interpolations were provided in square brackets. Kate Field's capitalization was left untouched, even when she was inconsistent and wrote *Autumn* in one place and *autumn* in another. Her ampersands and habitual use of *mss* for *ms* were retained.

Each of Kate Field's letters is preceded by a heading that identifies the recipient, followed by an abbreviation (enclosed in parentheses) that designates the published source or manuscript collection in which the letter may be found. A list of these sources and their abbreviations follows this preface. To keep the editorial notes within bounds, emphasis was laid on the significance of an item (e.g., a person, magazine, organization, event) at the time the letter was written rather than on the past or future history of the item, except, of course, where such history was relevant. Unless the context is sufficiently explanatory, an item is identified in the notes when first encountered.

In the search for information about women who were recipients of or mentioned in Kate Field's letters, a well-known phenomenon made itself felt. Though some women—for example, Elizabeth Cady Stanton, Olive Logan, Adelaide Ristori, and Harriet Beecher Stowe—were far better known than their husbands, the reverse was typically true. Wives, preponderantly, have slipped into darkest obscurity. Thus, though Kate Field developed friendships with as many women as men, the men are frequently easier to identify than their wives, sisters, or other female relatives. At any rate, if a person's birth and death dates do not appear in the text, it may be assumed that they could not be found.

Abbreviations

At the present time, the known extant Kate Field autograph letters are located in the thirty-one institutions identified in the following list. Also listed are two publications containing letters that no longer exist in manuscript form. The abbreviations in the list are used throughout this book to identify the sources of letters that were chosen for inclusion in this selection. These abbreviations also identify the sources of the letters listed in the Calendar of Additional Kate Field Letters (Appendix A).

B&E   Buffalo and Erie County Public Library, Buffalo, New York. Grosvenor Rare Book Room. James Fraser Gluck Manuscript Collection.
BC   Barnard College, New York, N.Y. Wollman Library. Overbury Collection.
BPL   Boston Public Library, Boston, Mass. Department of Rare Books and Manuscripts. Kate Field Collection.
BU   Baylor University, Waco, Tex. Armstrong Browning Library.
CHS   Cincinnati Historical Society, Cincinnati, Ohio.
CU   Columbia University, New York, N.Y. Butler Library. E. C. Stedman Papers.
CWS   Charles Warren Stoddard. "Kate Field, Cosmopolite." *National Magazine* 23 (Jan. 1906): 361–72.
DU   Duke University, Durham, N.C. Special Collections Library. George Howard Shields Papers.
FL   Folger Shakespeare Library, Washington, D.C.
HC   Harvard College Library, Cambridge, Mass. Harvard Theatre Collection.
HF   Harpers Ferry National Historical Park, Harpers Ferry, W.Va.
HL   Huntington Library, San Marino, California.
ISEA   Iowa State Education Association, Des Moines, Iowa.
IU   Indiana University at Bloomington. Lilly Library.
LW   Lilian Whiting. *Kate Field: A Record.* Boston: Little, Brown, 1899.
MH   Massachusetts Historical Society, Boston, Mass. H. H. Edes Papers.
MHS-LFM
       Missouri Historical Society, St. Louis, Mo. Ludlow-Field-Maury Papers.

-S	Sol Smith Papers.
-T	Theatrical Collection.
MNP	Morristown National Historical Park, Morristown, N.J.
MU	Miami University, Oxford, Ohio. King Library. Walter Havighurst Special Collections. Whitelaw Reid Papers.
NH	New Hampshire Historical Society, Concord, N.H. Edna Dean Proctor Collection.
NL	Newberry Library, Chicago, Ill. Charles Hutchinson Papers.
NYH	New-York Historical Society, New York, N.Y.
PUL-D	Princeton University Libraries, Princeton, N.J. Donald and Robert M. Dodge Collection.
-H	Laurence Hutton Collection.
-P	Morris L. Parrish Collection of Victorian Novelists.
-W	Wilkinson Collection of Mary Mapes Dodge.
RBH	Rutherford B. Hayes Presidential Center, Fremont, Ohio. William and Mary Claflin Collection.
RC	Radcliffe College, Cambridge, Mass. Schlesinger Library. Strickland Autograph Collection.
TU	Tulane University Library, New Orleans, La. Howard-Tilton Memorial Library. Manuscripts Department. George Washington Cable Papers.
UC	Union College, Schenectady, N.Y. Schaffer Library. Special Collections. John Bigelow Papers.
UCB-H	University of California, Berkeley. Bancroft Library. Hilgard Family Papers.
-P	Phoebe Apperson Hearst Papers.
-M	Mark Twain Papers.
-W	Waterman Papers.
-UK	University of Kansas Libraries, Lawrence, Kans. Kenneth Spencer Research Library. Department of Special Collections.
UM	University of Michigan, Ann Arbor, Mich. Special Collections Library. Hugo Erichsen Methods of Authors Papers.
UR	University of Rochester, Rochester, N.Y. Rush Rhees Library. Department of Rare Books and Special Collections.
UV-C	University of Virginia Library, Charlottesville, Va. Special Collections Department. Lydia Avery Coonley Collection.
-F	Clifton Waller Barrett Library, Kate Field Collection (#7947).
WV	West Virginia State Archives, Charleston, W.Va. Boyd B. Stutler Collection.

Acknowledgments

For permission to publish manuscript letters of Kate Field, I am most grateful to the following libraries and institutions, and I am deeply appreciative of the courtesies of their curators of manuscripts: the John Bigelow Papers, Special Collections, Schaffer Library, Union College, Schenectady, New York; Boston Public Library; Armstrong Browning Library, Baylor University; the George Washington Cable Papers, Manuscripts Department, Howard-Tilton Memorial Library, Tulane University Library; the William and Mary Claflin Collection, Rutherford B. Hayes Presidential Center; the H. H. Edes Papers, Massachusetts Historical Society; the Hugo Erichsen Methods of Authors Papers, Special Collections Library, University of Michigan; the Kate Field Collection (#7947), Clifton Waller Barrett Library, and the Lydia Avery Coonley Collection, Special Collections Department, University of Virginia Library; Folger Shakespeare Library; the James Fraser Gluck Manuscript Collection, Grosvenor Rare Book Room, Buffalo and Erie County Public Library; the National Park Service, Harpers Ferry National Historical Park and Morristown National Historical Park; the Harvard Theatre Collection, Harvard College Library; the Walter Havighurst Special Collections, King Library, Miami University; the Hilgard Family Papers, the Phoebe Apperson Hearst Papers, the Waterman Papers, and the Mark Twain Papers, The Bancroft Library, University of California, Berkeley; The Huntington Library, San Marino, California; the Charles Hutchinson Papers, The Newberry Library; Iowa State Education Association; Lilly Library, Indiana University at Bloomington; the Ludlow-Field-Maury Papers, the Sol Smith Papers, and the Theatrical Collection, Missouri Historical Society, St. Louis; the Laurence Hutton Collection, the Donald and Robert M. Dodge Collection, the Morris L. Parrish Collection of Victorian Novelists, and the Wilkinson Collection of Mary Mapes Dodge, Manuscripts Division, Department of Rare Books and Special Collections, Princeton University Libraries; the George Howard Shields Papers, Special Collections Library, Duke University; the E. C. Stedman Papers, Rare Book and Manuscript Library, Columbia University; the Strickland Autograph Collection, Schlesinger Library, Radcliffe College; The New-York Historical Society.

I also wish to thank James W. Goodrich, Executive Director of the State Historical Society of Missouri, for permission to draw on my article on Kate Field in the *Missouri Historical Review* (January 1994).

In addition, I wish to acknowledge a particular debt to those who performed special services on my behalf: Shyamala Balgopal, Reference Librarian, University of Illinois Library, Urbana; Denison Beach, Librarian, Houghton Reading Room, Harvard University; Martha Clevenger, Archivist, Missouri Historical Society, St. Louis; Professor K. K. Collins, Department of English, Southern Illinois University at Carbondale, who kept turning up Kate Field items for me; Deborah Cordt and Angela Rubin, Humanities Division of Morris Library, Southern Illinois University at Carbondale; Professors N. John Hall, Regina Soria, and Donald J. Winslow for sharing their interest in Kate Field; the Kansas City Public Library and Vassar College Library, which combined to make the entire set of *Kate Field's Washington* available to me; Laura V. Monti, Keeper of Rare Books and Manuscripts, and R. Eugene Zepp, Reference Librarian, Department of Rare Books and Manuscripts, Boston Public Library.

Lastly, I thank those whose love has always encouraged me, especially my son, Mark Kressenberg, and my sisters, Libby McMurry, Martha McDougald, and Cathey Bowers.

Introduction

IN CELEBRATING THE Gateway City's bicentennial in 1964, the *St. Louis American* published an article to honor one of the city's most distinguished daughters. Paradoxically, its eulogy bore the title "Who Was Kate Field?"[1] Few readers then knew, and certainly fewer now know, the answer to that question. So much for fame and the Ozymandias effect. Only a century earlier, the *Washington Post* named Kate Field "one of the foremost women of America," and the *New York Tribune* called her "one of the best-known women in America."[2]

So the question remains: Who was Kate Field?

Kate Field's St. Louis Background

KF was born in St. Louis on 1 October 1838, a year after her parents had married. Joseph Matthew Field, her father, was an actor of such talent that William Charles Macready, the best English tragedian of his day, was irritated when they acted together in *Hamlet* because Field had outdone him in the judgment of their audience.[3] And her mother, Eliza Riddle Field, acclaimed as "one of the most beautiful and accomplished actresses of the American stage,"[4] had played Desdemona to Forrest's Othello, Ophelia to Macready's Hamlet, and Cordelia to Booth's Lear—"*the* Booth," as impresarios called Junius Brutus Booth—to cite a few of her nearly thousand roles. On their daughter's arrival, the Fields became regulars at three playhouses—in Mobile, New Orleans, and St. Louis—though at times they continued to tour eastern America to round off theatrical careers of some thirty years.[5] While in the Gateway City, they acted at the St. Louis Theatre, which Ludlow & Smith had built by subscription in 1837. A con-

---

1. *St. Louis American*, 22 Sept. 1964.
2. "What the Papers Said," *KF's Washington*, 5 Dec. 1894; *New York Tribune*, 31 May 1896.
3. *The Diaries of William Charles Macready, 1833–1851*, ed. William Toynbee (London: Chapman & Hall, 1912), 2:269.
4. James E. Murdoch, *The Stage, or Recollections of Actors and Acting from an Experience of Fifty Years* (1880; reprint, New York: Benjamin Blom, 1969), 124.
5. John M. Heidger, *Family Ties: A Biography of the Fields on the Frontier Stage* (Ph.D. diss., University of Missouri-Columbia, 1988).

temporary recognized that theatre to be the "first building for Dramatic purposes in the whole Valley of the Mississippi, and ... inferior to but very few in the Union."[6]

To enlarge his income, though he gave up neither acting nor playwriting, Joseph Field turned to journalism in 1840. He became the European correspondent for the *New Orleans Daily Picayune* and also published humorous verse sketches in it under the pen name "Straws." In 1844, together with his brother Matthew, who had been an assistant editor of the *Picayune,* and Charles Keemle, who had served on a number of St. Louis papers, Field founded the *St. Louis Daily Reveille.* The paper became so well known that Edgar Allan Poe asked Field to counteract a libelous attack made on him in the *New York Evening Mirror.* Field, who had met Poe on tour, was pleased to honor the request.[7] The newspaper prospered until the Great Fire of 1849 gutted the *Reveille* building. Given that misfortune, the Fields had little choice but to return to the stage. In 1851, however, Ludlow & Smith brought down the curtain for the last time at their St. Louis Theatre when the subscribers elected to sell the property to the federal government for a customhouse and post office.

In 1850 the Fields had begun to manage and act at the Royal Street Theatre in Mobile during the winter seasons. After the St. Louis Theatre was sold, Field organized a stock company to build a new theatre in St. Louis, which he named the Varieties, and served as its manager. The Varieties Theatre, leased to Field for thirty years, had a fine company and enjoyed an auspicious opening season in 1852. Its second and third seasons, however, proved unprofitable because two newly opened theatres provided severe competition, even to waging a price war. Seeing Belshazzar's augury on the wall, Field subleased the building and resumed his management of Mobile's Royal Street Theatre.

KF, having finished her schooling at Mrs. Smith's Seminary in St. Louis, studied with a private tutor before attending Lasell Female Seminary (an exclusive girls' boarding school in Auburndale, near Boston), at the expense of her millionaire uncle, Milton H. Sanford, Mrs. Field's brother-in-law. In later years KF remarked of her schooling: "All the mental discipline I received was between the ages of eight and twelve. But for a woman by the name of Smith I should not have had that" (*KF's Washington,* 8 Feb. 1893, 81).

In 1856 KF's father, at age forty-six, died suddenly of pneumonia in Mobile. Though heartbroken, KF's mother took over the management of the Mobile

---

6. J. C. Wild, *The Valley of the Mississippi: Illustrated in a Series of Views,* ed. Lewis F. Thomas (St. Louis, Mo.: privately printed, 1841), 23.

7. Sidney P. Moss, *Poe's Major Crisis: His Libel Suit and New York's Literary World* (Durham, N.C.: Duke University Press, 1970), 20–25. At one of the numerous events that raised money for the Poe monument—the only one to be installed at Poets' Corner of the Metropolitan Museum of Art—KF "delighted everybody ... with her droll 'Silent Song' " (*New York Tribune,* 12 Feb. 1881).

theatre for the rest of the season before joining her daughter, who had withdrawn from school and was living on her aunt and uncle's estate. To support KF and herself, she joined the Boston Museum Repertory Company, which her brother-in-law, William Henry Sedley, was managing.

Kate Field as Journalist and Author

At age twenty, KF, described by Frances Power Cobbe, the Irish author and reformer, as "tall and beautiful, with magnificent hair and column-like throat,"[8] went on a European trip with the Sanfords. Encouraged by her aunt—a singer herself—KF remained in Florence to study voice, for even as a child she had aspired to be a concert singer like the world-famous Jenny Lind. Meanwhile, to provide for herself and her mother, who joined her in Florence some months after the Sanfords had returned to Boston, KF began to write travel articles, first for the *Boston Courier,* then for the *New Orleans Daily Picayune,* the *Boston Transcript,* the Massachusetts *Springfield Republican,* and the *Boston Commonwealth*—travel articles that Cobbe called "some of the best letters ever sent to a newspaper" (Cobbe, *Italics,* 398).

KF could not have chosen a better time to be in Florence, for in that Renaissance city was the well-known English literary colony whose core included the Brownings, Walter Savage Landor, Isa Blagden, and Thomas and Frances Trollope, brother and mother of Anthony Trollope. KF, intelligent and vivacious, cheerful and lovable, was virtually adopted by the group, who introduced her to other distinguished literary visitors, most notably the reclusive George Eliot and her erudite consort, George Henry Lewes, as well as the bluff Anthony Trollope, with whom she established a lifelong friendship. A votary to the life of the mind, KF no doubt felt the exultation that Wordsworth expressed in *The Prelude*: "Bliss was it in that dawn to be alive, / But to be young was very heaven!"

When KF returned to Boston with her mother in 1861, she published in the *Atlantic Monthly* reminiscences of the famous friends she had made in Florence. And when George Eliot died in 1880, she wrote the novelist's obituary for the *New York Tribune.* She continued to publish articles in newspapers, including travel letters on the popular resorts at which she vacationed. Among these was Newport in Rhode Island, where many of America's literati also spent their summers—for example, Henry James *père* and Henry James *fils*, John Greenleaf Whittier, Harriet Beecher Stowe, Julia Ward Howe, Helen Hunt Jackson, and Thomas Wentworth Higginson. Indeed, during her career as a journalist, KF came to know almost every VIP in the United States and abroad. The names of

---

8. Cobbe, *Italics: Brief Notes on Politics, People, and Places in Italy* (London: Trübner & Co., 1864), 397.

those she knew would constitute a *Who's Who* and include, for starters, Stanley (who found Livingstone), Schliemann (who found Troy), Ristori, Gilbert and Sullivan, Greeley, Twain, and Dickens.

KF came to national attention by her reports on Dickens's 1867–68 American reading tour. Her sketches were so "lively, graphic, piquant, witty, humorous, and pathetic" that the *New York Times* (28 Sept. 1868) called them "Dickensesque," and the *Springfield Republican* (4 Mar. 1868) hailed them as "the next best thing to seeing and hearing the original." Her reports were quite adulatory, perhaps because of her parents' association with the novelist on his first trip to America in 1842. To welcome him, the Fields had enacted a skit called *Boz! A Masque Phrenological,* which Joseph Field had written to amuse Boz, the pen name Dickens had adopted at the time. KF even used her father's pen name "Straws" as the signature of her Dickens reports, mischievously adding "Jr." So popular were these reports that KF expanded them into a book, which she titled *Pen Photographs of Charles Dickens' Readings* (1868). One reader said *Pen Phonographs* would have served equally well. Years later Jeannette Gilder, editor of the *New York Critic,* recalled what the book had meant to her and, no doubt, to many other women: "One of the very first of contemporary women's names that I remember in connection with literature is that of Kate Field. A copy of her 'Pen Photographs of Charles Dickens' Readings' came into my hands as long ago as 1868; and it gave me a thrill, for I had heard that she was a young woman . . . and the name of a young woman on the title-page of a book seemed to me a great and glorious thing."[9]

In 1869 KF began to freelance for Horace Greeley's *New York Tribune.* Her articles so impressed Whitelaw Reid, the associate editor of the paper, that in 1870 he offered her a salaried position. Given her principles, she refused the offer, saying, "Don't you know that I can't be salaried on a journal because I *won't* write what I don't believe?" (*To Whitelaw Reid,* 5 Oct. 1870). True to her word, she remained an independent journalist. That was not the first time she turned her back on such temptation. When, during the Civil War, her millionaire uncle, who doted on her, insisted that she suppress her abolitionist views or be written out of his Will, she chose disinheritance.

As nothing succeeds like success, KF became a prolific writer, so much so that only a book-length bibliography can do justice to her enormous output and multitudinous interests—inventions, drama, music, art, literature, education, and politics being but a few of them. Among American magazines that published her work were *Scribner's Monthly,* the *North American Review,* the *Atlantic Monthly, Lippincott's,* and *Harper's Monthly.* Among English magazines were *Truth,* the *Theatre,* the *Examiner,* the *Westminster Review,* and the *Athenaeum.*

---

9. Gilder, "Kate Field: An Appreciation," *Critic,* n.s., 25 (6 June 1896): 402.

Of her journalism, a spokesman for the Columbia Historical Society (now the Historical Society of Washington, D.C.) said on an occasion memorializing KF: "She ... set herself to the task of repairing every flaw in our national armor ... [and] no line of American activity—industrial, esthetic, or institutional—escaped her attention, and none failed to receive benefit through her efforts."[10] KF likewise said of the purpose of her journalism, "It never occurred to me that this Republic is faultless, and that the way to correct evils is to conceal them or to pretend they do not exist. I have never enjoyed living in a fool's paradise."[11]

Despite her national reputation, KF regarded her entrée in the London *Times* in 1877 as the pinnacle of her journalistic career. "Is there anything to attain in journalism beyond this?" she exclaimed (*To Edmund Clarence Stedman*, 28 Nov. 1877). As it turned out thirteen years later, there was something: the founding of her own weekly newspaper, *Kate Field's Washington*.

KF's debut in the *Times* was her series on Alexander Graham Bell's new invention, the telephone. The series was extolled by Bell himself, who told KF that hers were the best articles written on his invention. In gratitude, he gave her stock in his company; and to demonstrate the apparatus to Queen Victoria, he chose KF to sing some Irish songs over the phone into the Sovereign's ear. As with her series on Dickens, KF developed these articles for a book, her *History of Bell's Telephone* (1878). The stock Bell gave her eventually earned her an estimated forty thousand dollars, almost half of which she lost in the Ladies' Cooperative Dress Association, a venture she herself had launched.[12]

KF typically developed books from her articles. *Hap-Hazard* (1873), another such book, was a collection of humorous essays about her travels at home and abroad. In *Ten Days in Spain* (1875), she reported her interview with the President of the Spanish Republic, her disgust with bullfighting, her frustration at Spanish officiousness, and the people she encountered in a country riven by civil war. The book, one of her most popular works, went through four editions, and James Russell Lowell, then the American Minister to Spain, asked KF to favor him with a copy. Two other such books were her biographies of *Adelaide*

---

10. W. J. McGee, "Memorial of Kate Field," *Records of the Columbia Historical Society* 1 (23 Mar. 1897): 174. KF was one of two women among the thirty-six founders of the Columbia Historical Society, who included Henry Adams, John Hay, Henry Cabot Lodge, and Melville Fuller, Chief Justice of the Supreme Court.

11. "Americans Through Tartar Spectacles," *KF's Washington*, 6 Dec. 1893, 353.

12. KF had become intrigued with London cooperative stores and, on her return to New York, proceeded to found her own cooperative to free women, as she put it, "from the thralldom of milliners and the extortion of shopkeepers" (*New York Times*, 24 Feb. 1880). The Samuel Clemenses, the William Dean Howells, the John Bigelows, the James T. Fieldses, and Julia Ward Howe were among those who purchased shares in the co-op. Unfortunately, KF hired a London marplot, one Anthony Pulbrook, to oversee the operation, which went bust after three years. In the meantime, KF suffered loss of health, loss of her investment, and some loss of face. The only thing she won was a verdict against Pulbrook.

Ristori (1867), the world-renowned actress who was considered superior even to Rachel, and *Charles Albert Fechter* (1882), the celebrated actor of the French and English stage.

KF published three works that did not derive from her journalism. Her travels in California resulted in a long chapter that John Muir requested and published as "North of the Golden Gate" in his beautifully illustrated *Picturesque California and the Region West of the Rocky Mountains* (1888). Among her best work, it showed her exacting regard for historical facts, a naturalist's eye for the flora of the California coast, an artist's eye for the picturesque, and a conservationist's concern for nature. Indeed, in later years she joined the successful campaign to establish Yosemite as a national park.

Planchette's Diary (1868) was another fresh work. A report of her experience with spiritualism—a mystery that fascinated any number of people, including Fenimore Cooper, William Cullen Bryant, Elizabeth Barrett Browning, and Horace Greeley—it involved an early version of the Ouija board called a planchette. Her final book, *The Drama of Glass* (1894), ostensibly a history of glass, actually served as an advertisement for the Libby Glass Company, whose exhibit KF had visited at the Columbian Exposition of 1893.

Kate Field as Lecturer

Famous as journalist and author, KF became equally famous as a lecturer. She was not, of course, the first woman to mount the lecture platform. Among others, Anna Dickinson, Lucy Stone, Susan B. Anthony, and Elizabeth Cady Stanton had preceded her. But these women had used the rostrum to advocate abolitionism or women's rights. KF used the platform not only to campaign for social reforms but to double, triple, and quadruple her income. Thus she became one of the first professional female lecturers and held, almost at once, "first place on the Lyceum platform."[13] As KF explained to Noah Ludlow, her parents' former stage manager in St. Louis, "I've gone into the Lyceum because it pays better than anything else." And she added, "There is no more reason why a woman should not lecture than that she should not sing or act. At least I shall try to make lecturing fashionable as well as profitable" (*To Noah Miller Ludlow*, 3 July 1869). KF was refreshingly honest: she detested the grubby life and loathed being dependent on anyone.

At first KF read her lectures, but once she became accustomed to the platform, she presented her programs in a unique way. She looked and behaved on stage like a society hostess receiving guests in her parlor. Attired in a Paris gown and adorned with jewels, her hair elegantly arranged in curls, she spoke to her

---

13. Edwin C. Godkin, "Woman in the Lyceum," *Nation* 8 (13 May 1869), 371.

audience conversationally in a cultivated voice. William Lloyd Garrison, the retired abolitionist editor, told his friends that "it was worth an admission fee just to see Kate Field on the platform, as she made so lovely a picture."[14] Another commentator amusedly remarked that "Kate Field was the only woman he ever met who could wear a pretty bonnet and a nice gown and at the same time talk of the equality of the sexes and the brotherhood of man in epigrammatic English" (*New York Times*, 3 July 1892).

Though praised for her stage appearance, greater praise was lavished on KF for her intellectual qualities. The *New York Tribune* (11 May 1869) noted with pleasure that she "supports her theory with arguments, scriptural, logical, economical, and social." The *Boston Transcript* (1 April 1869) was impressed with her "wealth of artistic and literary anecdote and allusion." The *New York Metropolitan Magazine* declared, "It is veritably an intellectual feast to listen to the wit, humor and eloquence of this woman on the lyceum platform."[15] In short, KF's lectures were enthusiastically received, mainly because, as the *New York Tribune* (11 May 1869) said, she "takes up her work with quietness and courtesy [and] . . . does not denounce, nor bully, nor demand."

KF developed seven programs, a number sufficient for her lecture tours. In the order in which she produced them, they were "Woman in the Lyceum," "In and Out of the Woods" (sometimes titled "Among the Adirondacks"), "Charles Dickens," "Mormonism," "Alaska," "The Intemperance of Prohibition," and "America for Americans." She delivered these lectures weekly, sometimes even daily, over a twenty-five-year period in such cities as Boston, New York, Washington, Chicago, St. Louis, Kansas City, and San Francisco, as well as in towns bearing names like Paw Paw, Weeping Water, and Lone Mound. She also lectured in England, Alaska, and Hawaii, and she addressed all kinds of audiences, from the literati of New York and Boston to Civil War veterans, from prisoners in Ohio to gold miners in Alaska.

Like other platform performers, KF had her critics. But then even the redoubtable Charles Dickens had his, in one no less than Mark Twain.[16] KF was even criticized for not lecturing on women's suffrage, for, apart from refusing to be pressured by suffragists, she did not believe that the right to vote should be universal. Rather, like Thomas Jefferson, she wanted citizens—men and women alike—to earn the franchise by virtue of character and education. Nevertheless,

---

14. Garrison was quoted by Edward Increase Mather, "Kate Field's New Departure," *Bay State Monthly* 3 (Nov. 1885), 433.

15. Quoted in *KF's Washington*, 11 June 1890, 384.

16. After hearing the "puissant god" read from *David Copperfield* and the *Pickwick Papers*, Twain remarked that Dickens's "pathos is only the beautiful pathos of his language—there is no heart or feeling in it—it is glittering frostwork." Quoted by Howard G. Baetzhold, "Mark Twain's 'First Date' with Olivia Langdon," *Missouri Historical Society Bulletin* 11 (Jan. 1955): 155-57.

at age fifty-five, she joined the women's suffrage campaign in dramatic fashion. While speaking before the Women's Press Congress at the Columbian Exposition in Chicago, she paused to call Susan B. Anthony to the stage and to pledge her support for the suffragist movement.[17]

KF's lecture on Mormonism was the first to come under fire—from a not unexpected quarter, the Church of Jesus Christ of Latter-Day Saints. While vacationing in the West in 1883, KF began a study of Mormonism that kept her in Salt Lake City for eight months. Among other things, she interviewed Mormon husbands and wives and church officials, after which she went to Nauvoo, Illinois, to question two of Joseph Smith's sons who still lived at the old Mormon settlement. Her study convinced her that the Mormon mutation to the American institution of marriage was the lesser evil: the greater evil was mandatory obedience to Mormon church law rather than to federal law, an obedience that portended treason to the United States. She instanced the fact that in 1857, when Brigham Young was territorial governor of Utah, he resisted replacement by President Buchanan, even issuing a proclamation that forbade federal troops from entering the Utah Territory and that required Mormons to disobey any federal law that conflicted with Church law.

While still in Salt Lake City, KF sent inflammatory articles on Mormonism to newspapers in the East. In consequence, she was summoned to trial by the Mormon Church, a summons she ignored,[18] despite the rumor that the "very Bishops and Saints" of the Mormon Church were threatening her life.[19] Undaunted, KF continued her anti-Mormon campaign even beyond 1894, when Congress made Utah the forty-fifth state of the Union, for she still demanded that Mormons put their allegiance to the United States above their dedication to the Church and that they renounce polygamy.[20]

KF's lecture on Mormonism received kudos from the press. Her remarks, in respect to "courage, vigor, honesty, and power," were declared to be "almost unprecedented on the lyceum platform," and her "invincible logic, graphic presentation and thrilling power" were said to hold "her audience spellbound" (Mather, "Kate Field's New Departure," 433). In Salt Lake City, where she had the chutzpah to deliver the lecture, she was "presented with a very beautiful gold and diamond badge by the loyal citizens of Utah" (LW, 462).

KF's lecture "The Intemperance of Prohibition" drew even greater fire because prohibitionists far outnumbered Mormons. Rather than teetotalism, she advocated temperance, for the same reason that her idol Dickens gave. Dickens

---

17. KF, "A Talk," in *The Congress of Women*, ed. Mary Kavanaugh Oldham Eagle (1893; reprint, New York: Arno, 1974), 77.
18. KF, "Leaves from My Diary," *KF's Washington*, 17 Jan. 1894, 84.
19. "The Death of Kate Field," *Overland Monthly* 28 (July 1896): 126.
20. KF, "The Forty-Fifth Star," *KF's Washington*, 25 July 1894, 49.

said that he could not "go along with those excellent persons [prohibitionists] in confounding the use of anything with its abuse ... because his neighbour is prone to make a Beast of himself by irrational excess in those things."[21] Though Dickens had no objection to spirits (gin, whiskey, rum), KF did, and she recommended wine as a reasonable substitute. Unfortunately, she did not appear to be without self-interest in the matter, for she was accepting payment from the California Viticultural Association to promote its wines. When that fact became known, the prohibitionists denounced her as "a drummer for a wine syndicate" and "a disgrace to womanhood" and even charged her with "dragging women down to prostitution." In a reply to her critics, KF acknowledged that she had indeed accepted payment, just as Frances Willard was accepting a salary as president of the Woman's Christian Temperance Union and as a lecturer on its behalf. Is every minister of the Gospel a hireling, she asked, because he fails to preach without payment? Her "conscience has never yet been for sale, but when it is, Prohibitionists may be assured that it will not be represented by a few thousand dollars." Nevertheless, unwilling to be the target of abuse, she relinquished her association with the California wine industry, though she continued to lecture on the intemperance of prohibition.[22]

Kate Field as Actress

At age thirty-six, KF proceeded to fulfill another ambition, one that was the desire of her childhood. That desire was to be an actress in the family tradition, though her mother had begun her career at age fourteen. Thus, to a crowded house, KF mounted the stage of Booth's Theatre in New York to debut in the role of Peg Woffington in Charles Reade's *Masks and Faces*, "one of the most difficult and exacting parts in modern comedy" (*New York Tribune*, 16 Nov. 1874). Though KF had surpassed her father in journalism, she could not approach him, let alone her mother, in acting, and the reviews were dismal. The *New York Times* (15 Nov. 1874) said: "It is difficult to imagine anything more unsympathetic than Miss Field's presence and delivery.... Her work lacked warmth, spontaneity, and force.... Unhappily Miss Kate Field is neither young nor handsome; her voice is inexpressive, and the frailty of her physique makes the acquisition of power in the future at least improbable." Even the *Tribune* (16

---

21. *The Letters of Charles Dickens*, vol. 5, ed. Graham Storey and K. J. Fielding (Oxford: Clarendon Press, 1981), 45–46.
22. "Kate Field on Prohibition: A Vigorous Reply to Some Recent Attacks," *New York Tribune*, 26 July 1889. Judith Ellen Foster, a paid lawyer on the staff of the Woman's Christian Temperance Union, conceded (*Tribune*, 28 July 1889) that KF had a perfect right to compensation, but no right to spread her views on wine, for "alcohol is poison." Also see the *Tribune* (17 July 1889) for an attack on the prohibitionists for their "campaign of personal defamation" against KF.

Nov. 1874), for which KF was periodically writing, had little forbearance for her performance. Calling her a "sparkling lecturer" and a "pungent and brilliant writer," the paper found her unsuitable for the title role, because she had an "intellectual" aspect rather than the "sensuous" one required for Peg Woffington.

Despite such reviews, John T. Raymond, a hilarious comic actor, employed KF two months later to perform opposite him when he played the eponymous character in Mark Twain's *Colonel Sellers*, a comedy Raymond had already made a favorite with audiences and would perform a thousand times all told. Two performances were scheduled to be given in Twain's hometown of Hartford, Connecticut, before the play was taken to Springfield, Massachusetts. Though *Colonel Sellers* played to sold-out houses in Hartford's opera house, KF did not escape critical barbs. While lauding Raymond and Twain, the *Hartford Daily Courant* said that KF could "hardly flatter herself as a great success"; yet as a novice to the stage, she was "entitled to charitable criticism."[23] Her performance in Springfield received such charitable criticism from the *Springfield Republican*, especially as KF had been a correspondent for the paper and was a longtime friend of Samuel Bowles, its owner-editor.

Though disheartened, KF refused to quit the stage. She performed in a double bill featuring *The Opera Box*, her own play, and *Gabrielle*, her father's play, which she had reworked. If anything, the review of her performance in the *New York Times* (10 June 1875) was more devastating than before: "If Miss Field were fifteen years younger than she is, she would enter the profession under serious disadvantages; her choice at present is wholly unwarranted by either natural fitness or talent.... The actors who appeared with Miss Field are entitled to our warmest sympathy, for their presence, unlike that of the audience, was not optional."

Unwilling to admit failure, KF during the next year sought to establish a reputation in England. For her London debut, she chose *The Honeymoon*, the play in which her parents had starred at the opening of Ludlow & Smith's St. Louis Theatre. To keep her venture a secret from the American press, she acted under the name Mary Keemle (her full name was Mary Katherine Keemle Field). To agreeable reviews, she succeeded well enough to remain on the English stage for four years, during which time she also tirelessly wrote for English and American periodicals.

While in England, KF wrote a musical monologue, with songs by George Grossmith, titled *Eyes and Ears in London*, in which she sang and danced. This parody of London life resembled the burlesque her father had written and performed in St. Louis, titled *Tourists in America*. On her return to America, KF staged the farce to rave reviews. The *Boston Journal* called her monologue one of

---

23. Quoted by Karl Kiralis, "Two Recently Discovered Letters: Mark Twain on Kate Field," *Mark Twain Journal* 20 (Summer 1980): 2.

the "most brilliant and sparkling [entertainments] that has been introduced in Boston for a long time," and the *Boston Evening Transcript* declared her performance "an unequivocal success."[24] When KF took her show on the road, the *New York Times* (10 April 1880), which had earlier reviewed her so devastatingly, now applauded her: "She does her work with grace and spirit" and her "monologue alone proves how really bright a writer Miss Field is [and] how observing a commentator." Vindicated at last, KF gave up the stage, though she added *Eyes and Ears* to her "lecture" repertoire.

Kate Field as Promoter of the Shakespeare Memorial Theatre

Charles Edward Flower, a brewer in Stratford-upon-Avon, wanted to fulfill a boyhood dream of raising a memorial to his former townsman William Shakespeare. For this purpose, he donated money to construct a Shakespeare Memorial Theatre, and he provided the picturesque building site by the river in Stratford. As fifty thousand dollars more was required, he asked KF to organize a fund-raiser. Having as much bardolatry as Flower, KF was pleased to launch a campaign for subscriptions, not realizing that her involvement would go on, day after day, for an exhausting nine months. During that time, she managed to persuade eighteen distinguished actors to perform Shakespearean pieces at London's Gaiety Theatre, arranged to have "musical fire" produced onstage from Geisler tubes (an early form of the neon sign), and climaxed it all by having songs from Shakespeare's plays conveyed by telephone transmitter to a receiver at the Gaiety.

She also wrote letter after letter to American and European friends, urging them to contribute money and engage in fund-raisers themselves. Hermann Vezin, for instance, contributed £10.10 and also performed at the Gaiety. Henry Irving, though objecting to the Shakespeare Memorial Theatre being built in Stratford rather than in London, sent 25 pounds. Henry Schliemann sent her one hundred dollars from Paris. And Harry Palmer, owner of the New York theatre Niblo Gardens, was only one of many who organized benefits for the Shakespeare theatre. In short, as KF said: "I attended to the advertising, printing, [and] business of all sorts. I sold all the stalls [at the Gaiety] . . . I got subscriptions, wrote all the letters, and then applied to the Post Office for a wire to Stratford as I wanted to station a Telephone-Harp in Shakespeare's house, 130 miles away [from London]" (*To William Winter*, 7 June 1878). But her enthusiasm for the Shakespeare project was unflagging, and her powers of persuasion were all but unfailing.[25] As the Dramatic Censor of England wrote to her, "Had you been one

---

24. These and similar encomiums appeared in a theatrical advertisement in MHS-LFM.
25. Though KF was his "most chosen friend," Anthony Trollope, for one, refused her request to contribute to the fund, largely because, as he said, "If there be any one who does not want more

of the original 12 apostles . . . you would have converted the whole world right off the reel, & have left nothing for the churches to fish for!"[26] Having helped to raise the fifty thousand dollars needed to finish construction, KF went to Paris to recover from exhaustion. But just as Shakespeare was memorialized by the theatre that Oscar Wilde called "one of the loveliest [buildings] erected in England for many years,"[27] so no less were Charles Flower and KF, who contributed so much to its coming into being.

Kate Field as Publisher

At age fifty-one, KF climaxed her career by producing a weekly newspaper, *Kate Field's Washington*, in the nation's capital. The venture became the remarkable success expected from an enterprising journalist of thirty years' experience and of extraordinary reputation. As the *New York Metropolitan Magazine* (7 June 1890) remarked: "The American who has not heard of Kate Field is certainly not a . . . conscientious reader of the newspapers, for one can scarcely pick up a sheet at random that does not contain at least one article from the pen of this gifted . . . and prolific writer. . . . She stands in the foremost rank of the world's newspaper women." Upon its first press run, congratulations were sent to KF from all quarters of America.

Though KF had a staff, she wrote most of the articles herself, some signed, others unsigned, and still others under pen names that her father had used, such as "Straws" and "Everpoint." Though she inevitably had to write such trivia as "Capital Chatter," her columns usually concerned serious topics, a few being Mormonism, Prohibition, the Columbian Exposition, International Copyright, the Arts, Education, and Health.[28]

One of KF's most important crusades involved persuading Congress to repeal the tariff on the importation of objets d'art on the ground that it restricted the purchase of foreign art works to the wealthy. She carried this campaign to cities throughout the country. In recognition of her tireless efforts, the French government honored KF in 1892 by awarding her the highest distinction it could bestow on an individual, French or foreign, for service to literature and art—the *Palmes académique* (Palms of the Academy). KF, however, refused the honor un-

---

memorials than have been already given, it is Shakespeare!" (Letter to KF, 11 Apr. 1878, in *The Letters of Anthony Trollope*, ed. N. John Hall (Stanford: Stanford University Press, 1983), 2:770.

26. Quoted by KF in *To William Winter*, 27 June 1878.

27. Quoted by Micheline Steinberg, *Flashback—A Pictorial History 1879–1979: One Hundred Years of Stratford-upon-Avon and the Royal Shakespeare Company* (London: RSC Publications, 1985), 8.

28. For more on KF's paper, see Maurine Beasley, "Kate Field and 'Kate Field's Washington': 1890–1895," *Records of the Columbia Historical Society* 49 (1976): 392–404.

til her work was consummated. That consummation occurred two years later when Congress repealed the tariff.

Not to be outdone by the French, newspapers throughout America proceeded to publish encomiums on KF. The eulogy in the *Washington Post* was typical: "In conferring upon Miss Kate Field the 'Academic Palm' . . . the French Republic formally recognizes, in a manner as rare as it is complimentary, one of the foremost women of America . . . who has not only rendered service to literature and art, but has been a leader of public thought." More satisfying to KF than this tribute was the plain remark in the *Boston Herald* that the French Academy "recognizes the power of woman in general and of woman editors in particular." KF's equally plain remark was, "That's the point exactly."[29]

In 1895 KF notified her subscribers that, pending recovery of her health, she was suspending publication of her paper. "Unfortunately," she explained in an interview in the *New York Tribune* (29 April 1895), "I cannot relegate my work to another, as personal journalism demands personal presence." She further explained in that interview what the journal had meant to her: "To have founded it was one of the good inspirations of my life. It has served the truth without fear and without favor. If its weekly appearance gave its readers as much satisfaction as it has given me, my goal has been reached." The Columbia Historical Society took the larger view in saying that to the "future historian of the national capital 'Kate Field's Washington' will be a boon. . . . The history of the nation cannot be written fairly without recognition of the journal and the shaping of public affairs through its influence" (McGee, "Memorial of Kate Field," 175–76).

The End of the Story

With her paper suspended, KF went to Hawaii to regain her health. To defray her expenses and satisfy an interest, she accepted an assignment from Herman Kohlsaat, the editor of the *Chicago Times-Herald*, to write travel letters from Hawaii with an eye to its possible annexation to the United States. But KF soon found her conscience would not allow her to sit in comfortable quarters and write secondhand reports. As she wrote in the last letter she sent to Kohlsaat, "Merely to sit down in Honolulu and pretend to know about these islands is absurd, and no Hawaiian would give a penny for my opinion did I not do what I am doing, nor would the people and congress in the United States."[30] What KF was doing was penetrating on horseback into the interior of the islands, where natives had never seen a white woman, sometimes covering twenty-five miles in

---

29. The quotations from the *Washington Post* and the *Boston Herald* and KF's remark appear in "What the Papers Said," *KF's Washington*, 5 Dec. 1894, 367.

30. This letter, together with detailed information furnished by Kohlsaat, appears in the *Times-Herald* (31 May 1896).

buffeting rain, for Hawaii had no railroad, nor for that matter any hotels or roads.

This regimen lasting five months debilitated KF, who at age fifty-seven had gone to Hawaii because of failing health, and she contracted pneumonia. And though she had a multitude of friends worldwide, she spent her last conscious hours in the presence of strangers. One of those strangers was Mabel Loomis Todd, the coeditor with Thomas W. Higginson of Emily Dickinson's two posthumous volumes of poems, as well as the editor of the poet's letters. Todd, on an expedition with her astronomer husband to study a solar eclipse, happened to be on the tourist steamer carrying KF to Honolulu for critical medical attention. Those final hours of KF, who was called "Kela wahine naanao" (that learned woman) by her Hawaiian friends, were recorded by Mabel Todd in *Corona and Coronet* (1898).

KF died on 19 May 1896 and was buried in Honolulu. However, some months later, her Will was found in the safe of the Shoreham, a hotel where she had lived when in Washington. In it she expressed the wish to be cremated and have her ashes deposited in Mount Auburn Cemetery at Cambridge, Massachusetts, between the graves of her father and mother. That wish her friends lovingly observed. Her body was disinterred and taken to San Francisco, where it was cremated, then her ashes were carried to Mount Auburn Cemetary and buried in a private ceremony. At her interment in Honolulu and at her funeral in San Francisco, this "most unique woman the present century has produced" (*Chicago Tribune*, 31 May 1896) was honored by the presence of the most prominent people of both cities, and the hundreds who could not attend, such as President Cleveland, sent floral wreaths. And now she lies in Mount Auburn with the illustrious dead who were her correspondents and friends when alive, among them the critic Edwin Percy Whipple, the publisher James T. Fields, the senator Charles Sumner, the actors Charlotte Cushman and Edwin Booth, and the authors Oliver Wendell Holmes, Henry Wadsworth Longfellow, and James Russell Lowell.

Chronology

1838   October 1: Born in St. Louis to Joseph Matthew and Eliza Riddle Field.
1843   Brother, Joseph Matthew Field Jr., born.
1846   Attends Mrs. Smith's Seminary in St. Louis.
1850   Brother Joseph dies.
1853   Enters Lasell Female Seminary at Auburndale, Massachusetts.
1856   Quits Lasell Female Seminary soon after her father dies and, with her mother, resides at her aunt and uncle's Boston estate.
1859   Arranges with *Boston Courier* to publish travel articles from Italy, then travels with aunt and uncle to Paris and Rome before settling in Florence.
1860   Adopted into the English literary colony in Florence.
      Joined in Florence by her mother.
      Broadens her journalistic market by publishing travel articles in the Massachusetts *Springfield Republican*, the *New Orleans Daily Picayune*, the *Boston Commonwealth*, and the *Boston Transcript*.
1861   Returns with mother to Boston.
      Publishes in magazines as well as newspapers.
1867   Publishes *Adelaide Ristori*.
1868   Publishes *Pen Photographs of Charles Dickens' Readings*.
      Publishes *Planchette's Diary*.
1869   Freelances for the *New York Tribune*.
      Launches lecturing career.
1871   May 26: Mother dies at sea on way to England.
      Arrives in England.
      Goes to spas in Germany and Switzerland for her health.
1872   Returns to New York.
1873   Returns to London; visits Paris and Spain.
      Publishes *Hap-Hazard*.
      Returns to New York.
1874   Launches theatrical career in America.

1875	Returns to England to prepare for theatrical career there. Publishes *Ten Days in Spain*.
1877	December: Promotes Bell's telephone in the London *Times*.
1878	Publishes *The History of Bell's Telephone*. Involved in fund-raisers for the Shakespeare Memorial Theatre in Stratford-upon-Avon.
1879	Returns to America.
1880	Tours in her musical monologue, *Eyes and Ears in London*. Founds Ladies' Co-operative Dress Association.
1882	Publishes *Charles Albert Fechter*. Summer: Visits England and France.
1883	Ladies' Co-operative Dress Association fails. Studies Mormonism in Salt Lake City.
1890	Launches *Kate Field's Washington*.
1893	Covers the Columbian Exposition in Chicago. Joins the women's suffrage movement.
1894	Publishes *The Drama of Glass*.
1895	Suspends publication of *Kate Field's Washington*. Seeks to recover her health in Hawaii.
1896	May 19: Dies in Honolulu.
1897	January 10: Buried in Mt. Auburn Cemetery in Cambridge, Massachusetts.

Part One: 1843–1859

~ St. Louis Childhood
Boston Schoolgirl
Trip to Europe

To Joseph Matthew Field (LW)
 KF's father (1810–56) was an actor and theatre manager in St. Louis, Mobile, and New Orleans; later, foreign correspondent for the *New Orleans Daily Picayune*; and still later, part owner of the *St. Louis Daily Reveille*.
[Jan. 1843] [St. Louis]

My Darling Papa;—
 I send you a lock of your little Katy's hair. You are to make a bracelet of it, and not give it away, but keep it for yourself. I shall expect you home next week and then I shall dance and sing all day. I send a kiss to my darling papa.

To Cordelia Riddle Sanford (LW)
 KF's maternal aunt (1824–1894), a former singer, was married to millionaire Milton H. Sanford (1814–83). She suffered severe episodes of lethargy and depression that eventually led to her being institutionalized.
Feb. 28. 1849. [St. Louis]

 You have requested me to write to you, and it gives me a great deal of pleasure to comply with the request. . . .
 I have been reading "Masterman Ready, or a Shipwreck on the Pacific Coast."[1] It is a very interesting story, but the worst of it is I cannot get the third volume. A gentleman whom I know has gone to California, and promises to send me two barrels of gold dust; if he should do so, I shall be very rich and shall do

Kate Field's father, Joseph
Matthew Field.
(Courtesy Trustees of the Boston
Public Library.)

great wonders, but I do not believe he will, so I need not make such great calculations about it. I have related to you all the interesting news I can think of.

    1. Novel by Frederick Marryat (1792–1848). The actual title is *Masterman Ready, or The Wreck of the Pacific: Written for Young People*.

To Eliza Riddle Field (LW)
    KF's mother (1812–71) was an actress. After marriage and the birth of KF, she tended to limit her circuit to St. Louis, Mobile, and New Orleans.
[1849]   [St. Louis]

    Is the theatre doing a good business now? I hope it is. Has any person written in my album? Is Father well? Are you in good health? I went to a Practising Party last night, and I had a great deal of pleasure. I love to dance so much. I never get tired. I think I am improving in Drawing very much. I am half way through Racine,[1] and I can translate very well, but the difficulty is to speak the language; I can read and write French and understand it nearly always when it is spoken, but the difficulty is for me to speak it. I saw two books at the store that I want. They are "Bleak House" and "Dombey and Son," in the same binding as my "David Copperfield."[2]

Kate Field's mother,
Eliza Riddle Field.
(Courtesy Trustees of the Boston Public Library.)

1. French dramatic poet (1639–99).
2. Novels by Charles Dickens (1812–70).

To Eliza Riddle Field (LW)
Feb. 22. [1851]   [St. Louis]

Dear Mother;—
I received a letter from you a few days ago, and would have answered it before, but have not had time. You said that Jenny [Lind][1] was expected in Mobile. If you meet her, tell her to call on me when she comes to St. Louis and take me to hear her sing. She will be here in March and you will not be up here, and I shall not hear Jenny Lind; it is too bad. How much will Father gain by Jenny Lind's being in Mobile? I am enjoying very good health. Give my best love and a kiss to Father, and tell him to come up soon. Give my love to all my relations. . . .

There was an explosion of a ferryboat here yesterday, and killed about 25 and wounded about eight. It was a dreadful thing, but you will read it in the papers.

1. Swedish soprano (1820–87); made her U.S. debut in 1850 under the management of P. T. Barnum (1810–91).

To Cordelia Riddle Sanford (LW)
[1851]   [St. Louis]

Aunt Corda, you do not know how foolish I am. I may know a piece of music perfectly, and if one asks me to play I make mistakes throughout the entire piece. I am trying to conquer it.

To Eliza Riddle Field (LW)
[1851?]   [St. Louis]

To my great joy, I took two letters out of the [post] office this afternoon, and both were from my best friend. You well know who that friend is. I shall indeed endeavor to profit by your most excellent advice, dearest mother. I have often thought of the spirit of my angel brother[1] being near me, and how grieved he must be when I have committed a wrong action; when I have shown my ugly temper to you, my Mother, whom I ought always to obey with cheerfulness; who has sacrificed everything for a child who, in return, has made her sorrow again and again for her disobedience. May the angel one, as well as you and Father, be able to find me gradually and gradually improving in disposition, and becoming less selfish. I do not want you to read the letter I wrote Christmas week; it was in a very ugly spirit, and I was sorry I sent it. I do not think as I wrote in that letter, and I am sure it shows no improvement in me.

I am sorry you did not receive my Christmas presents except that which Tom[2] gave you. He was very thoughtful. Did the birds taste nice? Did you give the children anything? I shall give John [Graham, KF's cousin] the five dollars to-morrow morning, in your name. I shall have to keep one dollar for myself.

1. Joseph Matthew Field Jr. (1843–50); died of cholera.
2. Unidentified.

To Cordelia Riddle Sanford (LW)
[1852?]   [St. Louis]

What do you think of Ole [Bornemann] Bull?[1] We do not hear anything of Jenny Lind now; I wonder if she will return to America. Do you think that [Henriette] Sontag[2] is equal to her? I am improving very much in music and French, so my teachers say. I have translated Racine and the first volume of Molière.[3] In Music I have [Henri Jérôme] Bertini's[4] Instruction Book, and my pieces are now sonatas by Chopin,⁵ which are very hard for me. My teacher does not allow me to play waltzes, polkas, or anything of that description. He has sent to Germany for a grand piano, which will be here early in January. What a loss Mr. [Jonas] Chickering must have sustained by the total destruction of his piano manufactory! Father has been gone six weeks; very nearly half the time of his absence has passed away. I think he intends opening the theatre here by the middle of March. Lola Montez⁶ is in Mobile now. Do you like [Maurice] Strakosch?⁷ Have you read "Uncle Tom's Cabin"?⁸ I think it is an entirely one-sided affair. She makes the colored individuals perfection. I should like to have such a little negro as Topsy. Would not you? The Pacific Railroad⁹ is in operation for fifteen miles and that great work is rapidly going on. How is Mr. Sanford's health? You must give my best love to him. I should like to visit you next summer and then go to the World's Fair in New York.¹⁰

1. Famous Norwegian violinist (1810–80); settled in the United States in 1852.
2. Stage name of German soprano (1806–54); gave concerts in the United States in 1852.
3. Pen name of Jean-Baptiste Poquelin, French comic dramatist (1622–73).
4. Italian pianist and composer (1798–1876); wrote numerous technical studies for the piano.
5. Poland's foremost composer (1810–49).
6. Stage name of Marie Gilbert (1818–61), an Irish-born actress and dancer who claimed Spanish descent. She was known as an international bad girl because of her affairs, including those, the rumors went, with Franz Liszt (1811–86) and Alexandre Dumas *père* (1802–70).
7. Bohemian impresario and pianist (1825–87); settled in New York in 1848.
8. Novel (1852) by Harriet Beecher Stowe (1811–96); sold 1,200,000 copies in sixteen months and crystallized American antislavery sentiment.
9. Later called the Missouri-Pacific Railroad. The first railroad west of the Mississippi River, it was built from 1851 to 1856 and ran from St. Louis to Kansas City.
10. Opened on 14 July 1853 to exhibit the industry of all nations.

To Cordelia Riddle Sanford (LW)
March 1853.   [St. Louis]

Well, Lola Montez appeared at father's [Varieties] theatre last night for the first time. The theatre was crowded from parquette [*sic*] to doors. She had the most beautiful eyes I ever saw. I like her very much, but she performed a dumb girl, so I cannot say what she may do in speaking characters or as a danseuse. She is trying to trouble father as much as possible. Madame Anna Thillon¹ is here, and will commence her engagement as soon as the countess² leaves. You must know that father has adopted the *starring system* this season. He has been very successful at Mobile. The [Royal Street] theatre there is still open. Father had a silver salver together with four goblets presented to him by the citizens of Mobile.

   1. English operatic soprano (1816–1903).
   2. Montez was made Comtesse de Lansfeld when she became the mistress of Ludwig I of Bavaria.

To Eliza Riddle Field (LW)
[1855]   [Lasell Female Seminary,[1] Auburndale, Mass.]

Have you or has Father read "Hiawatha," Longfellow's new poem? If you have not, do so and give me your opinion. I have just commenced it. They accuse him of plagiarism from the German, then again others say it is not worth the precious time devoted to the perusal. For myself the singular metre has a peculiar charm, and there seems to be an undercurrent of harmony breathing throughout it. I have read but a few pages, however.

   1. Exclusive boarding school for girls where KF studied at the expense of her millionaire uncle, Milton H. Sanford.

To Eliza Riddle Field (LW)
[1855]   [Lasell Female Seminary, Auburndale, Mass.]

I am to sing in two more choruses, one from "Macbeth"[1] and the other from Rossini. I am very well, and have finished the "Corsican Brothers"[2] with the exception of two pages.
   ... I am quite bewildered with the [Italian] language, but I shall make rapid progress with it.

   1. Opera by Verdi (1813–1901).
   2. Presumed to be *Les Frères Corses* by Dumas *père*, since KF was studying French.

To Eliza Riddle Field (LW)
[Dec. 7, 1855]   [Cordaville,[1] Mass.]

As I expected, I attended Thackeray's lecture[2] Friday night. I shall not yet pass my judgment, as we had a seat near the entrance, and I only heard about half [of what] he said. The lecture was by no means an extraordinary composition, simply pleasing, chatty, and conversational. Not at all historic, but this latter he acknowledged he avoided, from the fact that he did not aspire to the position of an historian, but a recorder of the manners and times of the age of the Georges. I thought his lecture a complete satire, and certainly I could not help feeling that he arrived at the most unamiable and uncharitable conclusions concerning the individuals upon whom he dilated as were possible to any human being. They say the opening one is the most inferior; hereafter I shall hear what I shall hear, and shall then give my impressions. Thackeray was conducted to the hall (which was crowded with the elite and literati of Boston) by James T. Fields.[3] Mr. Thackeray is no orator, merely a pleasant speaker, very easy in his manner. His voice is quite monotonous, though at the same time it does not weary you. It must arise from his being so perfectly natural.

1. The Sanford estate near Boston, named for Sanford's wife Cordelia (Corda). KF's mother had come to live there soon after her husband's death in January 1856.
2. The English novelist (1811-63) delivered lectures on "The Four Georges" during this, his second, U.S. lecture tour.
3. Fields (1817-81) was a partner in Ticknor & Fields, Boston publishers.

To Eliza Riddle Field (LW)
Dec. 16. 1855.   [Lasell Female Seminary, Auburndale, Mass.]

Sixteenth of December. This year will have soon passed away, and we shall have entered upon '56. How short is life in this world! How short in comparison with eternity, and yet it seems to me as though all our labor, all our strivings, were for earthly objects, as fleeting and uncertain as our own mortality. Whenever I think on this, I resolve to try to be a Christian, but my resolutions seem to fail, and I am the same uncharitable, restless spirit. There is always such a tumult going on in my brain that I never can decide what I am, what I will be, what I was created for, or what it is my ambition to be. I suppose I am what is designated as "rather queer."

To Eliza Riddle Field (LW)
[Late Dec. 1855]   [Lasell Female Seminary, Auburndale, Mass.]

My own dear, darling mother;—
I am homesick, very homesick, and how I long to see you and Father! It

seems to me as though the time would never come when I shall be with you once more. I can only reconcile by anticipating the pleasure which is in store for me, Providence permitting. I think there is something inspiring in looking forward to what will be. It urges me to renewed exertion in whatever I am engaged upon. My poor father, how often I think of him, confined to his room and suffering! May his health be speedily restored!

To Eliza Riddle Field (LW)
[Jan. 1856]   [Lasell Female Seminary, Auburndale, Mass.]

Yesterday Aunt Corda made me an offer as generous as it was surprising, yet one which I dread to accept and would not if I did not know the displeasure my refusal would cause Uncle Milton. It is to finish this year at Lasell, and to study music at their expense. Aunt Corda urged it so earnestly, and I remembered how last summer when at the St. Nicholas [Hotel in New York] I refused to take some bank bills that Uncle Milton threw into my lap, I hurt his feelings so that I dare not refuse again. And yet, dear mother, it gives me great pain to place myself under such great obligation to my aunt and uncle, and I shall not rest till I can repay them. I shall devote all my energies to singing with a view to making it a means of support. My French I could turn to account and might teach beginners, the same with my English. But I prefer the singing if I can make myself capable. I have often thought I would like to practise writing sketches with Father, if he would criticise them and tell me if they were in the least meritorious. But I have been away from him so much, and when he was last here he was so ill and so full of cares, that I did not dare to mention such a foolish and trifling occupation. Has he ever told you what he thought of my capacities,—where he thought my little talent lay? I have none, I can excel in nothing, I am good for nothing. Write me very often, dear mother, take good care of your health, and remember that you have a / Devoted daughter, / Katey

To Eliza Riddle Field (LW)
[Jan. 20, 1856]   [Lasell Female Seminary, Auburndale, Mass.]

The opening opera to-morrow night is [Verdi's] "Il Trovatore." Ah, woe, ah, woe is me! I shall be a model for despair if I do not hear [Donizetti's] "Linda de Chamounix" Friday night. Do you remember the two gold dollars that Father gave me to see Rachel[1] in *Adrienne* [*Lecouvreur*]?[2] I did not need the money then, and I have treasured them ever since, waiting for something to "turn up." I think that if I spend $1.50 upon the opera of "Linda," it will be a profitable investment. What is your opinion of the matter?

... Present my remembrances to Mr. Barney and Mrs. [Maria Pray] Williams.[3] Is it true that they intend visiting Europe? Ask them to remember me if they have an opportunity of collecting autographs or curiosities of any description. I wonder if it will ever be our destiny to journey over the old world. If wishing would accomplish it, such a consummation would soon come to pass.

   1. Stage name of Élisa Rachel Félix (1820-58), French tragic actress.
   2. Drama by Eugène Scribe (1791-1861) and Ernest Gabriel Legouvé (1807-1903), which KF had seen the previous year in Boston. Rachel performed in French; English reading texts were sold in the theatre.
   3. KF's father, as manager of the Royal Street Theatre, had contracted with the Williamses to perform in Mobile.

To Joseph Matthew Field (LW)
Jan. 23. 1856.   [Lasell Female Seminary, Auburndale, Mass.]

Something has turned up in reality. Let me tell you the news. Aunt Corda and Uncle Milton are to visit Aunt Charlotte [Cushman][1] as long as the opera remains in Boston; furthermore, we are all going next Friday night to hear Linda [de Chamounix], which character La [Elise] Hensler[2] is to sustain. The greatest curiosity is of course manifested to see her, the American Prima Donna.

Tableaux [at my school] are progressing. I am becoming exceedingly nervous about my part in the performance. It will be hard for me to commit "Come è bello"[3] to memory, as I have not yet learned a note of it. Oh, dear me! what will become of me? We have seen the proof sheet of programmes, which has quite a nice appearance. My name looks quite imposing in print. I think, talk, and dream nothing but tableaux, and this is the case with my three co-laborers.[4]

   1. American actress (1816-76). She had acted with KF's parents and played the lead in Joseph Field's adaptation of *Gabrielle; or a Night in the Bastille* by Dumas *père*. KF uses the word *aunt* here only as a term of intimacy.
   2. Soprano (1836-1929); had debuted at La Scala in 1855.
   3. "How beautiful"; aria in Donizetti's *Lucrezia Borgia*.
   4. On the morning of the performance held on 28 January, school authorities were notified that KF's father had died, but they withheld the news from KF until after the evening performance.

To Eliza Riddle Field (LW)
[Feb. 1856]   [Lasell Female Seminary, Auburndale, Mass.]

   Yesterday I took my first singing lesson. Signor Bendelari was very kind, and seemed very sorry for me.[1] Darling mother, I pray that we may never be obliged to be parted hereafter. Signor Bendelari spoke encouragingly of my voice.

   1. Because of the recent death of her father.

To Eliza Riddle Field (LW)
Feb. 26. 1856.   [Lasell Female Seminary] Auburndale [Mass.]

My precious Mother;—
   Once more at school. Oh, how strange everything appeared here! Each object wears a different aspect. So sad, so desolate, how different it was when I left it![1] Well, well, it must be so. It was hard for me to return, but you desired it, Aunt Corda and Uncle Milton urged it very much, and I have come. I cannot as yet fix my mind on my books, but I will try to overcome my feelings and thoughts and fix my attention upon my studies. I do not think I have yet told you of my lessons. They are Geometry, Rhetoric, [Lord Henry Home] Kames' Elements of Criticism, and (perhaps) Geography of the Heavens. I have no French or Italian now, so I can take more English studies. I have concluded not to continue Algebra, from the fact that I dislike it to such a degree that it positively makes me sick to open the book. It is of no use unless you intend to be a teacher, and if I am to be one, I [would] never attempt to teach mathematics. I have a natural distaste for all excepting Geometry. You know my propensity to scribble and read. I delight in studies of a literary nature. Father wished me to study astronomy, and so I wish to take up the Geography of the Heavens. Father's picture is hanging up before my writing desk, so that I am gazing upon his beloved face all the time. Oh, mother dear, I know that I am very ungrateful to complain. You, who have so much more cause, are making all efforts to gain the mastery over your feelings. I think I have done so too, but in writing to you I forget myself. Forgive me, and do not be anxious about me.
   With regard to father's debts, if it is a possible thing, let them all be paid. Will not something be realized from the properties of the [Varieties] theatre and the disposal of the lease?[2] You remember that father owns the Reveille building on Olive Street in St. Louis.[3] If the debts cannot all be paid *now, collect them*, if the parties are willing, and let us see what can be done in the future, if we live.
   If spiritual manifestations are true, what a source of comfort they will be to

us! We shall hear from Father from the Spirit world, but we must not give our confidence too readily, but receive all such communications with great caution. Were I in New York, I should seek the Misses Fox.[4] I know them to be honest and truthful in themselves. I do not speak on this latter subject to Aunt Corda or Uncle Milton, for they are averse to it and consider such belief as fanaticism. Nevertheless I am one to enquire and to believe that which my reason allows,— to believe *facts*. My father's mind was too strong to be led away by impositions or idle fancies and suppositions. He sought eagerly for Spiritual Truth, he studied earnestly, he found that which he sought, in Swedenborg.[5] I have read but little of Swedenborg, but *that little* has satisfied me. What noble lessons of humanity does he teach! Charity and love are his passports to Heaven. But to be liberal one should study the teachings of others of the established doctrines. One thing it seems to me I must believe,—in the Trinity. Do you accord with the Unitarian belief?

1. KF had left school for a month owing to her father's death.

2. The theatre, built in 1851, was financed by a stock company, which leased it to Field for thirty years at a yearly fee of fifteen hundred dollars plus taxes and insurance.

3. The *St. Louis Reveille* had been flourishing for five years when, on 17 May 1849, the so-called Great Fire destroyed the office and plant, though it spared the building.

4. The Foxes—Leah (1814-80), Margaret (1836-93), and Katherine (1841-92)—claimed supernatural powers. Their séances impressed James Fenimore Cooper (1789-1851), William Cullen Bryant (1794-1878), Horace Greeley (1811-72), and George Bancroft (1800-1891), among many others. In 1888 Margaret admitted they had practiced fraud, but she later recanted her admission.

5. Highly influential Swedish scientist, theologian, philosopher, and mystic (1688-1772).

To Noah Miller Ludlow (MHS-LFM)
Ludlow (1795-1886) was an actor, theatre manager, author, and partner with Sol Smith (1801-69) in Ludlow & Smith, the company in which KF's mother and father had acted in New Orleans, Mobile, and St. Louis.
Sept. 16. 1858.   Cordaville [Mass.]

Dear Mr. Ludlow;—
Mother received your kind letter two days since and as I am her business man (very poor salary however), I hasten to reply. Aunt Sarah [Riddle Sedley][1] has obtained an engagement with Borrow [manager] of the Howard Athenaeum [Theatre in] Boston for the season, consequently though deeply obliged to you for your consideration must forego a visit West or South. Mother thanks you many times for the interest you have manifested in her plans, or at least desires

and trusts something satisfactory may be effected with the St. Louis or Mobile managements. Should Mr. [George Percy] Farren [a theatre manager] desire to engage her she would like to be advised of the terms he may offer. There is a *possibility* of Mother not receiving Mr. [S. B.] Duffield's[2] letter on account of its Boston direction, however she will make inquiries for it. You do not refer to any probability of an opening at Wood's People's Theatre [in St. Louis].

We are still in little Cordaville and the prospect of *Europe* is gradually lessening as Uncle Milt's responsible man has "give notice." Of course he would. Such good fortune as a trip to the Land of Song could not possibly befall me. No plans have been laid and we are trusting to Providence, the best thing to do under the circumstances....

We are pleased, more than pleased that you and Aunt Corney[3] derived so much enjoyment from your Eastern tour....

I remain just the same as ever, / Mary Kate Field[4]

I write *Mary* because Mr. St. John[5] much prefers it to a nickname like *Kate*. Equinoctial storm, am enjoying most dolefully.

1. Actress (1811-61). As a child she acted with KF's grandmother, Mary Lapsley Riddle. After marriage to Sedley, who was known on the stage as W. H. Smith, she adopted Mrs. W. H. Smith as her own *nom de théâtre*.
2. Manager of the Metropolitan Theatre in New York; former manager of the Mobile Theatre.
3. Ludlow's daughter Cornelia, widow of Matthew C. Field (1812-44), KF's uncle, who had been associated with the *New Orleans Daily Picayune* and the *St. Louis Daily Reveille*.
4. KF's given names were Mary Katherine Keemle.
5. Unidentified.

To Eliza Riddle Field (LW)
[Jan. 1859] [Paris][1]

To-day I have been to the Hotel des Invalides, where repose the ashes of the first Napoleon. I can give you no description of the grandeur of this chapel and of the splendor of the new sarcophagus, in which the remains are to be placed, but not for two years. Louis Napoleon is a great man, without doubt. He is determined to leave the Napoleon stamp upon every great work in France. I do not see who is so well fitted to govern this nation as himself. The French need a master. Yesterday the Legislative Session opened with a speech from the Emperor. Not one word in reference to America.

1. In January 1859, the Sanfords—KF's aunt and uncle—took her to Paris, Rome, and Florence.

Joined by her mother after the Sanfords returned to Boston, KF headquartered in Florence until October 1861.

To Eliza Riddle Field (LW)
[1859] [Rome]

    I like it, I love it, and I only wish I could remain here for months. The weather is charming, the sky is so blue. The carnival was glorious, and I was in it all the time, and what fun I did have. I was in a carriage with a boy's hat on, the only one in the Corso.[1] I have just sent a letter in rhyme[2] to the "[Boston] Courier." I am having singing lessons with [Carlo] Sebastiani, and if I only enjoy these for a month, it will still be a great gain.
    ... Last Sunday I went with Miss Cushman, Miss Stebbins, Hattie Hosmer, Mr. Ward, a young sculptor, and Mr. Ned Cushman,[3] to a picnic at Hadrian Villa (six miles out of Rome). We had a glorious day among the ruins, the mountains, and the wonderful sky. The country around Rome is made for drives and rides.

    1. Via del Corso, the main street of central Rome. With its fashionable shops and cafés, it usually attracted crowds.
    2. Unfound.
    3. The actress Charlotte Cushman, her nephew Ned, and American sculptors Emma Stebbins (1815–82), Harriet Hosmer (1830–1908), and John Quincy Adams Ward (1830–1910).

To Eliza Riddle Field (LW)
[1859] [Rome]

    Miss Cushman wants me to go to England this Spring, but I want to study with [Pietro] Romani[1] in Florence. Miss Stebbins is a noble woman, and has certainly a great talent for sculpture. The Brownings[2] are here, and have been all winter. [Nathaniel] Hawthorne and President [Franklin] Pierce have just arrived.[3] Rome agrees with me so much better than Paris. Then the green fields, the ruins, the paintings, the sculpture, all the life I love so much. If only you were with me, darling mother. There may be a bright future for us.

    1. Composer (1791–1877); taught singing at the Istituto Musicale in Florence.
    2. Robert (1812–89) and Elizabeth Barrett (1806–61).

3. Hawthorne (1804–64) had written the campaign biography of Pierce (1804–69) and had been rewarded with the consulship at Liverpool.

To Eliza Riddle Field (LW)
[1859] [Rome]

Miss Cushman says [Manuel] Garcia,[1] in London, is the finest teacher in the world and urges Uncle and Aunt to leave me in England. I am crazy to be at work. I want to see what effect the change of climate will have on my voice, and I am so anxious to be independent, and have my dear little mother in a position worthy of her tastes and talents. I shall never feel comfortable until I am my own mistress and have an occupation. Not that I do not enjoy the present; not, indeed, that I do not appreciate my opportunities; but I feel that if anything is to be done, now is the time, and Aunt Corda has become willing that I should go on the stage as a profession. I am afraid there's no chance for me, but I hope for the best. Rome is no place for music, Naples is better, but I want to study in Florence with Romani.

... President Pierce called on us yesterday. He was very polite, but does not seem to be a man of much fun.

1. Famous voice teacher (1805–1906) who numbered Jenny Lind among his better known students.

Part Two: 1859–1861

Florentine Days
The Brownings,
the Trollopes, Isa Blagden,
and Literary Visitors

To Eliza Riddle Field (LW)
[1859]   [Florence]

I could not possibly show one [of my travel letters][1] to him [Browning], he is too great. But to show you what kind hearts Mr. and Mrs. Browning have, I send you two notes that they sent me yesterday with [Walter Savage] Landor's[2] autograph. I wrote them a few lines thanking them for a letter of [Edward Robert] Lytton's.[3] To Miss [Isa] Blagden[4] Mrs. Browning writes of me as "*dear Miss Field.*"

   1. Apart from her juvenilia in the *New Orleans Daily Picayune* and the *St. Louis Daily Reveille*, KF's first venture into journalism was her travel letters in the *Boston Courier*. (Travel letters were a popular feature of most American newspapers.) From 1860 to 1865, KF kept a scrapbook of her travel letters from Italy, as well as those from New York and Newport, which were published in the *Weekly Picayune*, the *Boston Transcript*, the Massachusetts *Springfield Republican*, and the weekly *Boston Commonwealth*. The scrapbook of 143 pages is now in BPL.
   2. English author and poet (1775–1864).
   3. English poet (1831–91), son of Edward George Earle Bulwer-Lytton (1803–73), the novelist.
   4. English novelist, poet, and generous hostess (1816–73). Her Villa Brichieri overlooking Florence, on which she had a long lease, was a second home to English and American birds of passage, including KF. Blagden, a Eurasian, was romantically involved with Robert Lytton.

To Eliza Riddle Field (LW)
[Jan. 1860]   [Florence]

Mr. Browning is the person whose good opinion I am most anxious for, and to whom I am already very much attached. He feels music, and I should like to sing before him. There is something about him that I fancy marvelously. Last night he said to me, "You are very ambitious; you are the most ambitious person of my acquaintance." I laughed and asked him how he had arrived at such a conclusion. "Oh, I can tell by your eyes," he said. "How so?" I asked. "I can detect it in their glisten," he replied. "Well," I said, "it is no great crime to be ambitious, is it?" "No, indeed," he returned; "I admire it; I would not give a straw for a person who was not."

To Eliza Riddle Field (LW)
[Jan. 1860]   [Florence]

You are mistaken when you think I can take care of myself. I don't like to; I want some one to love me, to take an interest in me, some one to whom I can say, What do you think? some one to kiss and tease and scold me.

To Eliza Riddle Field (LW)
[Jan. 1860]   [Florence]

Every Monday evening we go to the Trollopes[1] and there meet a half dozen Italians, politicians, literati, etc. [Francesco] Dall' Ongaro gave me his new book of poems[2] and looked unutterable things at me, but he can't make an impression to save his life. Last Monday slavery was attacked, and I, an American, in the mingling of Italian, French, and English, had to maintain my country against seven adversaries. Foreigners cannot understand the "peculiar institution," and that it is no child's play to free 4,000,000 blacks. The English, the very creatures who forced it upon us, are most bitter against us. Mr. [Thomas] Trollope is such a fine man.[3] His wife is promiscuously talented, writes for the Athenaeum, composes music, translates, etc., but does not go very far in any one thing. What do you think Mr. James Jackson Jarves[4] said the other day? "It is impossible for you to lie. You have a tell-tale face." And then again, "I should like to see you when you are thoroughly smashed" (meaning in love). "Why?" "Because you will love with so much earnestness and passion." We were all talking about love. I could not but laugh and think how differently you viewed me, as one devoid totally of sentiment and passion. People here think me so full of passion and truth.

1. Thomas Adolphus Trollope (1810-92) and his wife Theodosia Garrow (1825-65). Thomas's mother was Frances Trollope (1780-1863), best known for her *Domestic Manners of the Americans*, and his brother was Anthony Trollope (1815-82), famous for his novels in the *Barsetshire* series.

2. The book by Dall' Ongaro (1808-73) to which KF refers is *I Volontari Della Morte* (The Volunteers of Death, 1860), a ballad about the Italian-Austrian War of 1859.

3. KF's friendship with Thomas Trollope is recounted by Zoltan Haraszti in "Kate Field and the Trollope Brothers," *More Books: Being the Bulletin of the Boston Public Library* 2 (July 1927). Suffice it to say, as Haraszti reports, that when Trollope was writing *Lindisfarn Chase* (1863), he wrote to KF about the central character of the novel, whom he named Kate: "The 'young woman called Kate' will be as charming as my skill could make her. You do not think that I could make a Kate, and make her anything but the dearest creature ever born!"

4. American author and art collector (1818-88); settled in Florence in the 1850s.

To Cordelia Riddle Sanford (LW)
[Feb. 1860]   [Florence]

I am almost happy. I believe at last I have a mother.[1] . . .

Your letter gave me more than one twinge about the heart, but I must, I must, I must submit to destiny, so I'll no longer implore for that which will not be granted. You know how I long to embrace you—here let it end.

. . . Mrs. [James Jackson] Jarves has asked me to go to the masked ball at the Veglio, which I hope to do, as much to see [it as] to write a [travel] letter about [it] as anything. James T. Fields and wife[2] are here, and I have made their acquaintance. She is very pretty and has been more than kind. He tells me he knew dear father, and speaks of the pleasure he had in reading my [travel] letters [in the *Boston Courier*]. Learning that I no longer write for the "Courier" he said, "You're just the person for the '[Boston] Transcript.' [Henry Worthington] Dutton[3] must have you. Suppose you send him twenty letters for $150, and later on you can ask more?" I agreed gladly. How good he is. I write twice a month for the "[New Orleans Weekly] Picayune" at $5.00 a column.[4] Mr. Fields is an inimitable story-teller. They go to Rome to-morrow, as do the Stowes.[5] I like Mrs. Stowe the more I see her. Robert C. Winthrop[6] and family are here. Americans are always the belles of the occasion. Not yet singing, I am obliged to learn self-denial; not a bad thing for me, as I expect my life to be anything but a bed of roses.

1. The Sanfords had returned home and KF's mother had joined her in Florence.
2. Annie Adams Fields (1834-1915), Boston hostess well known for her literary salon.
3. Senior proprietor of the *Boston Evening Transcript* (d. 1875).
4. KF's contributions to the *Transcript* and *Picayune* are in her scrapbook (see *To Eliza Riddle Field*,

[Florence, 1859], n. 1). KF's first travel letter in the *Picayune*, signed "Sempre Avanti" and datelined "Florence, February 4, 1860," was published on 4 March 1860; her first travel letter in the *Transcript*, signed "Fie" and datelined "Florence, March 3, 1860," was published on 27 March 1860.

5. The world-famous author and her husband, Calvin Ellis Stowe (1802–86), professor of Sacred Literature.

6. Former U.S. representative, Speaker of the House, and senator (1809–94).

To Cordelia Riddle Sanford (LW)
[Mar. 1860]   [Florence]

There is a young American here, Mr. [Elihu] Vedder,[1] very talented and very poor, to whom I do wish somebody would give an order. I have translated a sonnet of [Giovanni Battista] Niccolini[2] into blank verse; very blank, I fear, as it is my first attempt. It is about the Pope and Rome, of course. I've sent two [travel] letters to the "[Boston] Transcript" under the *nom de plume* of "Fie."[3] Do you think it good? I was at a loss for a name; Mother thought it as good as any. I think you will be delighted with Milan—people so fine—Cathedral so beautiful—La Scala so grand—and Liberty so new there. But poor Venice! It would make my heart ache to visit Venice while the white coats of Austrians hover over her like birds of prey.[4] Last evening we were at Miss Blagden's,—Mother and I meeting Miss [Frances Power] Cobbe,[5] Hattie Hosmer, Emma Crow[6] and young [Ned] Cushman, the great Charlotte's nephew; and we all laughed immoderately at nothing, as people always do whenever Hattie Hosmer is present. Emma Crow tells me that Mr. Browning paid me a tremendous compliment the night before she left Rome. I was dying to know what, but modesty forbade. Still this much is pleasant to me and may be to *you*. The Brownings return in May. Miss Cushman does not visit Florence *en route* to England, so they say. Miss Stebbins is at work upon her Lotus Eater, and has completed a wonderful bust of Miss Cushman.

1. American painter (1836–1923). Mrs. Sanford commissioned him to paint KF. The portrait, however, has vanished. A reproduction appears as the frontispiece in LW.

2. Niccolini (1782–1861), Tuscan poet, was best known as a tragedian.

3. In KF's scrapbook (see *To Eliza Riddle Field*, [Florence, 1859], n. 1).

4. Refers to the Italian-Austrian War, which ended with the Treaty of Turin in March 1860.

5. Irish author and crusader for women's and children's rights (1822–1908).

6. Daughter of Wayman Crow, former Missouri state senator and founder of Washington University in St. Louis.

To Cordelia Riddle Sanford (LW)
[June 1, 1860] [Florence]

Last night we went to the Trollopes and there met the authoress of "Adam Bede,"[1] and Mr. [George Henry] Lewes, the Life-of-Goethe man.[2] Miss Evans, or Mrs. Lewes, is a woman whose whole face is of the horse make; but there is something interesting about her, and you feel impressed with her importance. They say she converses finely, she is very retiring—and talked all the evening to Mr. [Thomas] Trollope. I liked Mr. Lewes, who is a very ugly man, but very charming in conversation, so that you forget his looks, and Mr. [John] Chapman,[3] who is a regular good-natured, obstinate John Bull though a young man. I thought to myself, "Shall I ever have the pleasure of looking upon you in the light of *my publisher*?" The Leweses intend to make Florence their home, returning here in the autumn.[4] I hear that Dickens is making more money than ever, has provided handsomely for his wife, and lives very quietly indeed.[5] It is reported of Mrs. Stowe that, having desired to know Dickens, he gave a large dinner party for her, and received her acceptance. Later the Duchess of Sutherland desired her company and Mrs. Stowe went to her, leaving Dickens out and sending him no apology. She called upon him afterwards and he refused to receive her.[6]

1. Novel (1859) by George Eliot, the pen name of Mary Ann Evans (1819–80).

2. George Eliot's consort and one of England's most brilliant intellectuals (1817–78). His *Life of Goethe* had appeared in 1855.

3. Publisher (1821–94); first to publish Eliot (her translation of Strauss's *Life of Jesus*, 1846); also owner of the *Westminster Review*, which Eliot helped to edit and for which she wrote.

4. KF discussed these and other literati in "English Authors in Florence," *Atlantic Monthly*, Dec. 1864.

5. Dickens purchased a house for his wife and paid her alimony of six hundred pounds a year, as the terms of their legal separation required.

6. Though the Duchess of Sutherland was Stowe's sponsor in London, the story is apocryphal.

To William Warland Clapp (HC)
Clapp (1826–91) was editor-owner of the *Boston Saturday Evening Gazette*.
June 16. 1860. Florence

Dear Sir;—

It may be that you have not forgotten me. I certainly have not forgotten *you* and now write to inquire if you wish a correspondent from Italy. I like Boston and [Boston] papers [that are] not absorbed in coming and going Presidents, and should like to write you once a week at the rate of $10 per letter.

For a sample of the little that I can do, I refer you to twenty letters lately published in the Boston Transcript under signatures of "Fie!" and "Somebody Else."[1]

I can promise you variety in Literature, Art, Politics and *Religion* as all four subjects are now undergoing a revolution. If my services are desired please address to the care of Emmanuel Fenzi & Co. Bankers, Florence.

1. In KF's scrapbook (see *To Eliza Riddle Field*, [Florence, 1859], n. 1).

To Cordelia Riddle Sanford (LW)
[1860]   [Florence]

I have seen a photograph of [William Wetmore] Story's[1] bust of Theodore Parker,[2] which I do not like in the least. Young [Joel Tanner] Hart,[3] the sculptor here, is, they say, making a much better likeness of him. Miss Cobbe has a cameo medallion of Parker, and Mr. [Thomas] Trollope one in plaster. The Brownings have returned, looking well and like angels. What think you, dear? They brought me a beautiful pair of Roman gold sleeve buttons, a copy of [Mrs. Browning's] "Poems before Congress" [1860], and photographs of themselves, also a large one taken from Hamilton Wild's[4] pretty painting of Penini[5] on his little pony. Is this not dear of them? They have received mother very kindly, and last night we took tea with them in company with Mr. Landor. Mr. Landor, they say, was quite cross until I came. They also say I always put him into a good humor. In going to the table he came up to me and said, "Now were I a young man, I should offer you my arm." "Why cannot you as it is?" I asked. "With delight, if you will accept it." And so we marched to the table. In taking our seats, Mr. [John] Chapman came forward to occupy the place next me, whereupon Mr. Landor exclaimed, "Don't come between me and Paradise," and down he sat. It's the first time I was ever told I was *Elysium* Field. Do you take [the joke]? Dear Mrs. Browning whispered, "I hope you appreciate the compliment, Kate." The old man, speaking of years, said, "I wish I were dead and buried." "Buried or not, Mr. Landor, you will always live," cried I, very much to his amusement. Miss Blagden and I noticed that his beard was cut. "Yes, I cut it myself. Ah, willingly would I exchange my hair for yours," said he to me, mine being curled. "Most willingly would I exchange the outside on *my* head for the inside of *yours*, Mr. Landor," retorted I, and again he laughed heartily. "Pray tell me, Mr. Landor, how many times does a man fall in love during his life?" "Well, every time he sees a pretty woman," and at this witticism he shouted lustily, then resuming, "Not that I ever was as fickle as that. Oh, no, I never loved but *twice*. I married to get rid of love, but found *this did not answer at all*." Once speaking of women, he said, "Women are all good. I never knew but two bad women in all my life—ah, stop, stop,—I mean *three—I forgot my wife*."[6]

    1. American sculptor (1819-95).

    2. Boston Unitarian minister (1810-60); sat in his last days for Story. Story also made the medallion of Parker, which embellishes his tombstone in Florence's Protestant Cemetery.

    3. Hart (1810-77) had made busts of Presidents Andrew Jackson (1767-1845) and Millard Fillmore (1800-1874), among others.

    4. Landscape and portrait painter (1827-84).

    5. "Little Pen," the Brownings' pet name for their only child, Robert Wiedemann Barrett (1849-1913). *Wiedemann* was the maiden name of Browning's mother.

    6. The Landors' marriage was so embittered that for the last twenty-three years they communicated only through third parties.

To Cordelia Riddle Sanford (LW)
[1860]   [Florence]

I have just finished "The Mill on the Floss"[1] and am perfectly content with it. It is vastly superior to "Adam Bede" in my eyes. The ending has really made me melancholy. It seems to me there is much in my character like Maggie's, and that I shall have just such a struggling existence, I mean morally and mentally.

    1. Novel (1860) by George Eliot.

To Cordelia Riddle Sanford (LW)
[Aug. 1860]   [Leghorn,[1] Italy]

We have seen Ristori[2] in Judith, Mirra, Medea,[3] and in farce. Our delight is intense—a more fascinating creature I never saw, and her comedy is as fine as her tragedy. You could not have seen her to advantage, for I prefer her to Rachel. She is more melodramatic, I grant, but she has greater passion; her love is real love. Rachel was not so superb in the softer passions, nor had she the beautiful figure and lovely face of Ristori. A more mobile expression I never saw; her blue eyes look any color to suit the feeling of the moment, and when she smiles, disclosing pearly teeth, she is angelic. I am transported with her, and regret that we are not able to see her again. What a glorious effect would be produced with Ristori and [Tommaso] Salvini[4] in the same tragedy! We have no actors in America; we have no criticism. Italy produces both spontaneously; but a bad Italian actor is the most atrocious conception on earth. Ristori looks more like an American than an Italian,—she is so exceedingly fair and feminine off the stage. I hope Edwin Booth[5] will study the French and Italian schools of acting, and will remember to be natural. Give my love to Miss Cushman when you see her next, and tell her that I sympathize in her admiration for beautiful, good Ristori.

1. KF and her mother had gone to this seaside resort to escape the summer heat of Florence.
2. Italian actress (1821-1906).
3. *Judith* by Pablo Giacometti (1816-62); *Mirra* by Vittoria Amedeo Alfieri (1749-1803); *Medea* by Legouvé.
4. Salvini (1829-1915) had acted with Ristori when he joined her company in 1847.
5. American tragedian (1833-93), best known for his Shakespearean roles; brother of John Wilkes Booth (1838-65), whose assassination of Lincoln in 1865 would cause Edwin to leave the stage for two years.

To Cordelia Riddle Sanford (LW)
[Oct. 1860] [Florence]

I don't know what it is to be free from—not exactly pain, but uncomfortableness. I am not unhappy about myself, however, but about [Giuseppe] Garibaldi![1] His declaration that the Two Sicilies shall not be annexed to Piedmont until he has marched through Rome sounds like a hot-headed boy. The sooner Italy is consolidated, the better will be her position with other Powers....

I've finished the first two volumes of [Edward] Gibbon,[2] and am quite fascinated with him. I am beginning to wake up to a sense of my enormous ignorance, and perhaps if I live I may know something in the course of a few years. After all, considering that I could not do anything in July and August, my time has not been entirely thrown away, for besides carrying on a large private correspondence, I have read [Elizabeth Barrett Browning's] "Aurora Leigh," [Robert Browning's] "Men and Women," "Bacon's Essays," [Hawthorne's] "Transformation,"[3] [Thomas Hughes's] "Tom Brown's School Days," [Anthony Trollope's] "Three Clerks" [and his] "The Bertrams," [George Eliot's] "Scenes of Clerical Life," [Napoleon III's] "Des Idées Napoleoniennes," and the two volumes of Gibbon's, besides dipping into various other books, reading Italian newspapers, writing twelve [travel] letters to [the] "[New Orleans] Picayune," that account of watering-place life that I sent you, and thirty pages of a *something* at which

I am now experimenting. I know this is nothing, but it is an improvement on the Kate Field of old. Three months of last year commencing to-day I did nothing except lie on a sofa and be miserable.

    1. Italian patriot and soldier (1807–82); conquered the so-called Two Sicilies (Sicily and Naples).

    2. English historian (1737–94); famed for his *History of the Decline and Fall of the Roman Empire* (6 vols., 1776–88).

    3. English title of *The Marble Faun* (1860), a novel whose locale is mainly Rome.

To Cordelia Riddle Sanford (LW)
[Oct. 1860]   [Florence]

Anthony Trollope is a very delightful companion.[1] I see a great deal of him. He has promised to send me a copy of the "Arabian Nights" (which I have never read) in which he intends to write "Kate Field, from the Author," and to write me a four-page letter on condition that I answer it. The Brownings returned day before yesterday. I sent her a bouquet yesterday and intend calling to-day.

    1. KF met the novelist at his brother's Villino Trollope; so began his richest friendship ("she has been my most chosen friend," he declared in his *Autobiography* [1883]), which ended only with Trollope's death. Though Trollope did not save KF's letters (he was not a saver of letters), KF preserved a number of his. For those letters, see N. John Hall, ed., *The Letters of Anthony Trollope*, 2 vols. (Stanford: Stanford University Press, 1983).

To Cordelia Riddle Sanford (LW)
[Nov. 1860]   [Florence]

We are to furnish the rooms ourselves, the [Thomas] Trollopes kindly volunteering to lend us some furniture to start with, and it is by far the most economical way to live in Florence. The furniture soon pays for itself and the remarkable decrease in the rent for unfurnished apartments is a consideration. Our situation, so near the dear Trollopes, will be a great comfort to us, and the Piazza [Independenza] is by far the healthiest locality in the city.

To Cordelia Riddle Sanford (LW)
[Dec. 1860]   [Florence]

I made only two gifts, one to Beatrice Trollope[1] and a camellia to Mr. Landor. The old man made us a visit the next day and presented me with *the only copy he possesses* of his works, in two large volumes. They are filled with his corrections and doubly valuable on this account.[2] Was it not kind of the poor old man? A few days previous he sent us some very fine grapes. The world may say what it pleases of Mr. Landor. I cannot but feel a sympathy for him, and certainly his errors have fallen most heavily on himself.[3]

 1. The Thomas Trollopes' daughter, usually called Bice.
 2. No one has yet found these volumes. In her will, KF willed "all my books left in boxes" to her cousin George Riddle (1851–1910), son of Edward Riddle (1820–1888), KF's maternal uncle, but none of them was named.
 3. At age eighty-five, the poet, infirm and somewhat mad, had a libel action pending against him, which threatened to bankrupt him. On advice of John Forster, a barrister, who predicted an adverse verdict should he stand trial, Landor left England and at length came to Florence, where Browning settled him in a cottage near the Casa Guidi and managed his finances.

To Cordelia Riddle Sanford (LW)
[Jan. 1861]   [Florence]

... There still remain three young artists, [Albert] Baldwin,[1] [Charles Caryl] Coleman,[2] and Oliver [Ingraham] Lay,[3] all three New Yorkers. Mr. Baldwin will never be an artist, but he is a noble character and very well educated. His father is very wealthy. Coleman is poor and has great feeling for art,—he is very clever in landscapes. Oliver is one of the handsomest and most charming young fellows that I have ever met. He is remarkably mature for his years, is well educated, talks well, argues with originality, is well read, and very imaginative....

 1. The man KF contemplated marrying.
 2. Painter (1840–1928); his portrait of Landor is now in the Boston Public Library.
 3. Portraitist (1845–90); painted KF's mother.

To Cordelia Riddle Sanford (LW)
[1861]   [Florence]

There are all good reasons for returning home, but there are still more powerful ones for remaining here. I assure you we have not the money to live out of Italy. Here we can exist comfortably within our income, which were it tripled would not insure us a respectable living in America. Were I strong and healthy, and could submit to many inconveniences fighting my own way, it would be different; but I am equal to nothing of the kind,—the greater part of my time is passed in an easy-chair. Distances are so great in New York that I never could walk; and where I pay a dime here for conveyance, I should pay a dollar in America. No, dear; much as I wish to see you, whom I miss more and more as I grow older, much as I wish to have Mother surrounded with her own particular interests and family, we cannot leave Italy.

To Cordelia Riddle Sanford (LW)
[1861]   [Florence]

You are good enough to say that if we are in need of the *nécessaire* you will accommodate us; but you forget that your money is in reality Uncle Milton's; and you forget that he would not respect me, nor I respect myself, did I become still more indebted to him when his feelings towards me are as they are.[1] Put yourself in my position and ask yourself if I am not right. Were we able to live independently of you in America, and there was a hope of my being able to refund the sum advanced, the inducements to return home would be so great that your proposition would be accepted; but there is no such hope, I am sorry to say. *You* know that my feeling towards Uncle Milton has ever remained the same.

1. Sanford was unhappy with KF's travel letters, as some of them urged abolition at a time when the States were involved in civil war. He threatened to disinherit her if she did not desist. When KF disobeyed him, Sanford carried out his threat.

To Cordelia Riddle Sanford (LW)
[1861]   [Florence]

Mr. Landor comes to see me every day, bringing me flowers, books, etc.; and although I have the very highest respect for his intellect and derive advantage from his visits, yet I do grudge passing every morning to such comparatively small profit. I console myself by thinking that I am pleasing an old man, and therefore making myself useful.[1] He sent me yesterday all the manuscript scraps in his possession, which I am to edit and publish after his death. What will Mr. Forster's biography say to this?[2] I endeavored to persuade him [Landor] otherwise; but he insisted, and I was obliged to accept them in self-defence. Mr. Landor's praise of me is too extravagant and absurd to mention. Let us hope that I may never offend him, and thereby become quite as black as I am now white, as is the case with his attached friend Forster.[3] But, Aunt Corda, Mr. Landor is a great man, the cleverest mind I have ever encountered, as well as being the most wayward,—wayward in temper and fancies. There is much good in him. His latest donations to me are a Virgil, a fine Latin dictionary, and Aubrey de Vere's[4] poems, that I fancy greatly.

1. Much as she disliked the task, KF permitted Landor to teach her Latin. Elizabeth Barrett Browning recognized KF's indulgence of Landor. From Rome she wrote: "So, Kate, you are learning Latin, & communing with Mr. Landor,—and he feels as we all do, that you are clever, dear & good & that the more we have of you the better" (LW, 129).

2. In his *Walter Savage Landor: A Biography*, 2 vols. (London: Chapman & Hall, 1869), John Forster (1812–76) drew (with acknowledgment) on KF's three-part article "Last Days of Walter Savage Landor" (*Atlantic Monthly*, April, May, June 1866), alluding to its author as "a young lady" (526).

3. Angry with Forster, Landor had terminated their correspondence for the last four years. For one thing, Forster, a barrister who had never practiced law, had caused Landor to retract his "libels" in the suit pending against him, an act that made him legally culpable and that forced him out of England for fear of bankruptcy (see *To Cordelia Riddle Sanford*, [Dec. 1860], n. 3). Also, in preparing a new edition of Landor's *Hellenics*, Forster had been delinquent and the book was published with so many misprints and errors that Landor felt violated.

4. Irish poet (1814–1902).

To Cordelia Riddle Sanford (LW)
June 29. 1861. [Florence]

Darling,

I am sick, sick at heart, for dear Mrs. Browning is dead. The news was as sudden as it is dreadful, for though she has been quite ill for a week past, yet her health has always been so feeble that I firmly believed she would rally as of yore. I believed that God had more work for her on earth before he called her to fill a glorious place in Heaven. During her illness I have not seen her once, as she was unable to converse, but I went every day, and always the report has been more encouraging. Two days ago we saw Mr. Browning, and he like myself deceived himself by founding hopes upon her powers of endurance. Yesterday Mrs. Browning said that she felt better, read a little in the "Athenaeum" and saw Miss Blagden as late as eight o'clock in the evening, who left her with but little misgiving. This morning, at half-past four, she expired unconsciously to herself with the words, "It is beautiful," upon her lips. Poor Mr. Browning was entirely unprepared for the terrible blow. When she raised herself to pronounce her dying words wherein she expressed the glorious life which was opening upon her, he thought it was simply a movement premonitory to coughing. I have not seen him, but Miss Blagden, who is constantly with him, says he is completely prostrated with grief. The poor boy wanders about the house, sad and disconsolate, hardly realizing that his angel mother is no more. We went to the house the moment we heard of Mrs. Browning's death, but could be of no use. All that we did was to buy flowers and consecrate them by placing them around all that is left of one who was too pure to remain longer in this world. They have cut off all her hair, and the emaciated form was heart-rending to look upon. I almost regret that I have seen her in death, only that I do not wish to shun the house of mourning. I am sufficiently callous as it is. Her last act to me was one of kindness, insisting upon our going up to [Blagden's] Villa Brichieri with Mr. Browning in a carriage. Almost the last thing that I did in her presence was to kneel before her, and say that when near her, I always longed to be at her feet—and she was so gentle and kind, so loving and unassuming. Her character was as perfect as God permits in the flesh. What Mr. Browning will do, I don't know. His nature is so excitable that at first I feared the consequences; that in the end this terrible loss will chasten and perfect him, I trust and pray. He who has never had any heavy affliction is now to feel its rod of iron, iron that remorselessly enters the heart and lacerates in the name of the Highest. I cannot realize what has befallen us and the world. The almost last link that binds me to Florence has been sundered, and I long more than ever to be away. Mr. Browning will surely leave Italy, and I should not be surprised did he seek a home elsewhere. Italy and his angel wife are one. Or perhaps for this very reason he will be the more ready to remain. I doubt this. Now I know nothing more than that she is dead, to-morrow we are to learn if anything can be done, and are to do it if called upon. I cannot help perceiving that Dr. Wilson, who was called in owing to the absence of [E. G. F.] Grisanowsky,[1] and who is most forbidding in physiognomy and is said by some to be a humbug, has hastened Mrs. Browning's death by resorting to a violent practice which her weak body was thoroughly incapable of enduring. He began by frightening her, telling her what a fearful state her entire system was in,—a fine way to treat an imaginative person. Grisanowsky knew her constitution, and it does seem most unfortunate that he should have been absent. Since the medical murder of Cavour,[2] I have begun to distrust all doctors in Italy. Dear Mrs. Browning had reached the age of fifty, and had labored long and nobly for humanity, therefore we must be resigned, and think that her release from a long-suffering diseased body is Heaven's reward for a pure, religious life, religious in the truest sense. I can never forget her, and hope that her memory may lead me to better things than have yet been my aspiration. I thank God that I was permitted to know her, that I can claim her as a friend, that I may look upward for one more tie binding me to a life hereafter.

1. Elizabeth Barrett Browning's physician (1824-88), a Prussian who practiced in Italy and became a familiar of the Browning-Blagden circle.

2. Camillo Benso, Conte di Cavour (1810-61); premier of Sardinia and leader in the struggle to unify Italy. As with Mrs. Browning, his physician was absent at a critical time and the substitute doctor summoned to his bedside bled him to the point of death.

To Cordelia Riddle Sanford (LW)
July 1. 1861. [Florence]

Dearest Aunt,—

I have been completely upset for the last three days,—the death of Mrs. Browning has unfitted me for doing anything. We have just returned from her funeral. We have seen all that is mortal of her buried in the beautiful Protestant burial-ground outside of Florence's walls, where lies Theodore Parker. The service was according to the Episcopal form. No discourse. Her life had been a sermon; she needed no other. It was agonizing to look on Mr. Browning—he seemed as though he could hardly stand, and his face expressed the most terrible grief. The poor boy stood beside him with tears in his eyes, and when I glanced from them to the pall where their loved one's remains lay, it seemed as though the sorrow was too much to bear. I yearned to go to Mr. Browning and weep with him that wept. The scene was made impressive in spite of the minister; it was very short, and we were hurried away by Mr. [Thomas] Trollope. A lovely wreath of white flowers and a laurel wreath were placed upon the coffin. The funeral was managed by a friend of the Brownings, and so managed that no one knew anything about anything. Orders were given in the greatest confusion during the three days, and up to this morning I was told that no ladies were to be at the grave. However, Mr. Browning expressed a wish that Miss Blagden should be present and all other friends that desired to; therefore at the last moment I sent word to those whom I knew would wish to attend, and in this way there were sorrowing women to mourn for a great woman. The funeral would have been meagre without them. I thought that Mr. Landor ought to have been there, and had I known that the service would have been so short would have gone for him. The Storys came up from Leghorn; young [Edward Robert Bulwer-]Lytton, Mr. Trollope, the Powers,[1] and others paid the last tribute to her memory. There were very few Italians; they were invited to attend, but with their usual indifference abstained from doing so, indifferent to one who loved Italy with her whole soul and labored for it with her whole intellect! England and America will mourn if Italy does not. Mr. Browning is almost heartbroken; last night he did nothing but rush through the house. He says that he will sell everything, settle up everything, and leave Italy forever,—only return to be buried beside his wife.[2] He will probably go almost immediately to Paris, where his father and sisters live. God be with him! My hold upon Italy has gone. The Brownings were dear to me; she was a guiding light, and will ever remain so, wherever I may be.

    1. Hiram Powers (1805-73), American sculptor, and his wife, Elizabeth Gibson, had settled in Florence.
    2. Browning was buried in Westminster Abbey.

To Cordelia Riddle Sanford (LW)
[July 1861]   [Florence]

    Mr. Browning has a very severe cold, and the other night he thought he was dying, being attacked by a fit of strangulation. Miss Blagden says the change in his face is marvellous. God help him! I love him more now for *her* sake. He has just written a reply to my note of sympathy, which I copy for you. "God bless you and yours for all your kindness, which I shall never forget. I cannot write now except to say this,—and, besides, that I have had great comfort from the beginning. I know you are truth itself in all you profess to feel about her. She also loved you, as *you* felt. I shall see you soon and talk to you; meantime ever remember me as your affectionate R. B." It is a great comfort to have this note,— to be told again that she *loved* me. Oh, Aunt Corda! hers was such a beautiful spirit that the tears flood up from my heart whenever I think of her, which is very, very often. We went to her grave two days ago. I could not feel that *she* was there. I hope she will think of me sometimes in the other world, and out of her love for humanity influence me for good. I did worship her as a glorious type of womanhood,—unselfish, suffering, loving, grand. She is not dead to me; but the absence of her dear face is hard to bear. I am trying to write upon her, but feel how unworthy I am for such a task. We shall probably go up to Miss Blagden to-day. She is very gloomy, of course. To me Florence is one vast camposanto [cemetery]; my hopes in it are dead. It seems as though there was to be a break up of everything.
    We passed several evenings at [Blagden's] Villa Brichieri before coming away. Mr. Browning is very subdued, very dear, and has been more than kind to us. He gave mother a favorite shawl that belonged to dear Mrs. Browning, and me a locket that she had before she was married, and of which she was very fond. In the centre is a crystal, in which is her hair shaped in two hearts. The gold around it is a serpent, emblem of eternity. I cannot tell you how much I value this souvenir. We went to [Browning's] Casa Guidi to take a last farewell of it.

Everything was just as she had left it,—the half-opened fan, the last "Nazione" that she had read, the open desk on which she had written all her poems. It was sad, very, very sad! I felt far worse than when standing at her grave. An artist here has sketched the drawing-room in oils, and has made a most satisfactory picture, not as a painting, but an account of the minute detail. He has put in everything, and the sketch brings the dear room right before you. Mr. Browning is to have it photographed, and has promised me a copy of it. He, Penini, and Miss Blagden leave to-day for Paris if all the furniture of Casa Guidi can be packed or sold in time. Miss Blagden has gotten release from her villa, stored her furniture with Mr. Trollope, and intends to pass a year at least in England. Mr. Browning does not think he shall ever return to Italy,—at least not to Florence. He says he shall never have a home again, but rove about the world. He said he might come to America some time or other. So there is nobody left in Florence but the Trollopes. You can fancy how changed the place must be to me. Dr. Grisanowsky, however, returns in the fall. I have met Lytton, the poet, several times. He talks exceedingly well, and is by no means a snob. I like to hear him converse, for there is no doubt about his being exceedingly intellectual, and he puts forth his best powers before Mr. Browning, whom he adores; but I don't like the man as a man. Although under thirty, he has the broken-down appearance of a *blasé* man of fifty. You can read dissipation in his face and in his stooping figure and shuffling gait. He is weak in character, and this one sees most readily in his poetry. There is nothing vigorous about him, nor is there anything lofty in his aspirations. There never was greater contrast in persons, as well as mind, as between him and Mr. Browning. I pity Mr. Lytton, for he has misused his life; but there is an inherent want of truth and candor about him that prevents him from ever obtaining the respect of honest, earnest natures. . . .

To Cordelia Riddle Sanford (LW)
[July 1861?]   [Florence]

I have sent it to the "Atlantic,"[1] but of course it will not be accepted, notwithstanding I said I would take no money for what was written as a tribute of love.

    1. KF's essay "Elizabeth Barrett Browning" (*Atlantic Monthly*, Sept. 1861).

Part Three: 1862–1871

⁓ Returns to America
Achieves Fame as Journalist,
Lecturer, and Author

To Theodore Tilton (B&E)
Tilton (1835–1907) was assistant editor of the *Independent*, a New York Congregationalist weekly. In 1863 he succeeded Henry Ward Beecher (1813–87) as editor.
Nov. 6. 1862.   Tremont House. Boston

Dear Sir;—

With doubts about the propriety of the thing, I submit to you an article written for a Boston magazine but received too late to be inserted immediately, and therefore useless. I don't know whether it is good enough for the "Independent" and even if good enough whether you will consider it worth the time spent in cutting down, as I suppose it would need pruning for a "weekly."[1]

As I am entirely unknown to you I will say that as a European correspondent I began to write three years ago for Boston and N. Orleans journals[2] and more recently (among other things) have written an article on Mrs. Browning that appeared in the Sept. Atlantic of last year, and a criticism on Anthony Trollope's "North America," published in the "Continental Monthly" of last September.[3] I mention all this as a reference that I may ask you whether there would be any chance for me in the "Independent" did I occasionally write short articles on leading subjects, provided such articles met your approbation. I hope you will not think me bold in thus writing to you. I am a beginner and have to fight my own battles and venture in the hopes of gaining. I am prompted to address you because I have seen and heard you when you have spoken in Boston,[4] and *know* you as having written an appreciative memorial to my dear friend, Mrs. Brown-

Kate Field as journalist.
(Courtesy Trustees of the Boston Public Library.)

ing.⁵ I thank you for that memorial. There are few men, *no* Englishmen, who would have done equal justice to her genius.

Hoping that in asking for a reply I am not intruding too much upon your time I am / Truly yours / Kate Field

I enclose stamps for return of manuscript as all the chances are against me.

1. The *Independent* was a weekly newspaper rather than a magazine. As it published only one full article per issue—Beecher's weekly sermon—nothing by KF was published in it.

2. The *Boston Courier,* the *Boston Evening Transcript,* and the *New Orleans Daily Picayune.*

3. Discussed by Carolyn J. Moss in "My Most Chosen Friend: Kate Field's Review of *North America,*" *Trollopiana* 23 (Nov. 1993): 15-19.

4. Tilton was a popular lyceum lecturer who crusaded for emancipation and the women's rights movement.

5. Tilton's memorial appeared in *Last Poems by Elizabeth Barrett Browning,* the fourth volume of a five-volume series (New York: J. Miller, 1862-63), each volume of which bore its own special title. This series was pirated from the three-volume edition published by Chapman & Hall (London, 1862).

To Mary Davenport Claflin (RBH)
Wife of William Claflin (1818-1905), businessman and politician who became governor of Massachusetts in 1869.
June 29. 1863. Nonantum Hill [Newton, Mass.]

Dear Mrs. Claflin;—

We [my mother and I] expect to start for Sharon [Springs][1] next Thursday morning and before I leave I want to appeal to your good husband in behalf of a friend of mine (Mr. Trollope of Florence) who writes to me for *autographs.* Now, as Mr. Claflin is in the way of politics and politicians, it seems to me he might give me a [Charles] Sumner[2] and a few autographs of some Washington big wigs. Can he? Don't ask him if he is very much bothered.

I have sent you a review of Mrs. Browning's Essays[3]—it is not very good but it may give you a little more insight into the Essays should you read them. In case you can get me autographs I will tell you that my address for the present is care of Mr. Sanford, Tremont House [in Boston]. Can't you persuade Mr. Claflin to come to Sharon instead of going to Saratoga? We'll get you rooms. Sulphur [Springs] is a great deal nicer than Congress water.

1. Popular New York spa.
2. Sumner (1811-74), a U.S. senator, was among the first in the Senate to advocate emancipation and equal rights for blacks.
3. KF's review "Mrs. Browning's Essays on the Poets," which had appeared anonymously in the *Christian Examiner* (July 1863). KF reviewed Elizabeth Barrett Browning's *Essays on the Greek Christian Poets and the English Poets* in the fifth and final volume of *The Works of Elizabeth Barrett Browning* (see To Theodore Tilton, 6 Nov. 1862).

To Noah Miller Ludlow (MHS-LFM)
Feb. 13. 1868. 108 W. 27th St. New York

Dear Mr. Ludlow;—

Many thanks for introducing us [mother and me] to your Seven Sisters.[1] We were much pleased to make their acquaintance. I write now to say that I shall return the compliment by sending you my book on Dickens[2] as soon as it is issued. I enclose the publisher's circular.

Desirous that the little book should sell in the South where Dickens the actor is not known,[3] I want if possible to have said book noticed in the newspapers. If I send you several copies will you hand them to editors in New Orleans and Mobile who will be likely to give some heed to the book? I should think The

Picayune and also Mobile papers to whom father is so well known. What do you think about it? Please be good enough to write me a few lines on the subject.

I hope Sophy[4] received a song that I sent her lately.

We shall break up next spring, store our furniture for the summer (rents being awfully high), go into New England and return to New York late in the autumn. At least this is our present plan.

Mr. [James E.] Murdoch[5] called on us today. He looks wonderfully well and has a most powerful voice in the Reading Room.

... I should be glad to have the book announced before its appearance.

1. *The Seven Little Sisters Who Live on the Round Ball That Floats in the Air* (1861) by Jane Andrews (1835–87).
2. *Pen Photographs of Charles Dickens' Readings: Taken from Life* (1868).
3. Dickens, still on his American reading tour, had excluded the South from his itinerary.
4. KF's cousin, younger daughter of Cornelia and Matthew Field, and Ludlow's granddaughter.
5. Actor and lecturer (1812–93); had acted at times with KF's mother.

To Agnes Claflin (RBH)
Daughter of Mary and William Claflin.
April 10. 1868.   8 Walnut St. Boston

... I *do* wish you had heard Dickens the last evening he read here.[1] His heart was in his mouth and in his eyes and when he made his farewell speech, the audience *choked up*, positively. I never heard anything so feelingly delivered. ...

1. On 8 April 1868 Dickens gave his last reading in Boston before concluding his reading tour in New York on 20 April. KF recorded the event in her diary: "Dickens['s] last night. [His program included] Dr. Marigold and Mrs. Gamp. Great house and great enthusiasm. Mrs. Wales, florist, sent an exquisite basket of flowers; from Mrs. [Annie] Fields a palm leaf inlaid with flowers; I a lovely little basket of pansies. On the card I wrote:—A little western flower / That's for thoughts. It was a memorable night" (LW, 182). In *A Midsummer Night's Dream* (II.i.165–67), Oberon tells Puck that he had "mark'd . . . where the bolt of Cupid fell / . . . upon a little western flower, / Before milk-white, now purple with love's wound." In the language of flowers, pansies symbolize thoughts. If KF was taken with Dickens, the feeling was mutual. On 3 January 1868 he sent her this note: "My dear Miss Kate Field,—I entreat you to accept my most cordial thanks for your charming New Year's present [a basket of violets]. . . . But I must avow that nothing in the pretty basket of flowers was *quite* so interesting to me as a certain bright, fresh face I had seen at my readings which I am told you may see when you look in the glass" (LW, 382).

To Charles Dickens (BPL)
April 14. 1868.   108 W. 27th St. New York

Honored Sir;—

In Boston, last week [after your reading], I had sufficient courage to tell you that I owed you so heavy a debt as to be unable to pay even the interest, and you were kind enough to say that you would give me a receipt for the whole amount. Will you think me presumptuous if I ask you to write this receipt beneath the accompanying engraving [of yourself]? Without it, I shall be bankrupt; with it, I shall be more than ever, / Gratefully, / Kate Field

To Albert Baldwin (LW)

Identified but unnamed by Lilian Whiting (LW, 190) as the wealthy American artist KF met in Florence (see *To Cordelia Riddle Sanford*, [Jan. 1861]). Regina Soria provided his name in *Elihu Vedder: American Visionary Artist in Rome* (Rutherford, N.J.: Fairleigh Dickinson University Press, 1970), 31. Soria added: "It is quite evident from letters in the Vedder Archives that Vedder and the other young men in Florence knew of Baldwin's infatuation [with KF]." Whiting remarked that "a large package of his [Baldwin's] letters are among the voluminous records of her [KF's] life" (LW, 190). Except for two fragments published by Whiting, however, Baldwin's letters have disappeared—at least they are not in the Kate Field Collection presented by Whiting to the Boston Public Library.
May 31. 1868.   [108 W. 27th St.] New York

It is five months since I received your last letter, and you undoubtedly imagine that my silence has been owing to disgust or indignation. Neither. I was at first disgusted, naturally, and therefore put your letter aside until I should be perfectly cool. The coolness came much before leisure. I have been so engrossed in business, people, and things—Dickens, especially, about whom I have written a series of photographs in book form[1]—that I have never seen the moment until now that I could sit down and tell you my opinion of you and your letter.

First let me tell you that I renewed our correspondence after a year's cessation because I heard you were very ill, and because I at that time could write to you, having no other feeling toward you than that of a friend. I supposed you would understand this from the fact of my writing at all. It seemed to me consequently that your letters were anything but friendly, even brutal at times, but I so believed in your honesty and principle that I gave you the benefit of the doubt and laid all the shortcomings to bad health. We are the slaves of our nerves.

The letter you wrote last December ought to have been written in 1862. You were a moral coward not to have written it then. Now you know you were; therefore I shall say nothing further because I don't care. That episode has passed out of my life, and is as dead to me as if it were buried six feet under ground. The friendship I entertained for you is very sensibly diminished by knowing more of your real character, but I have, at the same time, a certain respect for a man who even at the eleventh hour will voluntarily enter the confessional and show himself in his true colors.

By not writing that letter you made me fancy that I had allowed myself to be much more interested in you than you were in me. This is what made me so indignant *with myself* that ever since I have been trying to make the *amende honorable* by showing you that I was, after all, nothing more than a friend, that I had recovered from the delusion, after considerable mortification. Now I know that I was no such fool, that you were deeply interested in me, as I had reason to suppose at the time. I was young then and inexperienced, but not so inexperienced as to fancy myself admired without any foundation. This has always been the mystery to me,—that I, who never imagine I am making impressions, who give men the widest possible margin and rarely believe a word they say—when it comes to sentiment—should have made such an idiot of myself.

Your tardy letter assures me that I was not this idiot, and my regard for my own common sense is much greater than it has been for six years. I thank God that you did not remain longer in Florence and that I did not tarry in Paris, for had you offered me your hand, I should have accepted it, believing you to be other than you are,—and been cured. When my eyes open they open very wide. I am not one to submit tamely to wrong, and separation if not divorce would have been the inevitable consequence of such an ill-assorted union. You do well to say that you will never marry. No woman should be subjected to such a miserable fate. As a single man, infidelity hurts no one but yourself, provided you have honor enough to confine your flirtations to those who are educated in the art. I have no sympathy with flirtation. It must be a very cold nature that can play with fire. Neither do I admire fickleness. But your nature in no way concerns me, and pray don't imagine that I am lecturing. I am simply giving my opinion of you and your letter. It is unavoidable, and is given for the very last time.

I am not the Deity and having no claims to perfection do not intend to visit anathemas upon your head. You undoubtedly have many admirable qualities, and so long as you live I shall have hope of you. I believe that the time will come when you will be tired of your present order of exercises, and will care for more earnest friends. If you desire to retain me as an earnest friend, you can. I shall never flirt with you, never entertain you flippantly, *never go down to your lower nature.* You must come to me with the best there is in you. I will never tolerate any more cruel, unkind letters. Now we understand each other. If you choose to accept my terms, you can. If you do not care to do so, why, we will part. If ever I meet you it will be in the kindliest manner, for I shall always wish for you health, happiness, and ultimate regeneration. There is something of divinity in you, and the sooner it develops the better for you. You may laugh, but if you have a heart it will be more inclined to weep that a beautiful dream has vanished into such thin air.² / Yours earnestly, / The Once Mistaken

    1. *Pen Photographs of Charles Dickens's Readings: Taken from Life* (1868).

    2. Five months elapsed before Baldwin replied: "Your offer of 'earnest friendship' is magnanimous; but permit me to observe that friendship can only exist between *equals*. If I ever attain to your level, I shall eagerly accept your generous offer" (LW, 193-94). In 1871 KF recorded in her diary that "this man has made a long journey to ask my forgiveness and declare his love, and I have refused him" (LW, 193).

To Thomas Wentworth Higginson (BPL)
    Higginson (1823-1911) was a Unitarian minister, versatile author, and colonel of the first regiment of black soldiers during the Civil War. He and Mabel Todd were Emily Dickinson's first editors.

Oct. 15. 1868.   Charlestown [Mass.]¹

Dear Col. Higginson;—
    It was so very good and kind of you to send me that copy of Mary W[ollstonecraft]'s "[A Vindication of the] Rights of Women" [1792]. Believe that I am grateful. It was just the book I wanted and, of course, you being a Special Providence, gave it to me. Every now and then I shall say a prayer to you, just as the Catholics do to their patron saints.

    Don't I begin to look back upon the quiet of Newport with a sort of envy? I've been whirled about the suburbs of Boston to such an extent that I'm beginning to feel very much as if I were performing on the trapezes; but it's at an end now and my yesterday's work was room-hunting. I think I must have mounted a mile of stairs, all told, and for what? To inspect dirt, discomfort and the odors of Arabia *In*felix [infelicity].

    We have about determined to engage board at a very nice (new) hotel in Charlestown Square, provided the proprietor "appreciates us very highly" and reduces his prices. We are now in the diplomatic phase and know not what the day may bring forth. If I am not settled soon I shan't have any mind worth "improving." One thing, in *my* farming, no *draining* is necessary.²

    I thank you too for the criticism on my rhymes. It is not severe enough I fancy, but I'll try to take your excellent hints.

    I heard Emerson³ Monday night and was wofully disappointed. It seemed to me a lecture on anything but Art, with neither beginning, middle nor end, with nothing to take hold of and really not such a deal of axiomatic thought. Then his manner of delivery drove me wild. He stumbled over his words, he said *doo*ty, stat*ue*s for stat*ue*s and other horrid things, lost his place twice and once I thought he'd look in his boots for the mss. Not one murmur or round of applause throughout. I never suffered such agony and Mrs. Fields owns up that Emerson *never* gave her so little. The audience was a regular brain party.

Sunday night I met Lowell,[4] &c &c. and Thackeray's daughter [Anne] at the [James T.] Fields's. She was queerly dressed but seemed to be nice. Mr. [Herman] Merivale[5] was there and entertained me the whole evening. Today he is coming to say "goodbye."

You don't know how Mr. Fields praises your story. I am on the *qui vive* to read it.

Mother joins me in love to your wife. Don't we wish *we* had a farm and sold quinces and rang our own bells.

1. KF and her mother were staying in this Boston suburb with Edward Riddle, KF's uncle.
2. Refers to Higginson's complaint about his farm.
3. Ralph Waldo Emerson (1803–82), who, by his publications and lectures, became the father of American Transcendentalism. At sixty-five, judging from KF's observations, he had begun his slide into senility.
4. James Russell Lowell (1819–91), poet, literary critic, and Harvard professor of French and Spanish.
5. English playwright (1839–1906).

To Mary Louise Booth (HL)
Editor of *Harper's Bazar* (1831–89).
Nov. 11. 1868.   St. James Hotel. Boston

Dear Miss Booth;—

If I have not before replied to your kind letter, my silence has been in no way owing to forgetfulness. Life, as you know, is so crowded that it is impossible to be one's self. Every night do I groan in spirit, saying, "I have done those things which I ought not to have done, and have left undone what I ought to have done."[1] I know I'm a miserable sinner, but I also know that I shall never be anything else in *this* world. What another existence may have in store for me I can not tell, although Planchette[2] promises lots of agreeable society and sympathetic communing. Planchette tells so many lies however, that I dare not hope. Apropos, don't be disgusted if Mr. [Justus Starr] Redfield[3] obeys my instructions and sends you a brochure of mine which he will issue next week, entitled

Planchette's Diary / Edited by Kate Field.

If the Bazar makes fun of it, I shall be almost as obliged as if it treated the Diary with serious consideration.[4]

I wish you would send me those papers containing the articles you were to have shown me in New York. The last attack [on me] from the Sorosis[5] occurred in September when I was considered (*in print*) to be Becky Sharp's[6] superior in shrewdness and impudence and was altogether about as horrible a woman as you would like to encounter in Broadway! Of such is the kingdom of Sorosis.

Here [in Boston] there is a woman's Club worth talking about, to which men as well as our sex are eligible and which gave a reception the other night. The best women in Boston are members, its objects are most praiseworthy and its success undoubted. I am a member *but I belong to no committees*. To be a passenger is better than to be captain, as I have found to my cost.

I am here for the winter but expect to be in New York during next month when I hope to see you. If you meet Mrs. [Anne Charlotte Lynch] Botta[7] give her my love and address, and ask her to let me know how she is. . . .

1. "We have left undone those things which we ought to have done; And we have done those things which we ought not to have done." This quotation appears on page 6 of all versions of the Book of Common Prayer under "Morning Prayer."

2. A three-cornered or heart-shaped board with pencil attached that supposedly spells out messages under spirit guidance.

3. New York publisher (1810–88); issued KF's *Planchette's Diary* in 1868. In her book KF reported messages she supposedly received from her dead father; hence, "Edited by Kate Field."

4. *Harper's Bazar*, 26 Dec. 1868, remarked: "Mr. C. H. Webb in his witty article ["Confessions of a Reformed Planchettist"] in *Harper's Monthly* for December, calls Planchette an animated humbug, while Miss Field vouches for its gift of prophecy, though often a lying one."

5. First professional women's club in America; founded in 1868 by KF, Fanny Fern, Alice Carey, and Jenny June in consequence of being barred from the all-male Press Club Dinner held at Delmonico's to bid farewell to Dickens.

6. Character in Thackeray's *Vanity Fair* (1847–48).

7. New York author and literary hostess (1815–91); her husband Vincenzo was Professor of Italian at New York University. Among those who attended her salon were Poe, Emerson, Bryant, Greeley, Trollope, Thackeray, and Matthew Arnold.

To Theodore Tilton (UV-F)
March 17. 1869.   St. James Hotel. Boston

Dear Mr. Tilton;—

Nearly a year ago you and I talked about my lecturing. I am now about to make the plunge. On the 31st of this month I am (D.V.)[1] to appear at Chickering Hall. Subject—"Woman in the Lyceum."[2] The essay has been read before several critics, before the Women's Club, and they are pleased; so I am to make the venture. If I succeed it would be pleasant to have a good word from *The Independent.* What say you? Col. Higginson might do it if he comes from Newport to hear me as I hope he will.

Of course my success depends upon myself, but the Press is a power.

1. *Deo volente,* "God willing."
2. An argument for a woman's right to lecture as a career.

To Mary Elizabeth Channing Higginson (BPL)
Wife (d. 1877) of Thomas Wentworth Higginson.
April 5. 1869. St. James [Hotel]. Boston

Dear Mrs. Higginson;—

I am very grateful for your and the Colonel's congratulations,[1] and wish I might have had a glimpse of your handwriting for the first time in my life.

Yes, I have not failed; at least this can be said. When such different men as E[dwin]. P[ercy]. Whipple,[2] [James T.] Fields, [John Turner] Sargent,[3] Governor Claflin, Dr. [Samuel Kirkland] Lothrop,[4] *Col. Greene,* (*Post-Democrat*), [Arch] *Selwyn* the [owner and] manager of Selwyn's Theatre, all the representatives of the Press, and men and women who went to hear me *in spite of my subject* were all unanimous in praise, there really must be something in it. The [Boston] Transcript notice was written by Mr. Whipple, and he believes *all* he wrote. I could not ask for more. I enclose the letter to the Springfield Republican. It would do me no harm to have it copied into a Newport paper. Edward [Smith] King[5] wrote it.

Mr. Fields got up the paper of invitation, in consequence of which I repeat my lecture next Monday afternoon. *Can* not Colonel H. come? I've a ticket all ready for him and *it* begs him to accept it. Will he?

There is some talk of my going to [lecture in] Newton [Massachusetts]; that will be decided tomorrow. The Parker Fraternity talk of engaging me for next season I believe, and a Mr. Richmond [a lecture agent], one of Beecher's pillars (who heard me) says he will take all the risks if I will go to New York and Brooklyn this season. He was intent upon my leaving *presto* but I know New York and I'd rather wait until I have had more practice. My desire is to lecture in Worcester and Springfield, then to go to New York (where I am to visit my aunt) [and there] first try Brooklyn, and then if possible make a venture in the Union League theatre, after which I am promised a success in Buffalo by David Gray of the Courier (Buffalo) who volunteers to manage everything. This accomplished, retire for the season, write two or three lectures, put an agent on the scent and see what turns up.

Mr. [Henry A.] McGlenen, the business man of Selwyn's theatre, has managed for me so well that I think I'll let him do my work. He is very much interested in me, is very cool, shrewd, understands the public, and takes no end of trouble to accomplish his purposes. However I'll take counsel before deciding and bear Medbury [a lecture agent] in mind.

I'd like to try myself on a Newport audience. Is there any chance? I'd come down if a hundred people at $1.00 a ticket were collected in a good-sized parlor, and I'd read the essay to you in private besides, if you cared to hear it.

I sit down because the essay is thoroughly colloquial and there is no earthly reason why I should stand until the end, when I rise with good effect, they say.

It is too bad that we are not to hear the Colonel tonight. I had prepared a puff for him to be sent to the *Mail* (N.Y.) for which I now correspond.

This letter is all about myself, but as you have brought it upon yourself you must forgive me.

Hoping the wheels of housekeeping run smoother, and with regards to the Colonel. . . .

1. On hearing of KF's successful debut as a lecturer with her "Woman in the Lyceum."
2. American literary critic (1819-86).
3. Boston Unitarian minister (d. 1877).
4. Lothrop (1804-86), a Harvard Doctor of Divinity, was minister of Brattle Square Church in Boston.
5. King (1848-96) was a journalist with the *Springfield Republican*; he later joined the *New York Herald*.

To Henry A. McGlenen (HC)
Theatrical agent; later, business manager of the Boston Theatre.
May 5. 1869.   Westminster [Hotel]. New York

Dear Mr. McGlenen;—

I didn't make much money Monday night, but I *did* make a great deal of reputation.[1] Beecher introduced me in the sweetest way and Theodore Tilton, Dr. [Richard Salter] Storrs[2] and the newspaper men pronounce me a real success. I enclose such notices as I have seen. "More remains behind."[3] No influence was employed in Brooklyn to get me an audience and I am amazed that 500 people—intelligent people—collected together. Next time I'll charge a dollar [a ticket]. You don't catch me doing the 50 ct. business again in a big town where I am known.

The sale of tickets for New York begins tomorrow—at Union League Club, Rullman's [brokerage] in Wall St. and Beer & Schirmer's [music store]. I'll have my friends this time. In Brooklyn I read to strangers, but they made the most demonstrative audience I have had yet.

How about Providence?

I told Mr. Moore[4] to telegraph you on Monday night.

Mrs. Stowe was very complimentary.

1. KF had lectured on "Woman in the Lyceum" at Henry Ward Beecher's Plymouth Church.
2. Storrs (1821–1900) was an author, lyceum lecturer, and Congregational minister at the Church of the Pilgrims in Brooklyn.
3. Echo from *Hamlet* (III.iv.179): "Thus bad begins and worse remains behind."
4. Presumed to be George Henry Moore (1823–92), Executive Committee Secretary of the New-York Historical Society. Moore may have wanted to arrange for KF to lecture at the Society.

To Mary Aurelia Anthony (HC)

Wife of Andrew Varick Stout Anthony (1835–1906), art director for the Boston publishing firm of Fields, Osgood & Co.

May 7. 1869.   Westminster [Hotel, New York]

Dear M. A.;—

I've been keeping very respectable company lately, but I don't feel any the better for it; which shows what an awful creature I am. When Beecher introduced me to the combined intellect of Brooklyn,[1] I felt like a fool, but the feeling seemed to agree with the occasion, as the verdict passed was in my favor. I really don't understand why people are so much pleased. I wouldn't be if *I* were the audience. I'd find all manner of fault. The New York papers came out strong in my praise the next day, and this I am told is an extraordinary compliment. Such notices of a Brooklyn amusement are most unusual. So much for having friends at court. The Herald kept silent, but today it gives me a good paragraph.

[Euphrosyne] Parepa-Rosa[2] did not pay expenses the other night in Brooklyn, and I did. So I suppose it *was* a success.

Dear me! I wore that everlasting blue and white dress which the reporters turned into *green* and white. And my hair is *black* and I am *just eighteen*. Now I didn't pay for this last item, believe me.

But, I *am* to have a new dress for Monday night—a very pretty white muslin. Oh, I'm quite content about clothes. I've had a present of a black silk walking suit and a very stylish hat, black, with *field* flowers, lace and Roman ribbon. My uncle is behaving like an angel of light.

I think that I shall have a good house on Monday. The Union League Club[3] is interested and I seem to have unknown friends. People *are* so very good to me, but I was just the same person two months ago. Yet none of these new found admirers would have dreamed of helping me had I sat at home and stared poverty in the face. This success *is all* a satire to me. I remember those who liked me before I read an ordinary essay in public.

Yesterday I dined at the Bottas with Whitelaw Reid, the intended successor of [John Russell] Young on *The Tribune*.[4] He is a *young* man and a clever man; good looking and looking good—I *think* he is honest. I sat beside him at table and we "got on" very fast. *He* is my friend on *The Tribune. He*, not Young, has superintended my notices, and I fancy that my opportunities on The Tribune will be much greater when J.R.Y. retires into a disreputable obscurity. Horace Greeley is my friend, they say.

At the Botta dinner were the Ripleys[5]—who sail for Europe next Wednesday—Mrs. [Lucia Gilbert] Calhoun[6], the [Justin] McCarthys,[7] &c. Mrs. Calhoun has shown herself as kind as kind can be, and has received orders from The Tribune to do me into an editorial for next Tuesday morning. Look out for it.

Mother is not well, neither am I. This knocking about without a place to call "home" is not to my taste. But some people require a lot of discipline, and so I accept the inevitable.

New York is gay, but I haven't made up my mind that I like it as well as Boston. I *seem* to have more friends here, but the weather is diabolical. Thanks to the always good Mr. [James R.] Osgood[8] we have a $40 per week suite of rooms for $3 per day, and Mr. Ferrin[9] & his clerks are as polite as if they made lots of money out of me. This virtue is touching.

Perhaps I may run on to Boston for a few days during Anniversary week.[10]

This letter is full of myself and I am disgusted. Repay me in the same and believe me / Ever yours sincerely / Kate Field

Mother sends regards. Ask your boy what my name is. There's nothing like *object* teaching for persecuting children.

1. To give her lecture "Woman in the Lyceum" at his Plymouth Church.
2. English soprano of Romanian descent (1836-74).
3. Organized during the Civil War to promote the Northern cause; now a conservative social club.
4. Reid (1837-1912) was associate editor of the *Tribune*. Young (1840-99) was the *Tribune*'s managing editor. Young had been publicly exposed as a violator of the Associated Press's bylaws, and Greeley was planning to dismiss him and replace him with Reid.
5. Louisa (b. 1832) and George (1802-80). The latter succeeded Margaret Fuller (1810-50) as the *Tribune*'s literary critic. Their marriage was a second one for the widow and widower. As Louisa was thirty years younger than himself, Ripley first offered to adopt her as his daughter.
6. Journalist (b. 1844); like KF, associated with the *Tribune*. Her enthusiastic review of KF's lecture on "Woman in the Lyceum" appeared in the *Tribune* on 11 May 1869.
7. He was an Irish journalist, historian, and novelist (1830-1912); married to Charlotte Allman (d. 1879).
8. Osgood (1836-92) was a junior member of Ticknor & Fields. He became a partner in Fields,

Osgood & Co. on Ticknor's retirement in 1869 and founded his own publishing house, J. R. Osgood & Co., in 1871.

    9. Manager of the Westminster Hotel.

    10. The thirty-sixth anniversary of the founding of the American Anti-Slavery Society.

To Mary Aurelia Anthony (HC)
May 11. [1869]   [Westminster Hotel, New York]

Dear M. A.

Am *not* going to [lecture in] Providence [R.I.]. Decided to run no risks late in the season. A decided success last night.[1] Crowded house. "The most brilliant audience I ever saw in New York" said Mr. Ripley who congratulated me this morning. Very fashionable and intellectual; not demonstrative in consequence. But I was assured, as in Boston,[2] that I *had* pleased. An awful ordeal and I am glad that it is over. Horace Greeley there, [name indecipherable], [Henry Theodore] Tuckerman,[3] Bottas, McCarthys, [the Robert Ogden] Doremuses,[4] Prof. Horsford,[5] Whitelaw Reid, Fields etc. Notices in Tribune, Herald & Sun.

    1. KF's first lecture in New York; held at the Union League Club Theatre.

    2. Where KF had debuted as a lecturer.

    3. Popular American littérateur (1813–71), best known for *America and Her Commentators* (1864).

    4. Doremuse (1824–1906) was a Professor of Chemistry and the president of the New York Philharmonic Society.

    5. Unidentified.

To Mary Aurelia Anthony (HC)
May 21. 1869.   Westminster Hotel. New York

Dear M.A.;—

"What has become of me?" I really don't know. I *feel* as if *something* ought to happen.—An earthquake for instance,—but the world goes on about as it did before I got into the papers as a "female lecturer." That word "female" always gives me a spasm and to be called a *female* where *woman* would do vastly better, makes me indignant. But then I am always indignant about something, which proves how I am not a philosopher. . . .

We shall return to Boston immediately after the races[1] (June 13) and remain there until we plunge into the [Adirondack] Wilderness [on 5 July]. Where we shall be the Lord only knows. I *won't* go to the South End [of Boston] again. It is disagreeable and unhealthy *entre nous*. Don't tell.

Our remaining here is good for mother and for me too I think. We required a change of scene and air. The climate here is better for mother. Then we have better food and the fresh air of the [Central] park, to which we drive constantly, is invigorating. Aunt Corda is very sweet and my uncle is as good as she is. It is very nice to be petted you know, and I can't get along without it very well. Everybody I meet is friendly—more so than ever before,—and I feel that lecturing has not hurt me in the world's esteem. No one is more surprised than myself, for I had anticipated attack and slight. I have had all sorts of offers, over some of which you would die laughing if it were fair to tell you about them, but it isn't.

No I was not at the Women's Bureau[2] although the papers said I was. Fear of meeting Sorosisters[3] kept me away. I can't take hypocrites by the hand and not be one myself. As for the Equal Rights meetings here! They made me sick at heart. I went one evening and heard Olive Logan, Rev. Antoinette Brown Blackwell, Phoebe Couzins and Mrs. [Mary Ashton Rice] Livermore.[4] Olive Logan is the only disgusting woman *as a woman* that I have ever seen on the Women's platform. Others may be unladylike, vituperative, ungraceful, ugly, but they are true self-sacrificing and *in earnest. Miss* Logan (who is a married woman with two children whom she gave up all right to, in order to get a divorce from her husband without any difficulty), was dressed in the *loudest* style, squirmed as if she were preparing to dance the can-can, had all the wretched little affectations of a school-girl of fifteen, ogled the audience which she addressed with the utmost familiarity, talked trash and told—to my knowledge—no less than three lies. She had the impudence to say that her Boston audience refused to sit out her lecture *because she was a woman*. Her egotism far exceeded [George Francis] Train's[5] and her attack upon the stage was indelicately worded and her mannerisms were those of a fourth-rate actress. Her stock in trade is first, unparalleled assurance—secondly, an excellent voice—third, a good presence. She is a disgrace to the ranks she has joined and Mrs. [Elizabeth Cady] Stanton and Miss Susan B. Anthony will never make converts of *ladies* as long as such examples of unwomanliness are set up on a rostrum for the judicious to scout at. I, for one, have withdrawn even my moral support. I want no suffrage for myself if the world is to witness such howling spectacles. There is enough for good women to do, quietly.

Do go to the Boston Women's Convention and see what *they* do.

Think of Dickens not being able to read again for months. How disappointed the Fieldses will be![6]

Your birthday eh? Well, I'll send you those gloves and some photographs when Mr. Osgood comes on, if he will be good and take them. Mother sends regards. How I have rambled on!

The King is dead! Long live the King! Young is disgraced. Whitelaw Reid ascends the throne. Reid is Western and a friend of [William Dean] Howells.[7]

1. In Saratoga, where Sanford, KF's uncle, raced horses.
2. A New York house near Fifth Avenue donated by the wealthy Elizabeth B. Phelps to serve as a

Whitelaw Reid, managing editor of the *New York Tribune*.
(From *Harper's Weekly*, 1 July 1871.)

center for women's organizations. Phelps closed it down after a year because of the constant conflict between conservative and radical women's groups.

    3. Members of the Sorosis Club who no longer met at the Women's Bureau because of such radical agitators for women's rights as Elizabeth Cady Stanton (1815-1902) and Susan B. Anthony (1820-1906).

    4. Lecturers on women's rights.

    5. Train (1829-1904) was a Fenian lecturer who made himself a laughingstock.

    6. When Dickens returned to England, he "read" in London, then in the provinces. By May 1869, when Annie and James T. Fields visited Dickens, he had concluded his tour and was not at all well.

    7. See *To Mary Aurelia Anthony*, 7 May 1869, n. 4. Reid hailed from Ohio, as did Howells (1837-1920), the novelist, magazine editor, and literary critic.

To Whitelaw Reid (MU)
June 21. 1869.   Boston

Dear Mr. Reid;—

    Your telegram was very thoughtful and exceedingly welcome—as you can imagine my nervousness at so new a business[1]—and I am delighted that you were content. I have written four letters in all [about the Peace Jubilee],[2] one more than you suggested, but I couldn't stop in the middle of things and I hope you will print the remaining two. *Now* I could write a sound article on the real good and significance of the Peace Jubilee.

I hope Mr. [John Rose Greene] Hassard[3] found me as agreeable as I found him. He is a gentleman and was most courteous. All the newspaper officials treated me splendidly. That *World* man ought to be hung. Is lying wit? I never nibbled a pink pencil in my life, and as for the Old Testament?—

In a scrawl on Saturday p.m. I asked whether you'd take the débris of the Jubilee, or Class Day at Harvard, or Ida Lewis in a life boat at Newport.[4]

Will you be good enough to send me a check for Jockey Club leader, and Jubilee letters, as I am going to the Adirondacks July 5th and need all I can get for my outfit.

I suppose you will not come on to gaze at the remains of the Coliseum.[5]

My expenses [for covering the Jubilee] were: carriage for ball $5.00, shows 1.00, messenger l.00, for letters to midnight mail 7.00.

1. KF had recently become a freelance correspondent for the *Tribune*.
2. The Jubilee, held 15-21 June 1869, was called the "grandest musical enterprise the world has ever witnessed," with popular and classical music performed. The chorus consisted of ten thousand voices accompanied by a thousand instruments (*Harper's Weekly*, 19 June 1869).
3. Hassard (1836-88) was the *Tribune*'s arts critic.
4. KF's suggestions for articles. Lewis, living with her father, the lighthouse keeper at Lime Rock off the Rhode Island coast, was celebrated for rescuing shipwrecked mariners in her lifeboat. Before an audience of two thousand admirers, Lewis was presented with a new lifeboat, a gift from James Gordon Bennett, Jr., assistant editor of the *New York Herald* (*Tribune*, 5 July 1869).
5. Erected for the Jubilee.

To Whitelaw Reid (MU)
June 25. 1869.   Boston

Dear Mr. Reid;—

... July 5th I go to the Adirondacks to be absent until August. Then I *may* pass a week with my aunt at Saratoga, after which I retire to a row-boat (D.V.) in Newport Harbor.

Do you want anything more of me this Summer in case any of these places offer material? And if you do, will you write a little note to the effect that I am a Tribune correspondent? It gives one more facilities than can be had by an unprotected female in the character of a private individual.

Ida Lewis does not perform until July 4th. Too late for me.[1] Check all right. / Yours truly / Kate Field

... If you would know how he [Charles Frederick Briggs] loves me, read

Table Talk in July Putnam['s Monthly Magazine].[2] Mrs. Calhoun told me that he did not hear my lecture. There are men—and—men.

>   1. KF's plan to go to the Adirondacks with her mother conflicted with Lewis's lecture on her experience in rescuing seamen.
>   2. Briggs (1804–77), editor of *Putnam's*, published a put-down of KF's "Woman in the Lyceum" under his pen name, "Harry Franco."

To Noah Miller Ludlow (MHS-LFM)
July 3. 1869.   Boston

Dear Mr. Ludlow;—

Answering your last letter by sending a newspaper, I have found no time to treat you with more courtesy until now, and *now* I am driven to death. Tomorrow we leave for the Adirondacks to be absent for one month, after which we expect to go to Newport. Mother goes too, as she never *will* desert Mrs. Micawber,[1] but how she will enjoy black flies and camping out, is a question to be solved hereafter. Our regular address is Care of Fields, Osgood & Co. Boston, and if you *do* carry out your intention of coming to the East, be sure and let us know. Our silence will mean that we are still in the Wilderness.

Many thanks for your photograph and for the account of your complimentary benefit which was flattering, certainly. Mother says she would have acted for you, had she been in St. Louis.[2]

Yes, I've gone into the Lyceum because it pays better than anything else, and I am tired of grubbing along. They say I have been very successful and I believe the general verdict is that I lose none of my womanliness in the effort. There is no more reason why a woman should not lecture than that she should not sing or act. At least I shall try to make lecturing fashionable as well as profitable. Our love to all. Mother is tolerably well and sends greeting from the bottom of a trunk.

>   1. A character in *David Copperfield* who remarks that she "never will desert Mr. Micawber."
>   2. KF's parents had both acted for the theatrical company of Ludlow & Smith.

To Whitelaw Reid (MU)
July 4. 1869.   Boston

Dear Mr. Reid;—

The very generous "certificate"[1] has arrived and I hope that I shall not bring discredit on *The Tribune*.

Now I write to ask whether you would care to let me review [John] Forster's biography of Landor. It is a big book and one not likely to interest many, therefore it has occurred to me that your regular critic [George Ripley] might be quite willing to turn it over to somebody else. My acquaintance with the old lion [Landor] is the only motive that would prompt me to touch the book.[2]

Should you accept my proposition, I must be allowed *time*. Landor will keep; at present I am incapable of thinking of him. Answer just as if I were not to plunge into the [Adirondack] Wilderness tomorrow.

I shall visit John Brown's[3] grave with *my* knapsack strapped upon my back, and hope to live to tell the *moving* tale.

If I do not, do you write a not unkindly obituary in The Tribune. Say that I did my "level best."

---

1. Letter certifying that KF represented the *Tribune*.

2. KF's unsigned review of the biography appeared on 17 August 1869. See also *To Cordelia Riddle Sanford*, [1861], n. 2.

3. Abolitionist (1800–1859); executed for attempting to capture the U.S. Armory at Harpers Ferry with the intention of arming slaves so that they might achieve freedom from their slaveholders. Brown was buried on his farm in the Adirondacks.

To Whitelaw Reid (MU)
Aug. 6. 1869.   Union Hotel. Saratoga Springs [N.Y.]

Dear Mr. Reid;—

Have just returned from the Wilderness weighing *14 lbs.* extra. I send you a matter of fact [press] letter because people are growling at [Rev. William Henry Harrison] Murray's fancy.[1] I'll try and send you some better ones, now that my mind is relieved of said fact.

My next [press letter] may be a Saratoga homily.

I leave here on Wednesday next, for Boston—then to Newport.

The racing men are laughing at your Saratoga reporter.

---

1. Refers to *Adventures in the Wilderness; or, Camp-Life in the Adirondacks* (1869), one of "Adirondack Murray's" many best-selling books on the subject. KF's three-installment letter on Murray's "fancy" and on her own adventures in the Adirondacks was titled "Among the Adirondacks" (*Tribune*, 12 and 14 Aug. and 3 Sept. 1869).

To William Claflin (RBH)
Claflin (1818-1905) had been elected governor of Massachusetts in this year.
Sept. 7. 1869.   Box 244. Newport. [R.I.]

Dear Governor;—

When I saw you in Saratoga I forgot to speak to you about an idea of mine that may interest you, or if you are too busy to think about it, you may be able to interest somebody else.

John Brown's farm at North Elba, Essex County, N.Y. is *for sale*. For sale with the bones of John Brown lying there! Several years ago Mrs. [John] Brown sold it to Alexis Hinckley whose sister married her son Salmon, desiring to join this son in the West and having no money for the purpose.[1] Alexis Hinckley lost his wife last Winter and wants to move away from a spot that is associated with so much sorrow. He offers the farm for sale at $2000. There are 244 acres and $1000 worth of forest trees upon them. Now would it not be a great thing for Massachusetts or a few Massachusetts men and women, or a number of them, to buy this farm and keep it sacred to the memory of John Brown? He loved it and one of his last instructions to his wife was to live there always. She has not been able to do so. How fine it would be to give her a home there for life, and in course of time erect a monument worthy of the greatest hero of the late war! Can not $2000 be raised?[2]

   1. This sentence is somewhat garbled. It is Mrs. Brown, not Hinckley, who desires to join her son Salmon.
   2. KF had visited the farm while in the Adirondacks. Governor Claflin proving unhelpful, KF appealed to erstwhile abolitionists, but they too were unhelpful. In disgust that Boston, once the seat of the abolition movement, was unwilling to honor the man martyred for the cause, KF wrote to Isaac H. Bailey, a New York businessman, who immediately, as KF reported, "went into the street and secured the necessary subscribers in fifteen minutes" ("John Brown's Grave and Farm," *KF's Washington*, 13 Jan. 1892). In consequence, the farm became a historic landmark and eventually (in 1896) part of Adirondack Park. Until 1964, according to an eyewitness report, a granite monument stood at the site with the inscription "In Memory of Kate Field / whose endeavors / saved this John Brown / farm from being sold / and lost to posterity" (Paul Juarez, "Who Was Kate Field?" *St. Louis American*, 22 Sept. 1964.

To Whitelaw Reid (MU)
Sept. 7. 1869.   Box 244. Newport [R.I.]

Dear Mr. Reid;—

. . . I am writing lectures and can't leave them inasmuch as I make my début in Boston Music Hall on Oct. 20th.[1] But if you don't want the [Adirondacks] letters when I am ready to write them, it will make no difference to me. I can make them into magazine articles.[2] The same with Ida Lewis whom I have seen and like. We are to row together some day. . . .

If the Revolutionisters[3] haven't the good sense and taste to respect people's idiosyncrasies they're not fit to lead a Cause. I won't be bullied on to any platform whatsoever and I won't speak except I have the field to myself. It is bad enough to be responsible for my own sins. My total abstinence from the [Women's Rights] Convention[4] was owing to business engagements. Of course this won't be believed.

No, I am afraid I shall not see New York for several months. My regards to it.

It is best to be a lizard on a sunny wall. I wish I were one this glorious day.

1. KF was to lecture on "Among the Adirondacks," which she sometimes called "In and Out of the Woods."

2. KF's magazine article titled "In and Out of the Woods" appeared in the annual *The Atlantic Almanac* (Boston: Fields, Osgood & Co., 1870).

3. Women associated with *The Revolution*, a radical New York women's rights weekly, founded in 1868 by Elizabeth Cady Stanton and Susan B. Anthony. Its motto was "Men, their rights and nothing more; women, their rights and nothing less."

4. The Convention had been held in Newport, Rhode Island, in August.

To Whitelaw Reid (MU)
Sept. 26. 1869.　　　　　　　　　　　　　　　　　　　　　　　　　　Newport [R.I.]

Dear Mr. Reid;—

. . . I should much like to know who advised you to have nothing to do with me, professionally.[1] The editors with whom I have disagreed have invariably been dishonest. And *I* am to blame for rebelling! If you are satisfied with me *I* am satisfied. My only ground of complaint against *The Tribune* is that it does not pay as well as the magazines I write for, and I complain of this for the sake of others as well as myself;[2] but you have nothing to do with this department, and you will find that although I don't like to be cut up any more than the rest of the gens irritabilité [irritable people], I am amenable to reason, and am frank in the expression of my good will toward the present managing editor of *The Tribune*. Those who represent me as a troublesome, quarrelsome person, do me the rankest injustice.

1. Reid had informed KF: "Somebody warned me not to engage you. 'You never can get along with her unless you give her her own way in everything. . . . ' I thought we might succeed better than the false

prophet predicted. After a summer's work, of which there hasn't been half enough, I'm satisfied. If you are not, you ought to be" (LW, 241).

 2. Reid replied that, although "our rates are below those of the magazines, we can furnish you fifty times the market that the magazines can" (LW, 242).

To Whitelaw Reid (MU)
Oct. 11. 1869.   [St. James Hotel] Boston

Dear Mr. Reid;—
 There's no fear of my coming out of the lecturing business "too strong-minded." I'm so weak-minded about it that my nerves are completely unstrung, and how I am to get through Oct. 20th [lecture, "Among the Adirondacks"], heaven only knows. If I succeed and my agent sends you a telegram, will you publish it in *The Tribune*?
 Another thing. In my wanderings I shall be likely to come across items for *The Tribune*. Do you feel inclined to give me such a letter of introduction as you gave me this Summer?[1] It would be an immense comfort to me in case I fell among strangers or thieves. I can't advertise myself and as I am forced to travel alone I want all the support I can get.
 On Nov. 9th I lecture in Steinway Hall before some Presbyterian body, so I shall see you sooner than I expected.
 I'm just from the Adirondacks having run up there for a hunt. I shot a fine buck, 200 lbs! It was shot legitimately. Nobody held him by the tail, and I had never before handled a rifle. If lecturing fails I'll take to the woods and bury myself alive.
 Why *will* people describe my bathing and boating dresses? Both are intended for oblivion. I wish I were too.

 1. Reid complied: "The bearer, Miss Kate Field, who has long been connected with 'The Tribune,' is to represent us this summer at various water-places, and other summer resorts. Any courteous kindness that may be extended to her will be gratefully appreciated by this journal. Whitelaw Reid, *for* Mr. Greeley" (LW, 240).

To Whitelaw Reid (MU)
[Nov. 1. 1869]   [St. James Hotel] Boston

Dear Mr. Reid;—
 Many thanks for the "character."[1]
 Next Saturday I start for New York and expect to arrive there Sunday morn-

ing from Troy. Do come and see me Sunday p.m. if you can for I want some moral support with regard to my lecture "Among the Adirondacks" which is to be delivered on Tuesday evening Nov. 9th at Steinway Hall before some Presbyterian body of which I have no knowledge. Whether said body knows how to manage the affair and whether the Press will be taken care of properly is unknown to me, and as I shall not be on the spot until too late to do much good, I am nervous in the extreme. Then the hall is horrid for sound. Nobody is heard in certain portions of it and I certainly would not select such a place for a parlor entertainment.

And what I most fear is the manner in which I may be treated by the Democratic Press. I close my lecture over John Brown's grave pronouncing a eulogy upon him, and I dread to have horrid things said about me.[2] The opposition press here is lovely, but I can't expect the same treatment elsewhere. Do what you can to help me along. I get a certainty [guaranteed fee] but I want a good house. Mr. [George Stillman] Hillard[3] heard my lecture and thinks well of it. *I* am disgusted with it already.

Be disengaged on Tuesday evening Nov. 9. I shall send tickets to you, Mr. Greeley, Mr. Hassard and Mr. [William] Winter.[4]

Don't let your reporter report the *matter* of the lecture.

Where is Mrs. Calhoun?

I shall visit my aunt Mrs. Sanford at the *Clarendon Hotel.*

Tell Mr. Greeley about John Brown.

1. Letter certifying that KF represented the *Tribune.*
2. KF noted in her diary that Osgood had read her lecture "Among the Adirondacks" and praised it highly but advised her "as a matter of policy, to leave out the peroration on John Brown." To that advice KF exclaimed in her diary: "Leave out the only portion that was a matter of conscience? . . . I sobbed like a child, and wanted to die. Then conviction took possession of me and said, 'Retain the peroration if you die.' So I wrote a letter to Mr. Osgood, telling him that my conscience forced me to hold fast to John Brown" (LW, 213).
3. Lawyer, statesman, and Boston man of letters (1808–79).
4. Winter (1836–1917) was the *Tribune*'s drama critic from 1865 to 1909.

To Whitelaw Reid (MU)
Dec. 11. 1869.   St. James [Hotel]. Boston

Dear Mr. Reid;—

I'd like to have you and Mrs. Calhoun dine with me at my aunt's (Clarendon Hotel) on Christmas Day if you have nothing better to do. What do you say?

Please answer this week and address to the care of Sam'l Bowles,[1] "Republican," Springfield, Mass. (*To be called for.*)

I expect to "bring up" there the last of this week after dashing wildly over various railroads [to lecture].

The [Albert D.] Richardson murder is atrocious, and the remarks of the Press thereon a disgrace to journalism.[2]

1. Bowles (1826–78), owner-editor of the *Springfield Republican*, published some of KF's articles.

2. In 1869 Richardson, a *Tribune* accountant, was collecting his mail at the office when Daniel McFarland shot him in the conviction that his ex-wife was having an affair with him. In a deathbed ceremony, Beecher married Mrs. McFarland to Richardson. Greeley's competitors, assuming sanctimonious attitudes, charged him with tolerating sexual looseness and afflicted him with a plague of reporters. McFarland was acquitted in a jury trial.

To Mary Aurelia Anthony (HC)
Feb. 9. 1870.   Chicago

Dear M.A.;—

I thank you heartily for copying my dear [Thomas] Hood.[1] I love the spirit of that man, and want to try and recite those two poems—some time or other—if I can. Don't say a word about the photograph. "It is more blessed to give than to receive."[2]

After all, Chicago was a great success they say. Nobody ever does well here the first time I am told, and I actually cleared $400.00! My expenses were heavy for I told Mr. [J. B.] Runnion to be mean in nothing. One half of my success is due to Mr. R. who managed me magnificently. The Press was on my side before, is still more so now, and the people follow. Why, I might be "the most remarkable woman in the country" if I lived out West, but I've no such ambition as Caesar, and had rather sit at the feet of others than have others sit at mine. The Westerners are hero worshippers with a vengeance and a very little ability goes a great way. One man calls me the "rising star in the East" and (in a letter) tells me not to be "mad" because he sends me some handsome sleeve buttons. And the further West I go, the more I love the East. I wouldn't live here—no-"not for Joseph,"[3] or any other man.

But what book-stores they have here! F[ields]. O[sgood]. & Co. flourish in magnificent quarters, presided over by a most civil gentleman who told me with much *gusto* how he had enjoyed sticking up one of Miss Kate Field's posters in his abode of royalty. People *are* very kind to me, and I don't understand it, for I have done so very little. Gov. [William] Bross[4] gets me passes over the [rail]roads, and his daughter [Jessie] is devotion itself. But I'm not well. I've a disappear in this longitude and Boston East winds are as soft as the wooings of Zephyrus.

Regards to all.

Chicago.
Feb. 9. 1870.

Yours ever,
Kate Field

Dear M. A.,

I thank you heartily for copying my dear Hood. I love the spirit of that man, and want to try and recite these two poems — some time or other — if I can. Don't say a word about the photograph. "It is more blessed to give than to receive."

After all, Chicago was a great success they say. Nobody ever does well here the first time I am told, and I actually

Sample of Kate Field's letter to Mary Aurelia Anthony, 9 February 1870.
(Courtesy Harvard Theatre Collection.)

bad throat and the worst is yet to come. The agent here has made my engagements regardless of distances and I am in despair. Tonight I take a sleeping car to Detroit. O dear! Won't I be glad when it's over? I might remain here with profit until April, but I don't wish to, moreover I'm down for private theatricals in Boston on March 11th. I've got into the scrape and now must keep my promise....

Do send me a letter to St. Paul (Minn).... I lecture there Feb. 19th and it's such fun to receive letters at a distance. All your failings disappear in this longitude and Boston East winds are as soft as the wooings of Zephyrus.

    1. English poet and magazine editor (1799-1845).
    2. From Acts 20:35.
    3. Derived from the Catholic custom of dedicating one's work with the statement "For Jesus, Mary, and Joseph," or, more commonly, "J.M.J."
    4. Bross (1813-90) was the former lieutenant governor of Illinois.

To Whitelaw Reid (MU)
April 5. 1870.   21 Joy St. Boston

Dear Brother-in-law;[1]—

You are "gooder" aren't you? The Tribs. came today and I do receive the old paper, and Miss [Phoebe] Couzins did come to hand.[2] *You* wrote that article.

I'll send another Leaf[3] as soon as I can. My aunt and uncle have just arrived to remain a little while, in addition to which I'm not very well and I'm bothered. But I'll be as expeditious as I can. At least you won't have me *too* often.

If every woman is going into the lecture room, I shall take to something else. It is becoming too vulgarly common.

    1. Rumor had it that Reid was engaged to KF's nonexistent sister.
    2. In *The Revolution* (a women's rights magazine) Couzins (1845–1915) criticized a *Tribune* woman reporter "with [such] great coarseness and indecency," Reid noted in "Pretty Little Miss Couzins, Et Al." (*Tribune*, 26 Mar. 1870), that "we cannot quote it without offense to our readers." He added: If Miss Couzins "wants to reform the social and political system of civilization, she should begin by radically reforming her grammar. Some rights have been withheld from women, but writing the English language correctly is not one of them."
    3. "Leaves from a Lecturer's Notebook" was published *Every Saturday* and in the *Tribune*. KF eventually published this series, together with another series titled "Americans Abroad" (written for *The American Register of Paris*), under the title *Hap-Hazard* (1873).

1862-1871 57

To Whitelaw Reid (MU)
June 11. 1870.   [21 Joy St.] Boston

Dear Mr. Reid;—
    ... Indeed I never did put my *faith* in Hartford and Erie [railroad stock]. Somebody else put my money there, which is vastly more important and now I'm resolving myself into a committee of ways and means. If you want to send me the payment on two columns and a half of Woman in the Lyceum, I won't be proud about acknowledging the receipt, although I don't particularly deserve it. I've ordered a new hat and some new boots.
    We are feeling badly about Dickens.[1] I have just read Dickens's very last letter to this country, written to [Charles Albert] Fechter.[2] There is no reference to ill health, saving that he had been dining out (*this is entre nous*) since January, having been living in London during that time, and having gone beyond his endurance was going home to rest. He *has* gone to rest. It is a sad loss to the world, but best for him.

    1. Dickens had died on 9 June.
    2. Tragedian (1824–79); born in London of a French father and Italian mother. He had come to the United States to act and remained there until his death. KF published two admiring articles about him (see *To Whitelaw Reid*, 2 Aug. 1870, n. 3), as well as a biography (*Charles Albert Fechter*, 1882).

To Whitelaw Reid (MU)
June 27. 1870.   21 Joy St. Boston

Dear Mr. Reid;—
    I received the check and I've spent all the money. Such is life.
    I wonder whether you'll make a paragraph of the enclosed and tell people that I am going to lecture about Charles Dickens and Actors and Acting? I've changed one subject since Dickens died as this is the time to talk about him.
    After July 1st my address will be Newport, R.I.
    As soon as Aunt Corda's house[1] is finished I hope you'll keep your promise [to visit us]. The dog days of August will make a few days in Newport rather agreeable—and my new [row]boat will be at your service.

    1. Said by the *Boston Journal* (9 Aug. 1870) to be the "most elegantly finished house ever built in Newport.... The location is on the Point and the lawn has a water front and sea wall."

To Mr. Mumford (HC)
   Theatrical agent.
June 27. 1870.   [21 Joy St., Boston]

Dear Mr. Mumford;—
   I have made a change in my programme. Instead of Mrs. Browning I shall lecture on Charles Dickens.
   Please make the correction.
   After July 1st address me at Newport, R.I.

To Whitelaw Reid (MU)
Aug. 2. 1870.   Newport [R.I.]

Dear Mr. Reid;—
   The ways of house-builders are inscrutable.[1] A house that ought to have been completed on the first of July still exhibits signs of chaos, but there are hopes of our moving into it next week. Of course we don't want to have our friends come until it is in tolerable running order, but I look forward to your visit (I meant to insert with pleasure), and hope you'll not fail me.
   Suppose I feel inspired to write a letter from Newport (*suppose*, no promise you know,)—does The Tribune want it?
   Would you like me to report the opening of Fechter's new theatre *The Globe* (which I named) on September 5th?[2] That's something I'd be willing to promise.
   See *Atlantic* (next) for twenty pages of biography[3] that helped to make me false to *The Tribune*.
   The papers declare that I'm a Mrs. [Mary] Musgrove,[4] that I'm engaged, that I'm always doing something extraordinary; all of which are lies.

   1. See *To Whitelaw Reid*, 27 June 1870.
   2. The opening of the Globe, under Fechter's management, was delayed until 12 Sept.
   3. KF's "Charles Albert Fechter: A Biographical Sketch" (Sept. 1870). In the Nov. 1870 *Atlantic* KF also published "Fechter as Hamlet."
   4. Character in Jane Austen's *Persuasion* (1818) who is "always thinking . . . of her own complaints" and "fancies herself neglected and ill-used."

To Whitelaw Reid (MU)
Sept. 14. 1870.   [21 Joy St.] Boston

Dear Mr. Reid or Mr. Reid's Proxy;—
   I am mortified to death at the mutilated appearance of my Globe [Theatre]

report in *The Tribune*. It is disgraceful to the paper and to me. It stops at the first act. I obeyed orders explicitly. I was not limited as to space, sent half my telegram at 10 1/2 and the remainder before 12 1/2 so that it was the same as if I had despatched the whole at 12 as directed. The performance was not over until after 12 and wanting to get ahead of the other papers I wrote up to the end.

In first telegram I sent word that the conclusion would be forwarded *after* performance.

Please tell me the reason of the contretemps, for I feel as if The Tribune had some great fault to find with me.[1]

Address as usual: Newport. R.I.

1. KF's second telegram was not delivered by Western Union until 2:30 A.M., after the *Tribune* had been put to bed.

To Whitelaw Reid (MU)
Sept. 16. 1870 [21 Joy St.] Boston

Dear Mr. Reid;—

Whenever you feel like coming to Newport, come. The latch is always out. Unless you will promise not to be disgusted with rainy weather, you had better come soon however.

I'm so cut up about the Globe letter [report] that I could kill somebody. I obeyed instructions to the letter, made the head telegraph man promise perfect devotion and then half of the column I wrote in my lap (the only thing to be done as midnight found the curtain still up) didn't arrive until 2:30! I hoped to have The Tribune beat the Boston papers and so you can fancy my feelings. There *are* chords. Now I want to redeem myself. Let me do Tom Hughes[1] who lectures in Boston Oct. 11th. He can't keep at it more than two hours, giving me oceans of time. Let me have a letter to him, find out what manner of man he is, get hold of his *mss.* and do something neat but not gaudy. What say you?

You refer to "matrimonial rumors" and hint at putting questions to me. You won't believe what I said in a previous letter, so consider that I am swearing on a dozen bibles when I tell you that the rumor connecting my name with a gentleman of your acquaintance is without the slightest foundation. We are the best of friends, appreciate each other "wery highly."[2] "Only this and nothing more"[3] and there never *will* be anything more. So you needn't ask me any questions and you can flatly contradict anything you hear to the contrary, "by authority." I wish people would sometimes tell the truth. What a surprise party we should enjoy.

Was my Globe [report] very flat for not being well rounded? I'm so sorry.

1. English author (1822–96); wrote *Tom Brown's Schooldays* (1857) and *Tom Brown at Oxford* (1861).

2. A Wellerism. Sam Weller (Mr. Pickwick's manservant in Dickens's *Pickwick Papers*) uses *v*'s for *w*'s and *w*'s for *v*'s.

3. The refrain of Poe's "The Raven."

To Whitelaw Reid (MU)
Oct. 5. 1870.   Newport [R.I.]

Dear Mr. Reid;—

Your letter about Miss [Isabella] Glyn[1] has just arrived and I have telegraphed my inability to tear up [to Boston] tonight, thinking you may desire somebody else to "do" the subject. As the matter is not "war" and as you do not desire telegraphing, I think that a calm résumé of Miss Glyn's abilities, after hearing her in several plays, would better suit The Tribune and do her more justice than an article written after one hearing. This hasty writing is false to art and as I love art I can't bear to take it in vain. If you say so, I'll do Miss Glyn next week. Going up for Tom Brown[2] I shall probably remain there although I can't bear to think of leaving my terrace for the dust and plunge of city life.

I will neither write Miss G. "up or down." How can you say such things to me? Don't you know that I can't be salaried on a journal because I *won't* write what I don't believe?

I suppose you have made inquiries about Tom Brown. Can you tell me who are R. W. McAlpine Gen'l Press Cor[respondent], Ed[itoria]l Rooms [*New York*] *Sun* and Geo. H. Stone Manager of N.Y. News Ass'n? They want me to lecture in New York and Brooklyn.

I began an editorial after you left, being stung by what you said of women reporters (do you remember?), but it was so passionate (not ill-tempered) that the words looked as though they might burn up the mailbag, and so I tore it up, anticipating you in the deed. But when I have a good digestion and a clear head and rest and time, I intend to write a story. The heroine a reporter. The hero an editor. The heroine shall fall in love with the editor. The editor shall fall in love with reporter but shall believe thoroughly in the miserable dogma that a woman lowers instead of elevates her womanhood by honest labor. Consequently the editor shall put away his best nature and marry a curled darling of Fifth Avenue whom he fancies realizes his ideal. The ideal shall open up an amount of well regulated falseness very startling to her husband, and the denouement shall end with some sort of catastrophe (perhaps destruction by fire of the editor's office) in which the editor's life is saved by the energy and magnanimous daring of the unwomanly reporter while the wife goes into the feminine swoon so indicative of the ideal character. You didn't know what a mine you fired, did you?

Somebody once told me that you were insincere. I shall contradict that statement. Mind you, I don't quarrel with this sincerity. I am only sorry that I must say of you, in this opinion of women, *Et tu Brute*!

Don't you wish that *I* had so many letters to write that you would have been spared this second sheet.

    1. Mrs. E. S. Dallas (1823–89), English actress who performed under her maiden name and was booked to read in Boston.

    2. KF's jokey name for Thomas Hughes (the author of the "Tom Brown" novels), scheduled to lecture in Boston on 11 October.

To Whitelaw Reid (MU)
Oct. 23. 1870.   21 Joy St. Boston

Dear Mr. Reid;—

    ... What do you think? J[ames]. G[ordon]. Bennett Jr.[1] has just written to me asking me to take charge of reviews of novels for The Herald and wants me to call at the editorial rooms! What is your opinion? I am loyal to *The Trib.* and so write for "an opinion as is an opinion." This is *entre nous*.

    I am to lecture here Nov. 16th—a matinee at Globe Theatre—introduced by Mr. Fechter. I wonder whether you'll think the occasion worth having anything written about in the *Tribune*.[2] Please read Hamlet in *Atlantic* for Nov. and abuse as much as you please.[3] ...

    1. Bennett (1841–1918), nominally the assistant editor of the *New York Herald*, was actually in total charge of the paper, as his father (1795–1872), the founding owner-editor, was dying.

    2. This was KF's first presentation of her lecture on Dickens, which she continued to give until her death. Fechter was managing the Globe. The *Tribune* (17 Nov. 1870) reviewed KF's lecture: "The applause which salutes her is only less enthusiastic than that with which she is summoned before the curtain after it has fallen upon her brilliant peroration." The *Tribune* also noted that in the audience were "the poet Longfellow ... James T. Fields of 'The Atlantic,' the Hon. George S. Hillard, E. P. Whipple, [and] the Rev. Petroleum V. Nasby [David Ross Locke]."

    3. KF's "Fechter as Hamlet."

To Whitelaw Reid (MU)
Oct. 27. 1870.   21 Joy St. Boston

Dear Mr. Non-Committal;—

    I wrote to you asking what I ought to reply to Mr. Bennett [about reviewing novels for the *Herald*] and sure enough you are as dreamy and irresponsible as the Delphic oracle. In consequence of which I reply to Mr. Bennett that I shall be in New York on the first of December and if he chooses to call upon me he can. I do everything on the square, so if you hear I'm writing for The Herald (which is not impossible, considering that a paper declares one of my arms broken and a lady called yesterday to tell me of a gentleman in California who writes that Kate Field is there and reads poetry to him every day!!)—you'll know the truth. . . .

Of course I'd like Mrs. [Louise Chandler] Moulton[1] to report my lecture [on Dickens for the *Tribune*], for there is much jealousy among my brethren here and some of them seem to owe me a spite because I have a little success. At least don't let an enemy write about me. My lecture will be submitted to friends of Dickens on next Sunday night and a verdict pronounced.

Don't worry your soul to reply to my onslaught concerning reporters unless the spirit moves. I shall be in New York before long if I live, and if I don't I shall know your thoughts without the bother of words. That's the fun of being a ghost.

1. Freelance journalist, author, and KF's friend (1835–1908).

To Whitelaw Reid (MU)
Nov. 6. 1870.   21 Joy St. Boston

Dear Mr. Reid;—

Monsieur Tonson come again![1] Don't you wish I wouldn't, but how can I help it when business is business? A man by the name of O. Sackett (declared by Anna Dickinson[2] to be a vendor of pea-nuts) of Kansas City, has written me various letters concerning his Western Lyceum Bureau, none of which have I answered. The cry is still they come and in the last he writes of Mr. Greeley saying that The Chief lectured for him on Oct. 6th, 7th and 8th, and that he, Mr. Greeley, spoke to O. Sackett of me. Now I should like to know how much of this is true and in what estimation Mr. Greeley holds O.S. As you can get more out of him than anybody else, I appeal to you.

My lecture is just advertised and I am as nervous as a witch. If Mrs. Moulton is to do me [for the *Tribune*], I'll send her tickets; if not, she must pay like a Christian. If nobody does me, will you (provided of course my lecture is a success,) let me send you a telegram, a short one, at my own expense? I begin so late that people fancy me out of creation.

James T. Fields has just heard my lecture and declares it "a wonderful success—that it could not be better." He has not made *one* suggestion.

1. A tag from *Monsieur Tonson: A Farce in Two Acts* (1821) by William Thomas Moncrieff (1794-1857), based on *Monsieur Tonson: A Tale in Verse* (1796) by John Taylor (1757-1832). The farce hinges on a Frenchman's mispronunciation of *Thompson*—the name of his persecutor—as *Tonson*. Unable to bear "Tonson's" harassment, the Frenchman keeps crying out in dread, "Here's Monsieur Tonson come again!" The tag was so familiar that Dickens had only to allude to it in *Sketches by Boz* (1836), chap. 5.

2. Dickinson (1842-1932) was a lyceum lecturer, suffragist, actress, and friend of KF and Reid.

To Mr. Mumford (UV-F)
Nov. 14. 1870.   [21 Joy St.] Boston

Dear Mr. Mumford;—
Feb. 15th will not answer for [my lecture on Dickens in] Bloomington [Illinois]. They have Anna Dickinson on the 17th.
Can you name another date?

To Whitelaw Reid (MU)
Nov. 18. 1870.   [21 Joy St.] Boston

Dear Mr. Reid;—
Are you so busy that you have not time to receive my thanks for the kindness which prompted you to give me so much space in *The Tribune*? You must let me thank you and you must let me tell you that Mrs. Moulton did *not* "gush,"[1] that Fields, Longfellow, and the best people of this city pronounced the thing [my lecture on Dickens] "tip top" and old actors (whose judgment I value more than all others) came to me with moistened eyes and patted me on the shoulder. Fechter wrote me a lovely note in French (he having been moved to tears) "Je suis bien heureux de votre *grand* succès—c'est un beau commencement."[2] Mr. [Arthur] Cheney, the proprietor of the [Globe] theatre, rushed to his private room at the close of the lecture, wrote me a charming note and enclosed the rent of theatre (previously paid) as the price of his ticket ($100.00), declaring himself still under obligations. This was the temper of the audience. The newspapers did as well as I expected. I'm a bit of a New Yorker, and I'm a dramatic critic, and I've dared to write about Hamlet, and so when the critics sit on me, they are not going into spasms. But they treated me well, even those who personally dislike me.
I enclose a sample of the letters I am constantly receiving. . . .

1. Moulton's review, "Kate Field at the Globe Theatre: A Brilliant Success," appeared in the *Tribune* on 17 November 1870.

2. I am very happy at your *great* success. It is a wonderful beginning.

To John Brown Jr. (HF)

Oldest Son (b. 1821) of the abolitionist. While his father went south with his followers to seize the U.S. Armory at Harpers Ferry, John Jr. stayed up North to secure volunteers, gather arms, and serve as communications officer, though nothing came of his efforts. Not unamusingly, he took the alias of John Smith.

Nov. 28. 1870. 21 Joy St. Boston

Dear Sir;—

I thank you heartily for your gracious offering of grapes and wish that I might shake hands with the man whose father is to me so great a hero. I have fine dreams of what the John Brown Farm is to be one of these days and I should like to have the promises signed, witnessed, and sealed, of your mother[1] that the noble grave which renders the Farm historic and because of which I and my friends bought it, should remain undisturbed.[2] Can you secure this promise?

I should much like to talk with you about your father. If you ever come East, let me have the pleasure of seeing you. I have very vague ideas of "Put-in-Bay."[3] Is it near Sandusky?

1. Mary Ann Day Brown (1816–84), John Brown Jr.'s stepmother.

2. In 1895 KF called on the members of the John Brown Association to authorize Henry Clews, the trustee who held the deed for the Brown farm, to gift the property to the State of New York so that it would forever be the center of Adirondack Park (*KF's Washington*, 23 Feb. 1895). In her will too (written in July 1895) she stated: "I bequeath my shares in John Brown's farm at North Elba to the State of New York, hoping the other stockholders will follow my example, that the farm may be the nucleus of... Adirondack Park." In 1896, two months after KF's death, New York officially accepted the gift, and the John Brown farm was incorporated into Adirondack Park, the largest park in the United States.

3. Island in Lake Erie off the coast of Ohio.

To Whitelaw Reid (MU)

Dec. 3. 1870. Hoffman House. [New York]

(While waiting for my baggage to turn up!)
Dear Mr. Reid;—

I wanted to ask several things and of course forgot them. Here are three of them.

Do you feel inclined to give me such a letter of credit from *The Tribune* as you most kindly gave me last season?

Can you tell me the best hotel to go to in Washington—the quietest? I hope to get into a boarding house. If not, I *must* go through the horrors of a hotel.

In my Dickens lecture I suggest the founding in America of a Newspaper

Fund. It seems to me a good thing to start and I should esteem it an honor to start it. The subject is worthy of a strong, earnest editorial. I'd like to write it myself were I not a tired sick creature, but if you think favorably of the matter, I will make the necessary extract from my lecture which should be the basis of the article and give or send it to you. In addition I should like to head the fund with $50.00. I'd like to give more but I cannot in justice to my hungry pocket and hungrier poor relations. What say you?

I wish you had not told me that my uncle had publicly stated that I was "able to take care of myself." It looks as if he felt called upon to find some excuse for letting me fight along unassisted, and gives people such a strange idea of me. Thank heaven that God helps those who try to help themselves. "And I believe in God and the angels Ever sence"[1] I have stood all alone.

It is strange reasoning this, that because a woman does not give up, *therefore* she needs no help! When swimming for my life it [I] would have been grateful had my uncle turned, looked into my face and handed me an oar to rest upon for a while. It has often been remarked that *it is the best swimmers who are most frequently drowned.*[2] I do not claim to be a good swimmer, but others insist upon it as a fact and—so much the more must my strength be taxed. In another world my uncle will know me better. I say this with no grain of bitterness. It is my last bit of nerves—the very last that I intend to exhibit (unless I *do* have "hysterics").

For lecturing now and then "Is a derned sight better business than loafing around" rich men.[3]

If you think favorably of the editorial I'd like it to appear soon after my lecture.

1. From John Hay's poem, "Little Breeches": "I b'lieve in God and the angels / Ever sence one night last spring / . . . And I think that saving a little child, / And fotching him to his own, / Is a derned sight better business / Than loafing around The Throne." First published in the *Tribune*, then in *Pike County Ballads and Other Pieces* (1871). Hay (1838–1905), who had been one of Lincoln's two secretaries, was Reid's assistant on the *Tribune*.

2. Variation of the proverb "Good swimmers are oftenest drowned," first collected by Thomas Fuller (1654–1734) in his *Gnomologia: Adages and Proverbs* (1732).

3. See the John Hay quotation in n. 1 to this letter.

To Whitelaw Reid (MU)
Dec. 6. 1870.   [Hoffman House] New York

Dear "Bear";—

I quote your illustrious self because you *are* a bear to go off to Washington when you knew perfectly well that you were the one person I was most anxious to have present tonight. I hate the person who intends to occupy your seat and I shall kill him a little for his mother. No amount of telegram copartnership in regret compensates for a vacant fact: It's mean.

I'm off for Phila. tomorrow 5 p.m. without my letter of credit from Tribune. When I have that in my pocket I feel armed for the fray. I've written to Mr. Tisdale to secure me a room at the Arlington House [in Washington, D.C.].

As you see all the papers and I see none, will you be a very good "bear" and just cut out anything you may see about my lecture? My Western agents want notices and I have none to send them. Let me see bad as well as good—if there be any of the latter.

Mr. [John Augustin] Daly[1] of Fifth Avenue Theatre agreed with Mr. Isaac H. Bailey to have me lecture there, Sunday. Dec. 18th. What do you think?

Two newspaper men said very nice things of you at Newark last night, and I didn't abuse you much. It appears however that you oppose Woman Suffrage because you have quarrelled with the author of Jenny Arc.[2]

    1. Prolific playwright and theatre manager (1838–99).

    2. The author of "Jeanne d'Arc," a lecture, was Anna Dickinson, rumored to be engaged to Reid. The reference to Jenny Arc is an inside joke. On one occasion a witless chairman introduced Dickinson by saying that she would talk on "John Dark, the most remarkable man of antiquity."

To Whitelaw Reid (MU)
Dec. 7. 1870.   [Hoffman House] New York

Dear Mr. Reid;—

It [my 6 December lecture on Dickens] was a success, although had I not been there, and did I take my coloring from The Tribune, I should consider that lecture a failure and my voice a myth.

The lecture is to be repeated Sunday Dec. 18th at the 5th Avenue Theatre. Do you believe Mr. Greeley would introduce me? Will you ask him? My address up to Sunday will be Arlington House, Washington. Monday or Tuesday I shall return to the Hoffman House.

To Laurence Hutton (PUL-H)
    New York drama critic (1843–1904); wrote some fifty chatty books, mainly on the theatre and his literary pilgrimages abroad. Hutton remained KF's friend for a quarter of a century and wrote an obituary tribute on her for the *New York Bookman* (Aug. 1896) in which he called

Laurence Hutton, New York author and drama critic.
(From *Talks in a Library with Laurence Hutton*, recorded by Isabel Moore [New York: G. P. Putnam, 1905], opposite 120.)

her "one of the cleverest, most self-contained, most self-sustaining women of her generation in any country."

Dec. 27. 1870.   21 Joy St. Boston

Dear Mr. Hutton;—

Why did you not let me thank you in person for your charming remembrance on Christmas Day? I sent my card to no one in New York because of overwork, but you should know that I am always glad to see you, and always glad to be found out. I wore the mistletoe [you sent me] on Christmas night and now it hangs over the Graphic's illustration of Dickens's Library.[1]

Do you know that your writing strongly resembles that on a card sent with an anonymous bouquet some days ago? If it *was* your writing, pray accept my hearty thanks.

1. KF refers to the *New York Daily Graphic* which, like the *London Graphic*, had introduced en-

graved rather than woodcut illustrations. KF, like thousands of others, associated Dickens with Christmas because of his annual Christmas stories.

To Whitelaw Reid (MU)
Jan. 18. 1871. Roundout [N.Y.]

Dear W. R.;—
(Which it stands for Woman's rights, n'est-ce pas?) . . .
I had a very good and interested house [for my Dickens lecture] last night, much to my surprise. I never dreamed that anybody would travel to 22nd St. and 9th Avenue. The Herald actually sent a reporter, but The Tribune couldn't give me a mention along with other lecturers. Such is life. What we want we never get. What we don't want is lavished upon us.
I send the note for Mr. [George Washington] Smalley,[1] as you told me to do. Can't you give me one or two letters [of introduction] for Cincinnati? I lecture there Feb. 4 and may be obliged to remain there several days. Is Murat Halstead[2] nice? I don't know anybody there. . . .
If I come to grief on this trip, won't you be sorry you didn't go to the Dickens?

1. Smalley (1833-1916) was the London correspondent for the *Tribune*. KF was planning a trip to London with her mother and wanted Smalley's recommendations for lodgings.
2. Halstead (1829-1908) was the owner-editor of the *Cincinnati Commercial*.

To Mary Aurelia Anthony (HC)
Feb. 12. 1871. Ironton. Ohio

Let this be a valentine.
"O lady! we receive but what we give,"[1] and to receive news of M.A. I take it that I must answer her welcome note received two weeks ago in Buffalo. Believe me this is the first moment I have had to give to anything but duty.
Travelling most of the time, I am overwhelmed with visitors the moment I arrive in town or city, and people are so kind and—shall I say it?—admiring as to force me into amiable sacrifice of the few spare hours I ought to give to serious writing. Mother gets a daily letter from me, business correspondence is religiously attended to and then I am driven out to a Soldiers' Home, or to a bridge or a view or a dinner or a something, and one scene succeeds another with such kaleidoscopic swiftness that my ideas are singularly mixed. I've threatened to

keep a journal, for really I have material for several readable articles, but so far have only threatened. Tomorrow I see a little peace and may accomplish something.

So far I still live. I have made every connection and fulfilled every engagement. I have had one sore throat but doctored myself and escaped serious inconvenience. My health is quite as good as it is in the bosom of Joy St.[2] And my head is less tired. I *can't* do anything in the [railroad] cars, not even think, which is a blessing, and at other times I am so occupied with affairs of the moment as to prevent me from having feelings and sich.[3] I don't know which is the real person, K.F. on the rampage with no thought but so much per night, or K.F. quietly plodding and being human at home. God fits the back to the burden and I seem to be able to carry whatever *must* be carried. I don't know but it is as interesting an experiment as can be devised to (as it were) regard yourself as a third person, set tasks for yourself and see how much you can stand. I don't know a more curious study than one's own personality. I've not yet guessed the answer to *my* conundrum.

Talking of conundrums, I met Mark Twain in Buffalo.[4] He is amusing but not inherently a gentleman I should say. He talks or rather drawls through his nose in an absurd manner but to marry such a voice or to connect such a voice with sentiment is to me incomprehensible. Yet this queer, original man with a disregard for things polite, has married a delicate little woman who thinks much of her upholstery and *will tolerate no smoking or drinking in her house*! He went to my lecture and I was somewhat curious to know what he thought of it, but all I heard was that he called me "an actress."[5]

Of course I see lots of people and the press men seem to know me for their own and call without introduction. One editor sent to Whitelaw Reid for a letter of introduction and his salutation was "Miss Field all the Press are in love with you and I want you to count me there too." I need not say that this young man is Western. But they are all hearty, with genuine streaks of originality and I like them all more or less. I see just enough of them.

At Syracuse a Grand Army encampment attended my lecture in a body and the commanding General brevetted me and pinned the G.A.R.[6] badge (made out of captured cannon) on my shoulder, making me promise that I would wear it whenever I lectured for the Grand Army. In Columbus [Ohio] I met several of [William Dean] Howells's friends who spoke of him with great affection, one young woman (now Mrs. Pearce) asking me to recall her to him as Miss Kelton. [Thomas Bailey] Aldrich[7] had an old friend in a Mrs. Sullivant who is pretty and formerly wrote poetry for him in the Home Journal. She wanted to know all about his wife. And à propos des bottes,[8] an editorial friend who has done me many kindnesses and won't take money, has asked me for the enclosed list of autographs. He wants a bit of Baby Belle[9] from Aldrich. Will he be angelic and send it to me for his admirer? And for the others I am going to ask you to tease

Mr. [James R.] Osgood when he is particularly good-natured and has nothing else to do.

The most interesting places I have seen are The Soldiers' Home in Dayton [Ohio] and the State Lunatic Asylum in Utica [New York]. Both are magnificent institutions and the one person who has really interested me since I left home is Dr. John P. Gray[10] [Superintendent] of the Insane Asylum. He is master of the situation and so impressed am I by his ideas that I shall make him a visit (D.V.) as I return home and go over the Asylum thoroughly. I shall lecture to the inmates. At the Soldiers' Home I was obliged to address eleven hundred wounded heroes and cried in spite of myself. It was one of the most pathetic scenes I ever witnessed. I'll tell you all about it.

But, my dear, I wouldn't live in the West for all the wealth of the Indies. It would be splendid misery. There is much to admire—and certainly I am treated with bounteous hospitality; people in five minutes treat me as though I were a bosom friend,—but there is too much spitting and *rawness* and too little culture to please me. Whenever I feel as though I knew something then I *know* that I am in the wrong place. Then the pronunciation is so torturing and fancy the Cincinnati and Louisville papers taking exception to *my* pronunciation when the people don't pronounce the names of their own towns correctly! However, the papers have generally treated me well. I enclose a few specimens of the reverse of the medal which I think you'll enjoy and which you are to preserve for me. The communications are taken from an Auburn (N.Y.) paper. Don't show them to mother, as they may annoy her. I have a good many enemies and they occasionally show the cloven foot in print. [William] Wirt Sikes[11] the agent &c of Olive Logan does all he can to injure me. One of his letters about me has fallen into my hands.

Where am I? In a little town 145 miles east of Cincinnati. I came up by boat last night and am lodged in a poor hotel the master of which plays the violin vastly better than he cooks. He is playing Beethoven this blessed moment (was formerly leader of a theatrical orchestra) and my injured stomach is crying aloud with anguish at the bad butter on the tea table.

Here I lecture tomorrow night for two enterprising young men. The next night in Portsmouth [Ohio] and after lecture I take the steamboat for Cincinnati (a filthy city) where I arrive at 7 a.m. and leave two hours later for Chicago, reaching there at 11 p.m. This is what may be called travelling. I doubt whether I return to Boston before April. My address from Feb. 17 to 24th is 202 Michigan Avenue, Chicago.

1. From Coleridge's "Dejection: An Ode."
2. Where KF lived in Boston with her mother.
3. KF was fond of this dialectical word popularized by Dickens.

4. Twain (1835-1910), having purchased a one-third interest in the *Buffalo Express*, had moved to Buffalo.

5. In his posthumously published *Autobiography* (1924), Twain commented on KF: "She went on the platform; but two or three years had elapsed and her subject—Dickens—had now lost its freshness and its interest. For a while people went to see *her*, because of her name; but her lecture was poor and her delivery repellently artificial; consequently, when the country's desire to look at her had been appeased, the platform forsook her" (157). Actually, KF lectured for twenty-seven years and on more than one subject. Twain liked neither KF nor Dickens (see Introduction, n. 16) as performers. Culturally, KF and Twain were a world apart, as were Dickens and Twain, which may account in part for his disgruntledness. As KF, for example, was annoyed by Twain's Western drawl, Twain was annoyed at KF's Bostonian accents. In any event, KF, let alone Dickens, typically drew enthusiastic audiences in the United States and abroad.

6. Grand Army of the Republic, a national organization of Union veterans.

7. Author (1836-1907); at the time, editor of the Boston weekly, *Every Saturday*.

8. Apropos of nothing.

9. In Aldrich's *Ballad of Babie Bell and Other Poems* (1859).

10. Gray (1825-86) wrote many books on insanity, edited the *American Journal of Insanity*, and received honorary degrees from French, English, and Italian universities.

11. Second husband (1836-83) of Olive Logan (1839-1909), actress and women's rights lecturer, both of whom KF detested. Logan required her third husband to be called Mr. Logan. For the contents of Sikes's letter about KF, see *To Whitelaw Reid*, 6 Sept. 1871.

To Mary Aurelia Anthony (HC)
March 2. 1871. Bloomington. Illinois

Dear M. A.;—

Your two welcome letters and valuable contents[1] in No. 2 have arrived safely. Accepting hearty thanks for your efforts in behalf of my aspiring friend.

(Talking of aspiring, I've been wept over today in Springfield by a former schoolmate whom I had entirely forgotten and who wanted me to open a correspondence and be a sister to her. She is very fat and dresses like like—like the—d—l, and I don't remember her now, but she calls me "Katey" and burst into tears in telling me how she had treasured a lead pencil I gave her when I was a child. I suppose she is sincere, but oh dear!)

And St. Louis! I don't exaggerate very much when I say that about one third of my audience (female portion) kissed me and called me "Katey."[2] My old teacher who used to shake me almost out of my shoes got up quite a little scene, and altogether I experienced novel sensations. Judges and old merchants, men who never heard a woman lecture, came because I was "little Katey" the daughter of my father.[3] It was strange, and very, very sad.

My dear, how can I protest against [Lecture] Bureaus when so dignified a journal as *Every Saturday* goes out of its way to laud [James] Redpath[4] in no less than two articles? When J. R. Osgood & Co. [publisher of *Every Saturday*] advertise him gratuitously, K.F. might as well attempt to speak disrespect[ful]ly of the equator.

Bret Harte? Well, I'm curious about him. I hope he'll keep until I arrive. I've my doubts about him. He was guilty of a most outrageous breach of decorum in Chicago and has killed himself there.[5] I doubt whether the mine he works is very rich in ore. They say J. R. Osg[ood]. & Co. intend to make all sorts of offers and get down on their knees to him with Atlantic Monthly in one hand and half a dozen banks in the other, but *I* don't believe what people say.[6] Bret Harte will find his level. He has done his best, I believe and won't get such another offer as Chicago was ready to make him.

My head is turned toward the East. I may be home the last of March. Find out for me as soon as you can who are the leaders, men and women, in the French Fair.[7] Mr. Osgood has my various addresses. Fechter is in Chicago. I shall see him tomorrow.

I had an offer to go South [to lecture] but was afraid to go alone. My companion did *not* meet me and I was not sorry. People must be very congenial to travel together.

It is raining, thundering and lightning like—blazes!

1. Autographs KF had requested for a friend.
2. KF gave her Dickens lecture in St. Louis on 28 February 1871.
3. The *Missouri Republican* (12 Feb. 1871) had announced KF's forthcoming lecture: "There will be an intense curiosity to see and hear Miss Field by the many who cherish pleasant recollections of her father—ever a prime favorite with the St. Louis public. . . . It is no exaggeration to say that this lady is now the most popular lecturer upon the boards."
4. Redpath (1833-91) founded the Boston (later, Redpath) Lyceum Bureau in 1868. Redpath's system featured one or two house-fillers like Twain, whom he paid well, and six or seven house-emptiers, like Olive Logan, whom he paid little, though he charged the lyceums an average of $100 a lecture. If audiences wanted to see such notables as Horace Greeley, Henry Ward Beecher, or Julia Ward Howe, they had to buy the rest of the package. KF foresaw that Redpath's exploitative system, widely adopted by his competitors, would destroy the lyceum movement. Thus she did her own bookings or, when too busy, hired an individual agent or used a lecture bureau that resisted the Redpath system. However, in 1885 she succumbed and enrolled in Redpath's Bureau, the name retained by Major James Burton Pond (1838-1903), who had bought out Redpath in 1875. A rare pamphlet, replete with blurbs from America and England, was published under the Redpath name to advertise KF's lecture series for the 1887-88 season and is now in the Howard-Tilton Memorial Library of Tulane University.
5. Author (1836-1902); as famous in his time as Twain and, indeed, Twain's mentor as well as his collaborator in the play *Ah Sin* (1877). The breach of decorum had to do with the newly founded *Chicago Lakeside Monthly*, whose proprietors had offered Harte fourteen thousand dollars and part ownership in

the magazine to be its editor. At a grand dinner held in his honor, a check for fourteen thousand dollars was put under his plate. When Harte failed to appear and no explanation from him arrived, the check was destroyed and the offer annulled.

6. The rumor was true. The *Atlantic Monthly*, owned by Fields & Osgood, had contracted to pay Harte ten thousand dollars for (in Harte's words) "exclusive publication of my poems & sketches . . . in your periodicals for the space of one year"—the most lucrative contract yet offered an American writer (Richard O'Connor, *Bret Harte: A Biography* [Boston: Little, Brown, 1966], 145–46).

7. Held to raise money to support the Paris Commune in its struggle against the National Assembly.

To Whitelaw Reid (MU)
March 4. 1871.   Chicago

Dear W.R.;—
 . . . My head is turned—toward the East. I lecture tomorrow in Toledo. And so on until I reach home. Unless it is settled that I lecture in New York, I must not return there, as it costs money. But I shall be sorry, which costs something better than money. New York is *the* place in America.

Have you heard anything from Mr. Smalley in reply to my inquiries concerning England? I can't conceive who wrote that thing from London.[1] Yet I have the idea of lecturing there and I *do* want to learn of a competent manager. I have learned down to the deepest depths of conviction that ability is one third and management two thirds.

I have been successful. I have had several poor houses, as everybody must have. I have had first-class audiences in quality and been praised by the best people. *In spite of this* I am more popular than I expected to be.

If you will print them, I hope to put together *Leaves from a Lecturer's Note Book*.[2] But they will not be offered before being written. I remember my Waterloo.

Tell Mr. [John] Hay that one of the most intelligent audiences I have had was in Springfield, where I heard of him.

If you have a message for me remember that March 14th I am in Buffalo: Buffalo Courier.

March 18th: Care of Dr. John P. Gray State Lunatic Asylum, Utica, N.Y. where I shall interview the maniacs. Don't you envy me?. . . .

Fechter is a success here.[3] Ha! ha! ha! ha!

1. "That thing" was a newspaper report that KF would lecture in London in the spring. "Women-lecturers," stated the report, "are almost wholly unknown here; likewise popular lectures. [Of] Specialists who address . . . special audiences there are some few." The *Missouri Republican* of 12 February 1871,

which had copied the report, added, "It is very plucky, then, for this bright, intrepid daughter of St. Louis to . . . beard the lion in his den of conservatism, stupidity and prejudice."

2. For KF's "Leaves," see *To Whitelaw Reid*, 5 Apr. 1870, n. 3.

3. Fechter was appearing in a series of plays, the latest of which was *Hamlet*.

To Whitelaw Reid (MU)
March 15. 1871.   Buffalo [N.Y.]

Dear W.R.;—

. . . As Mr. Greeley, you say, dislikes me ("Barkis is willin' ")[1] it may be very unpleasant for you to receive offers of articles from me. Believe that I would not wittingly place you in a disagreeable situation, and I have no desire to contribute to The Tribune outside of the desire to write for a journal edited by yourself. A certain other paper [*New York Herald*] gives me my own terms, and if *The Trib.* does not want me, I can go over to the enemy and make money by the operation. I say this preparatory to stating that *No Thoroughfare*, Dickens's, Collins's and Fechter's drama is to be brought out at Boston Theatre by Fechter on March 28th.[2] I expect to be at home (D.V.) Saturday March 25 and shall probably want to *do* the new drama. I'd like to do it for your paper if I am welcome and am permitted to speak my mind, and I'd rather not make a telegram of it. . . .

1. When Barkis, a man of few words, learns, in chapter 2 of Dickens's *David Copperfield*, that Peggotty is an excellent cook, he conveys to David Copperfield his desire to marry her by this cryptic message.

2. The drama derived from a Christmas story of the same title by Collins and Dickens (published in Dickens's magazine *All the Year Round* in 1867). Fechter was involved in presenting the play, not in writing it.

To Whitelaw Reid (MU)
March 30. 1871.   21 Joy St. Boston

If I'm a "goose" W.R., "you're another" of the male persuasion. Who wants you to be "bullied" out of being my "cordial friend"? Do you suppose *I* do? Don't you know better? Of course you do. That's a little bit of acting on your part because you know the friendship is not all on one side.

I didn't suppose you associated my name *and* my "sister's"[1] with those dreadful women, but there's nothing like being perfectly sure. Now I'm satisfied.

I sent the [review of] No Thoroughfare Tuesday p.m.[2]—hope it was acceptable, but do you know that I want to scratch your eyes out (in a Pickwickian sense) for telling me not to *gush*. If there's a thing I despise, if there's a word I abhor, it is *gushing*. I'd rather be accused of murder and arson. I *don't gush*. I honestly and *manfully* admire what is beautiful and I say so in strong language, giving my reasons for it. If you call my Hamlet article[3] *gushing* I give up the English language. I wouldn't praise [Christine] Nilsson[4] to save her from purgatory. I call the newspaper twaddle about *her, gush*. Someday you'll do me justice in this matter of criticism. I am not given to liking everything and everybody.

The French Fair [to support the Paris Commune] opens here April 11. All the *ton* [fashionable] run it. Do you want a notice?

I do wish Mr. Smalley could tell me of a nice lodging in London, reasonable in price. My mother is ill, has been so all Winter. She must have a change and I can devise nothing better than England.

1. Refers to her nonexistent sister (invented by gossipmongers) who was supposed to be engaged to Reid. "Dreadful women" refers to such women as Olive Logan and Victoria Woodhull, whose vulgarity degraded the women's rights movement in KF's eyes.

2. The review appeared in the *Tribune* on 30 March.

3. "Fechter as Hamlet," *Atlantic Monthly*, Nov. 1870.

4. Swedish opera singer (1843–1921).

To Whitelaw Reid (MU)
April 11. 1871.   21 Joy St. Boston

Dear W.R.;—

Rob't Collyer[1] of Chicago is delivering three Sunday evening discourses on Actors and *The Drama*. He sends them to me and I want to boil them down with remarks. Can I for *The Tribune*?

(*Confidential*. Enclosed is third review in *Herald*. I receive $50 per column.) "How is that for high?" I know you like slang. Yesterday's *Trib*. says so; therefore I use it.

Please send payment for [my review of] *No Thoroughfare*. It is over a column and a half. I wonder whether *The Tribune* will begin to treat me as well as The Herald.

Thanks for Mr. Smalley's letter. He is very kind in his offers of assistance [to find mother and me lodgings in London]. If my uncle fulfils his promise to me he will engage stateroom on board of Russia that sails from New York May 17th. I hope I shall see you before sailing.

The notice of Adelaide Phillipps[2] [in the *Tribune* of 9 April] was very nice indeed, and I am sure she was as much pleased as / Yours sincerely, / Kate Field

1. Collyer (1823–1912), an Englishman, was called to be minister-at-large to the First Unitarian Church in Chicago.

2. Phillipps (1833–82), a singer, had performed with the New York Philharmonic on 8 April. KF said she was the finest contralto in the world (*Tribune*, 27 Jan. 1868). KF's Aunt Cordelia, a singer herself, discovered the "rare musical genius" of Phillips when she was a child and gave her her first singing lesson (LW, 47). Later, encouraged by Jenny Lind, Phillipps studied voice in London with Garcia, Lind's teacher, with whom KF also planned to study.

To Whitelaw Reid (MU)
April 18. 1871.   [21 Joy St.] Boston

Dear W.R.;—

As you accept my paragraph accept also the cause of it. I want all the money I can scrape together, so don't be so magnificently oblivious when I ask to have payment for articles. $30 is the least *The Tribune* ought to pay for [my review of] *No Thoroughfare*. The other things are cheap writing.

I didn't mean articles on Collyer:—only one article, perhaps not a column. I *must* write it and I'll send it to you, and if you don't like it, you can return it. That's bearding an editor in his den, isn't it?

Yes, I shall pass several days in New York, and I expect my friends to be very good, as I may go down to the bottom of the ocean and become a mermaid.

To Whitelaw Reid (MU)
May 8. 1871.   [21 Joy St.] Boston

Dear W.R.;—

Please order my *Tribune* stopped on and after May 11th. On that date I leave here to lecture half way on the road to New York. Friday afternoon (D.V.) will find me at the Fifth Avenue Hotel in which men-agerie I must remain without my mother until Sunday morning. Friday's dinner I shall go without rather than face the animals [in the dining room]. If you will dine with me on Saturday at your favorite hour of half past six, I shall be delighted. Don't however, if the spirit doesn't move....

I'm beginning to be frightened, now that the day of sailing draws near.

Part Four: 1871–1873

Voyage to England
Death of Mother
Grief and Readjustment

To Whitelaw Reid (MU)
May 28. 1871.   Liverpool

Dear friend;—

My dear darling, my mother is dead. She died at quarter past ten on Friday night of congestion of the brain brought on by cold and nervous exhaustion.[1] The blow is so sudden, so unexpected that it seems impossible. I have been anxious about the sweet darling for some months; ever since that fever in Newport, and came to England because I believed this change would be the best for her. The doctor assured me I could not make a wiser move and yet as I too thought of England as good for myself, I feel as if I had murdered my own darling, for she would not have died on shore with the quiet of a room and the care of a homeopathic physician. O, it stabs me to the heart! I ought to have known by instinct that I was doing wrong. I felt something black hanging over me, the moment I reached the ship. I wrote a few lines to you in that mood, but I did not connect my mother with this mood. How blind is poor humanity! The dear was quite well the first two days, better than I, for I was sea-sick and she took care of me. She ate well, walked about on deck, and said she had never slept so well on board a steamer. Friday on nearing the Banks, she complained of cold feet, but as this was nothing unusual with her, I did not worry. Saturday she said she had caught cold. On Sunday she went to bed with a chill and nausea. I thought the nausea sea-sickness, but it was not. It ceased on Monday but as she had fever I sent for the doctor against her will. I dreaded to call in an aid in which I had no faith, but there was no alternative. He gave her medicine. I sat up with her on

Monday. She was restless, perpetually moving, clutching whatever she could. I followed her motions, holding her as best I could. Tuesday morning she was so terribly restless that the doctor, fearful lest she should wear herself out, gave her a quarter of a grain of opium. She slept quietly until Wednesday morning, when upon waking the heart-rending restlessness returned. The first days she complained of a great pain in her head and her left hand was swollen with inflammatory rheumatism. After that she was almost wholly unconscious, though on Wednesday when it was impossible for me to conceal my tears from her, she looked at me with troubled eyes, saying pitifully, "Darling, I can't help it." That and "Sister, sister," said in her feeble delirium were about her last words.

Wednesday night she was quieted somewhat by "valerian" but the restlessness remained. Thursday the same, although being quieter I thought she was better. I lay down from 1 to 5 a.m. on Friday and was waked up by Madame [Hermine] Rudersdorff's[2] maid, a kind, sympathetic soul used to tending ill people, who feared my mother was dying. The doctor had begun to give her brandy. The stateroom was so dark, so close, so horrible considering the situation that I said there must be a change. As we were nearing Queenstown I asked the people opposite (the Manafees[3] of Kentucky) who were to land at Q. to give us their room which was an outside one and commodious comparatively. They did so. The darling was moved on to the sofa and so exhausted was she as to seem dying. I gave her brandy and strong beef tea alternately (by order) every half hour, pouring it down gently for she was too weak to be raised. She breathed as a dog breathes in warm weather—short panting. It was pitiful, and yet even when we arrived at Queenstown and I telegraphed to [William John] Hennessy[4] in London to meet me at Liverpool, I had hopes of getting her on shore alive and seeing her well again. That was about 2 p.m. on Friday. At six I noticed a change. The darling showed repugnance to taking nutriment. An hour later the doctor said it was useless to cause needless suffering and I ceased giving her anything. The change began. The dear, sweet mother was two hours and a quarter dying, in a state of coma, so that she did not suffer, but O it was dreadful to witness. I can never forget those sweet features growing gradually more and more pinched, but there was no agony on the face. The forehead was smooth, the half open eyes bright.

The Doctor was with me and Madame Rudersdorff. Dr. Wallace was most kind. He has shown a tender heart throughout and has helped me to the best of his ability. Never breathe a word of my dissatisfaction with his treatment. He is young and inexperienced and I believe did not in the least understand the case, although I am told that from the first he did not believe she could recover, as the noise and agitation of the vessel were death to her. Dr. Wallace was obliged to leave yesterday, being called to a sick mother at Belfast; consequently I can not have a calm talk with him about my mother's condition. I greatly fear the effect of the intelligence upon my aunt, she being in so delicate a state, consequently I shall leave a note at the Cunard Office here, asking Dr. Wallace to call upon you in New York and tell you just what he thought about her physical condition, and if out of your questioning you can gather any comfort for me or Aunt Corda, write to both. My aunt's address is Mrs. M. H. Sanford. Box 28. Newport, R.I. If there be nothing consoling, only write to me who knows and can bear the worst.

While the darling was dying there was laughing, talking and singing on deck. Such is the consideration of the living for the suffering.

Now let me tell you a few plain facts that for the sake of others ought to be made public. What Mr. [Isaac] Bailey, Leonard Jerome[5] and Gen'l [Philip Henry] Sheridan[6] think of Capt. Cook of the Russia, you can soon find out. Miss Charlotte Cushman (supposing she knew the captain which she did not as she confounded him with Capt. Lott, former commander) told me to write to Capt. Cook, requesting him to give us seats at table "midship" as my mother was delicate. I wrote the note as soon as he reached port. Capt. Cook received it, as he told a passenger he had had a note from me, but he had no acquaintance with Miss Cushman. He took no notice of my request. Our seats were next to the last table in the stern where there was great motion. Capt. Cook never came near me. His table was filled with hearty, healthy, *wealthy* people, half of them young, stout men. From first to last Captain Cook never by visit or word expressed the slightest interest or sympathy in my mother's suffering or my grief. Not an officer, the kind doctor excepted, did his decent duty. It was the business of Capt. Cook to at least come to me at last and tender his services. He did nothing of the kind. The men that did come were Mr. Alexander[7] of Springfield (Mass), young Nathan Appleton[8] and young Jaffray.[9] Moreover, and here is a crying shame, there *is no such thing as a room fit for a hospital on board Cunarders*. A room on deck so called is too noisy. They take out 200 passengers, half of them in dark, stifled rooms and appropriate no quiet, airy apartment to the possibilities of disease! It is a crime against humanity. My soul cries out against it in the name of my dear mother and if you will put my facts into *a few plain words to the Cunard line of steam packets*, you will benefit others. A lady died just after leaving [Nova] Scotia only last week. What befalls steerage passengers, God only knows. It is all shameful. Do this for my sake. If I only could think I could do it myself. And tell Henry Sedley[10] about it. [page missing]

She supported [other actors] for several years.[11] She was a great favorite in Philadelphia, receiving presents and testimonials some of which I now have. She was the original Julia in the Hunchback in America, acting it with the author Sheridan Knowles[12] and when Fanny Kemble[13] performed first in Phila. she did Julia at one theatre while mother acted it at the other. Going South as a leading actress, mother became engaged to my father, Joseph M. Field to whose ability and accomplishments all the West and South will testify. As both remained out of New York, as my father died young and my mother retired from the stage fifteen years ago, the general public know less of them than of lesser people, but no one can act domestic drama as did my mother. Her Lucille [and] Thérèse in the Orphan of Geneva,[14] her Martha Gibbs in All That Glitters is not Gold,[15] the heroine in Advice To Husbands[16] & similar characters were lovely. She had the quick, impulsive feelings of the artistic temperament. And her Juliet that she often played to Miss Cushman's Romeo I have often heard lauded. Once my father said she acted Lady Macbeth (the sleep-walking scene) like one inspired. Mother was a person of inspiration, and if she had been brought up in the French school, she would have had equal art. [William Charles] Macready[17] liked her so much that he begged her to travel with him through the West, which she did. She was the only person he never scolded. She often supported the elder Booth[18] and acted in former years with Charles Kean.[19] In New Orleans, Mobile and St. Louis she was a great favorite. Personally very attractive many a man has told me how much they were fascinated by her. Her last appearance East in conjunction with my father was at the Howard Athenaeum in Boston autumn 1855 when my father was the first to produce Tom Taylor's[20] *Still Waters Run Deep* in which she performed Mrs. Mildmay and in which my father made so tremendous an impression as Hawksley as to crowd the theatre for six weeks, an unparallelled excitement for sixteen years ago.

As a woman, my dear mother was without fear and without reproach. If there is any good in me I owe it to her teachings and beautiful example. Unselfish, sympathetic, tender, she supported several of her family for years; she was a faithful daughter, a loving sister, a devoted wife and mother, a loyal friend. The poor always loved her. She was best appreciated in times of sorrow, and dependents always went to her for sympathy. Her loss to me is another world's gain. She needs no prayers. Her soul is fit for Heaven. God help me to approach her. *And she was an actress, Rev. Mr. [Justin Dewey] Fulton.*[21]

Will you please have inserted in New York papers and pay bills charging to my account a notice of her death? If I do not word it correctly, please change it.

Died May 26th on board steamship Russia of brain fever, Eliza Riddle Field, wife of the late Joseph M. Field.

Boston, St. Louis and News Orleans papers please copy.

If you do this, notify Aunt Corda. I ask you because it is in your way, and I want to spare my aunt as much as possible. I am now fearing to hear how it goes with her. I have written a different letter to my aunt; for she needs consolation. She must not know that I reproach myself for sailing or that Mother might have lived had she been on shore.

May 30

The doctor who embalmed her says it was too late to retain the beauty. The process ought to begin six hours after. This was not done until 24 hours. It is shameful to have no competent person on board these vessels. Two bodies were thrown overboard in the harbor from steamers the other day from San Francisco with friends waiting at landing.

Please go to Sarony's[22] and have him look up the negatives of photographs taken of my mother several years ago. They are not good but may help in a painting. Tell him to take good care of the negatives.

I shall ask Mr. [Octavius Brooks] Frothingham[23] to perform the funeral services and if he comes to you, read him this letter, all but what is private. I can not copy it. I have not the strength.

I am told Mr. Smalley is in America.

A few more words and you will be spared further infliction. . . .

I am seeing to everything. My mother's embalmed body will be sent to Boston in The Siberia on June 1st where the funeral will take place. When all is over, I shall go [on] to London and do what my dear mother would have me do; try to take care of myself and show my love for her by endeavoring to overcome my faults.

What of this letter can be made public, relate to Henry Sedley, Mrs. Botta, Mrs. [Mary Mapes] Dodge,[24] R[ichard]. W[atson]. Gilder[25] and such of my friends as are interested.

    1. KF and her mother had sailed for England on 17 May; her mother died on shipboard on 26 May.

    2. Russian dramatic soprano (1822–88); taught singing in Boston.

    3. Unidentified.

    4. Irish artist (1839–1917); had studied in New York. He and his wife Charlotte came to KF's aid and found lodgings for her near their London home.

    5. Unidentified.

    6. Union general (1831–88) still on active service.

    7. Unidentified.

    8. Appleton (1843–1906) was the son of Nathan Appleton (1779–1861), the wealthy cotton manufacturer, banker, and politician who gave Craigie House to Longfellow as a wedding present when his daughter Frances married the poet in 1843.

    9. Unidentified.

    10. KF's cousin, author, and New York journalist (1835–99).

    11. KF's mother began her dramatic career at age fourteen.

    12. English actor and dramatist (1784–1862); author of *The Hunchback*.

    13. English actress (1809–93); she had last toured America in 1868.

    14. *Therese, the Orphan of Geneva*; adapted by John Howard Payne (1791–1852) from a French melodrama.

    15. By the father-and-son team of Thomas Morton (1764–1838) and J. M. Morton (1811–91).

    16. By Charles Sears Lancaster (b. 1821?).

    17. Eminent English tragedian (1793–1873).

    18. Junius Brutus Booth (1796–1852); known as "*the* Booth" to distinguish him from his actor sons, Edwin and John Wilkes Booth.

19. English actor (1811-68); son of Edmund Kean (1789-1833), the great tragedian.

20. English dramatist (1817-80); most famous for *Our American Cousin*, the play Lincoln was watching when assassinated by John Wilkes Booth.

21. Baptist clergyman (1828-1901); denounced slavery, drinking, women's suffrage, and the theatre. In his sermon preached in Boston on Lincoln's death, the only fault he found with the martyred president was his love of the theatre.

22. Leading New York theatrical photographer; reputed to pay for the privilege of making exclusive portraits of celebrities (such as Oscar Wilde) and professional beauties. KF and her mother, as well as her father, were photographed by him.

23. Boston minister (1822-95).

24. Dodge (1831-1905) wrote the popular *Hans Brinker; or, The Silver Skates* (1865) and was editor of *St. Nicholas*, a New York monthly that exerted an important influence on children's literature.

25. Gilder (1844-1909), poet and author, was editor of *Century Magazine*.

To Whitelaw Reid (MU)
June 11. 1871.   Aubrey House [London]

Dear W.R.;—

... You have said nothing about my sending any correspondence from Europe. I know you have your regular men, but ill as I am in body and mind, I see numerous things untouched by your people. Shall I ever take advantage of my opportunities? For example, this week Leicester is to present a memorial to Mr. [Peter Alfred] Taylor (M.P.),[1] Sir Charles [Wentworth] Dilke[2] and the other M.P. who voted against the Princess Louise's[3] dowry, and I am to report the meeting, which is private, for Leicester. Here I see an article for The Tribune. Again you never have art, music or the drama fully treated; music never that I remember, and music is my pursuit now. The great [Manuel] Garcia is most complimentary to me but he refuses to teach me in my present exhausted condition. I am under medical treatment and am told that rest is absolutely indispensable if I ever desire to be well, so there is an end to hard work in which I hoped to forget my great loss.

Mr. Smalley is my benefactor in giving me Mrs. Peter Taylor [Clementia] for a friend.

I shall send the article tomorrow.

1. Taylor (1819-91) was a liberal MP for Leicester, at whose Aubrey House KF was staying.

2. Dilke (1843-1911) was a liberal MP for Chelsea.

3. Queen Victoria's daughter (1848-1939); betrothed to John Campbell (1845-1914), Marquis of Lorne, afterward Ninth Duke of Argyll; married to him in 1871.

To Mary Aurelia Anthony (HC)
July 19. 1871. [Aubrey House] London

Dear M.A.;—

What can I say? Your letter was very gratifying to me, and the knowledge that the beauty of my mother's character was appreciated by the few who gathered around her grave,[1] in some slight degree, consoles me for not being there. I tried to do her honor as far as I could, and it is comforting to hear that the service was touching and tender—that loving hands cast flowers upon the dear remains. I wanted honest, upright men to bear her to the grave, men who had expressed their regard for her, so your husband must pardon my having asked him to perform the painful duty.

It is *all* dark and sad. The shock came so unexpectedly and in so terrible a way! It will take me a long time to understand it;—to be able to do without her tender care and love,—a care and love that can never come again, [and] that this separation causes me to appreciate. I must believe in immortality, for if God be just, my mother must be blessed as she has blessed others. Sometimes I wish it were over with me too, there is so little to live for and so great a struggle is required to lead a true life.

Now I have no aim. The one who believed in me and encouraged me is gone, and I have little hope. Of course I keep up the fight but my heart is not in it and it *is* fight in this great Babylon where none but the strongest rise to the surface. Not that London has taste or special judgment, but here one must be as brave as Hercules or be supported by social power or degrading intrigue.

If I were well I should return to America immediately, as my duty would be to take care of my aunt, being as ill as she is—in another way—[but] I am prohibited from making any exertion. My malady is dyspepsia, an irritated mucous membrane, and a congestion of the larynx. The vocal chords are relaxed and were I in America it would be unsafe for me to lecture. Garcia, the great singing master, paid me many compliments but refused to teach me until I became strong. I have been travelling down hill for a long time but work seemed inevitable and I trusted to my endurance. Now the end has come. Next week I expect to join Mrs. [Laura Curtis] Bullard[2] at Ems. Then I may go to Aix les Bains near Geneva, having Lina Warren[3] for a companion. Later all is obscurity, but I hope Aunt Corda will join me in the Autumn. She needs the change and I trust that her husband will realize the necessity. I shall give up the house [we leased] in Joy St. and probably never again live in Boston, yet I hope to visit there of course and see my kind friends.

Hennessy was very kind and his wife and sister are sweet womanly women. I first took lodgings near them but the loneliness drove me well nigh distracted and Mrs. Peter Taylor, wife of the radical M.P., insisted upon my staying with her and so urgent is she for me to remain that I find it difficult to start for the continent. They have a lovely house with a beautiful garden on Notting Hill, Kensington—about four miles from the old City. I have met a good many people but few are sympathetic. I can not like English people unless they are exceptional, and this in spite of their kindness, for many have been good to me. My republicanism has waxed exceeding strong and my detestation of snobs and flunkeyism has become a mania. There is something patronizing in the air that irritates my nerves. This is not for public repetition mind you.

Hennessy has improved. [William] Bradford[4] has an immense parlor at the Langham Hotel, invites the nobility and is invited to dine with the Duke of Argyll. So goes the world. If you will work for *patronage*, you are likely to succeed here....

1. KF's mother was buried at Mount Auburn, alongside her husband. The inscription KF supplied for her mother's tombstone derived from the refrain of Elizabeth Barrett Browning's "The Sleep" (which, in turn, derived from Psalm 127:2): "He giveth His beloved sleep"—a line KF herself is reported to have murmured sometime before her own death (LW, 551).

2. A woman whose great wealth derived from Dr. Winslow's Soothing Syrup. In 1870 she purchased the failed *Revolution* from Elizabeth Cady Stanton and Susan B. Anthony for a dollar and turned it into a literary and society journal.

3. KF's school chum from the Lasell Female Seminary days who lived with her sister in Geneva.

4. Bradford (1823-92) was an American painter of marinescapes who exhibited in England and whose paintings were sold to the Duchess of Argyll, Baroness Angela Burdett-Coutts, and Queen Victoria, among others.

To Whitelaw Reid (MU)
July 28. 1871.   Aubrey House. London

Dear friend;—

Ill in body and mind, perplexed, torn by conflicting emotions, I have not replied to your kind letter of June 3d. I thank you for its friendly words and refer to the letter written in the moment of my greatest distress [my mother's death] as proof of my trust in your friendship....

I have lived years since I left America. I seem to be torn up by the roots and to be hopelessly drifting God knows where. I am prohibited [by my doctor] from returning to America for a year—during which time I suppose I shall be forgotten. I have given up all lecturing engagements; I have given up my house [on Joy St.] in Boston where I shall never live again; I have written to my aunt begging her to join me, as I do not see how I can exist here all alone (I have had enough of visiting). In all probability she and my uncle will join me in the Autumn.

Tomorrow I am ordered to Ems [Germany] for the waters. There I join Mrs.

Bullard. Later I expect to be in Switzerland with my old chum Lina Warren. I have invitations to visit Florence and Rome[1] but everything must be subsidiary to health.

Here the [Peter] Taylors have been most kind. Both seem to have taken a great liking to me. Indeed I can make as many friends here as I desire, but I prefer America. I never loved the dear country until now. I never realized how free it was. Mr. Smalley thinks me very foolish in my desperation at the social and political rottenness here, but I can't help it. My nerves are near the surface. . . .

I have done three things since I have been here. I have engaged an artist to illustrate a book compiled by me (the publisher's secret); I have arranged with Trübner to republish my Pen Photographs in the Autumn;[2] I have given my Dickens lecture at the Haymarket Theatre in the presence of thirty critics.[3] I did so against Mr. Smalley's advice, feeling that if I am to be exiled a year I must turn the year to some little account. As I have no intention of going about America lecturing as necessity obliged me to do the last two winters, and as I want an English reputation in order to take the rank I desire without overworking for it, I determined to give a rehearsal and listen to the verdict. That Mr. Smalley thinks much more favorably of the venture now than he did before, is a victory. He told me that he was "charmed." The newspaper men were loud in my praise and predicted a great success. So did the agent who had previously written to me about lecturing. Sir Charles Dilke said it was "a great treat." Mr. & Mrs. Taylor were delighted. They are very critical people and are very desirous to have me lecture in London. Miss Francis Power Cobbe has just written me a long letter saying that my lecture is "clever & brilliant"—"a great many points of it ought to be quoted as epigrams" &c. She winds up by saying "You have great literary powers which can not fail to be successful in pure literature. You have dramatic powers which would render you very successful if you went on the stage." She believes my lecture will have great success in the great towns outside of London, but is not sure of drawing money in London. Others, the Taylors, among them, believe in London. So I have done well to give the rehearsal (*it is sub rosa* and you are not to whisper it) and if I return in good health I may give a second rehearsal before a larger audience and then judge what is best to be done. It will be such a triumph to succeed in spite of all your predictions that I want to do it.

Do you know George W. Childs?[4] He is a great friend of [John] Walter[5] of The Times and Trübner said Walter will do anything for Childs who is now his guest and is to remain here for some time. *The Times* is the paper that never can be depended upon and Trübner advises me by all means to get a letter to Mr. Childs. Can you do it? I wish to present him with copy of [my] book and ask him to use his influence in securing Mr. Walter's presence at my second rehearsal if it is attempted. Don't call me mad, because the advice comes through a clearheaded man of business. Heaven knows I wish everything like management were unnecessary or could be done by somebody else, but it seems my fate to be forced to do everything for myself even when I am utterly unfit for exertion.

Another thing. A wild idea, I suppose you will call it. I see some one proposes to buy up the Adirondacks and make it such a pleasure ground as the world never saw. It is superb. The region is too far north for agriculture and will be ruined if all the timber is removed. The lakes will dry up and beauty gone that can never come again. I want to write something to this effect if you will publish it. Our John Brown farm[6] would be fine as a donation—a starting point in subscription. What do you think?

You wish nothing from me in correspondence I suppose. I am sorry. The little I may do I shall send to *Every Saturday.*

Will you tell Mr. Botta that I may go to Italy and that as he offered me letters [of introduction] I shall be very happy to accept them? Further, will you tell Sarony to be *very careful* of my father's portrait and photograph while I am away? I am worried about it. And also I'd like him to send me small photographs of myself. A few of each kind—as people here to whom I am indebted ask me for my photograph—and I can not sit here. If you will see that Sarony sends them it will oblige me. . . .

1. To visit the Thomas Trollopes in Florence and the Elihu Vedders in Rome.

2. Trübner brought out KF's enlarged edition of *Pen Photographs of Charles Dickens's Readings* in London simultaneously with Osgood's American edition, to protect the copyright.

3. The rehearsal was held on 23 July 1871 to invited critics, the most prominent of whom was Fanny Kemble.

4. Childs (1829–94) was a book publisher and owner of the *Philadelphia Public Ledger.*

5. Walter (1818–94) was chief proprietor of the London *Times*; his editor was John Thadeus Delane (1817–79).

6. See *To William Claflin*, 7 Sept. 1869, n. 2.

To Cordelia Riddle Sanford (LW)
[July 1871]   [Aubrey House, London]

. . . I miss mother and I am so tired and do so long to have some one know what ought to be done for me and to do it. Everything seems impossible, and yet the old story of supposing I am able to bear all, goes on. Dear, you tell me to spend the remainder of my life with you and to give up work. You ask whether I have not had enough of public life, and say that mother worried at my work. I have never overworked from desire. Necessity has been my master ever since childhood. I have never known freedom from care. I have never seen that I could be idle until now. Now I am alone and have sufficient money to authorize devotion to my best interests, which at present are assuredly health and relaxation. I certainly desire to be with you, but it is neither right nor expedient that I renounce my public career just as it is beginning. To do anything while I am ill is impossible. To work reasonably should I recover my tone is absolutely required of me. No one desired me to do certain things more than mother, and now if I live I long to realize her desires. But I long for home life, and I have no wish to repeat the experiences of the past two winters. Incessant travelling is most distasteful to me. I want to return to America, but as the physicians say "no," I ought to turn Europe to the best possible account. I am hedged in by the fact of loneliness. If I only had some one with me, I might do what now seems so difficult. The doctor says I am generally better, but I feel far from well. I sleep very little, and old troubles make me good for nothing. I am told to go up the Rhine to Wiesbaden, there to drink the waters which are prescribed, and then to go on to Switzerland. How I am to do this alone I can't see, yet if no one can be found, I must go alone. In Switzerland I shall be with Lina Warren, and the [Thomas] Trollopes want me to spend October with them, and the Vedders write urging me to go to them wherever they are, and then spend the winter in Rome.

To Cordelia Riddle Sanford (LW)
[1871] [London]

Dear, you say your only ambition for me is to see me *well* married. Do you think that so easy? I've had several escapes from matrimony, for which I thank God. A life of ambition is a terrible grind, you say. And how about most marriages? Are not they terrible grinds? Do you realize what would happen if I married and made a mistake? I do. I believe in love. I don't believe in being tied to a man whom I cease to love. Therefore the less said to me about marriage the better. If I marry, there's no knowing the misery in store for me, so don't think that the panacea. My observation makes me afraid of lifelong experiments....

You seem to think that ambition is the guiding star of my existence, and that I am sacrificing everything to it. Dear, it seems useless to argue the matter, yet you never were more mistaken in your life. With regard to the acts of my life (outside of health) of course, no one can decide but myself. If a human being possesses character and conviction, he or she is the best judge of what must be done. I *am* a person of convictions, and am as fervent in them as Charlotte Corday[1] when she became a murderer, or Jeanne d'Arc when she braved everything to lead France on to glory.

1. Royal sympathizer (1768-93); fatally stabbed Jean Paul Marat (1743-93), the French revolutionary leader, in his bath.

To Whitelaw Reid (MU)
Sept. 6. 1871.   Ems [Germany]

Dear W. R.;—
... Here I am alone in the stupidest place the imagination can conceive. Mrs. Bullard left three weeks ago; then I was consigned to the care of some German-Americans who departed ten days since, leaving me sole monarch of the Kaiser's apartment in the Kurhaus.[1] I am known for this little fact. Royal accommodations are none too good for American republicans. But the waters have been of great benefit to me and as the doctor says I have a fine constitution and that rest ought to bring back strength of nerve, I take heart. I look one hundred per cent better than I did. But it is very difficult for me to look on the bright side. Everything seems so unstable and were it not that I was born with an unusual amount of energy and pluck,—for which I am no more responsible than I am for the color of my hair and eyes—I should be desperate. ...

I have seen Smalley's letter about ocean steamers. It made me shudder to read my own words but you would not have printed them had it not been best. Need the matter stop there? Can you not send spies aboard to see what treatment is meted out to steerage passengers? They die on the passage and are thrown overboard like cattle, so I have been told. Do take up the subject if it is possible. I hope Mr. Bailey, Mr. Jerome and Gen. Sheridan were willing to have their names used.[2]

And there are those who have said cruel things about my remaining in London to lecture! Do these people think I am made of cast iron? *Could* I cross that ocean after such an experience? Even in crossing the channel I buried my face in my hands and kept the loathsome water from me. There must be a fatality about the sea. An uncle [Matthew Field], dearly loved, died and was buried at sea. My father's remains were sent from Mobile to Boston by sea. My mother— Will my homeward berth be equally narrow? I am so fearful of being instrumental in bringing about misfortune that I shall not ask my aunt to join me. If she comes of her own free will, I shall be thankful; but she writes that she suffers agony even in sailing about Narragansett Bay. People have died of sea-sickness. I shall urge no more and my uncle talks of sending a stable [of race horses] to New Orleans next Winter! He loves me not less but horses more.[3] I suppose we can not help our natures.

Will you tell me what Smalley wrote about the [Dickens] lecture?[4] You do not express an opinion, but I think if you look the matter all over, as I have tried to do, you will conclude that much can be gained by a success; and no success was ever attained without trial. I never wish to repeat my lecture experiences in America. I loathe the life and the majority of the country audiences. I did it for money. If I make a success in London I make a settled reputation (such flunkeys as we are! thinking the opinion of Europe of so much more value than our own!

I refer to the public) [and] can command higher prices and need only appear when I feel like it. In cancelling engagements at home, I have given up my income. To spend money and make none is a bad business, and under ordinary circumstances would be inexcusable. This is another reason for trying to turn an old lecture to account. If I make money here I need not draw upon my uncle, or invade my little invested capital, both of which alternatives I must otherwise resort to. Then I have calls upon my purse that I must heed—nothing forced saving by conscience. The legacy my dear mother has left is the care—to the strength of my ability—of a cousin[5] and five children, impoverished by the war and by the death of the father. At present I can do almost nothing for them. Success in England will mean much comfort and peace of mind to them. Again, if I return *without* lecturing, amiable critics will say it was because I couldn't and this will injure me. And lastly I want to succeed for the sake of America and American women. They can't abuse my voice or my *English*, at which my recent audience expressed much astonishment, and I'd like to show these John Bulls a few things. They can't read and they have no grace, and I am not afraid of them, having heard and seen quite enough to give me confidence. But what *is* needed is management, and knowing this I tremble.

... Since writing in July, I have had several letters from editors and others expressing an unusual amount of interest and faith in the experiment. One was from an agent who heard me and wants to manage the matter. In a letter rec'd from a friend in London (only yesterday) this agent is quoted as saying "She will do splendidly if she lets Woman's Rights alone." As I was born to be an artist and not a reformer—saving in trying to reform myself—there is no danger of my invading the province of others. In a recent *Revolution* sent me by Mrs. Bullard I read that Olive Logan was to return to England in the Spring and lecture under [George] Dolby's[6] management. As Dolby is to be in America this Autumn with a concert troupe, I wish you would find out in a roundabout way (if you can) whether this report is true. If so, the more reason why I should appear before her. After, I could not hope for anything; that is if people become as disgusted as they ought. And this reminds me that the worst enemies I have (I am sorry they are so ignoble) are O. Logan and W. Sikes [Logan's husband/manager]. Last Winter an agent put into my hands (and I travel with it lest I may need it) a letter written by Mr. Sikes devoted to my annihilation. The paper is stamped "Author's *Union*," bears as its motto "*Good will and good words*" (hypocrisy is the homage that vice pays to virtue)[7] is dated Sept. 19, 1870 and reads thus—"Let me say to you in all candor and in confidence that I believe you will be wise, if you have engaged Kate Field to lecture for you, to be sure and let her engagements come *after* your others. She will without doubt draw a good house, but if she does in Cin[cinnati]. and Dayton as she has done in all the other Western cities I have heard from, she will make a failure so complete that it will kill the house of any woman lecturer who comes after her. This is in strict confidence to you—for your own good as a manager—not to be repeated to the annoyance of any third party, but to be borne in mind by yourself if you want to make money this year. I was in Chicago, Detroit, Milwaukee and other cities where Miss Field spoke last year, and I heard the same story in every case—she *bored* her audiences, being no orator. The very editors who out of kindness spoke well of her lecture told me that she fell utterly flat. I should be sorry to have you open your hall with K.F. because it will frighten off all future audiences. I heard her in New York and I would not endure the misery of it again at any price. Keep this to yourself please, and profit by it."

Why have I copied this wretched letter? Because I learn from you that people say cruel things about me. Now I am away W. Sikes & Co. may repeat their slanders and I want some good friend to know what they have already tried to do.

I do not wear mourning. Will some call this heartless? My mother did not believe in it. I shall be escorted from here to Geneva by an old friend, though a young man [Albert Baldwin] who happens to be nearby (at Schwalbach) for his health. Will this be tortured into a scandal? I don't know what the world is made of.

... I see The Tribune almost daily. I have it sent from London and so keep au courant of movement. How you do go on about Free Love! Is there never to be a cessation of hostilities? And now good Henry James [Sr.] returns to the charge, and H. G[reeley]. comes to the rescue.[8] What *he* thinks is of little consequence but what *The Tribune* thinks is of very great consequence; therefore I am excessively sorry that Mr. Greeley and The Tribune should assert that a belief in Woman Suffrage is belief in Free Love. I can't understand it. Because adventurers take up Suffrage to win notoriety I don't see why you should denounce the honest believers in Woman's Suffrage. There never was a cause more badly managed, but that does not make the cause itself immoral. Mr. Greeley grows sentimental over his daughters [Ida and Gabrielle] and hopes that the grave may cover him before they lecture. Mr. Greeley is safe. His elder daughter, sweet soul, is the devoted slave of an insane mother. Moreover she stutters and can't lecture. The younger is very pretty, very heartless, very cold and a consummate flirt—so I am told by those who know her best. I dare say that I am a disgraceful spectacle but I'd rather have *my* daughter (if I am ever blessed with one) lecture than possess the virtues of H G's younger daughter. I'd believe in his sentiment more had he paid more attention to the training of his daughters. What is a father good for if he betrays his own home? Public men never seem to realize that their own children are their first duty. Mr. Greeley's slur upon women who lecture is an insult to some of his best friends, and insults, like chickens, come home to roost.

But Providence will settle these things. I do not worry my soul about them. What *has* hurt me is seeing Gail Hamilton's[9] slander of Georgina Hogarth copied into *The Tribune*; she one of the best of women and of whom that spitfire can know nothing.[10] How could you? And how *could* you copy once, *twice*, her attack on female journalists? You who employ so many of them, who have so many friends among them, who know that her statement is one-sided, and that worse could be said of male journalists! I don't understand it. I should feel like a traitor if I allowed such a paragraph to appear in a journal over which I had control. I have always been encouraged to write personalities. "Be as wicked as you dare" was the order received from an editor who engaged me to write from Newport. I disobeyed the order and was condemned. Murat Halstead wrote me a letter asking me to "show up" all the people I met abroad. I have never answered his letter and never intend to. Aside from my disgust of such things I fortunately can afford to be virtuous. How many women penny-a-liners can? I don't expect women to be angels. Poverty does not resist temptation as readily as a comfortable income can. Do tell me that you never sanctioned Gail Hamilton's slanders. She has as cross a pen as she has an eye. Ugly women always have the worst tempers. They won't forgive anybody anything. Look at her *Battle of the Books*[11] and then ask if she ought to be quoted on any subject!

... And that Joaquin Miller![12] The poem Myrrh is good, but the poet who can set his wife's, his daughter's and his own disgrace to music[13] is a very contemptible specimen of a man though his name be "among the princely few."[14] What conceit! In London he said that he wrote one of Bret Harte's best stories—name forgotten. Much of his success was due to his top boots and his rabid Southern sentiments. Has he changed his tone in the North? Robert Browning came to see me one day saying "I met that man Miller at dinner yesterday. Guess where—" Of course I couldn't. "At the Bishop of London's! He told me that his motive in visiting England was to see *me and the Houses of Parliament*! He lunched with me today." And this is all there is true of that grand dinner given by Browning to Miller! I think the man must be a clever humbug. However Hal Prescott says he is as much to the world as the discovery of California, and I suppose I am a fool. . . .

Sept. 9th

Mrs. Bullard has sent me *The Golden Age* with Tilton's replies to Greeley. I think Tilton has the best of it, and I think of Tilton as I did last Winter, so it is not prejudice in his favor.[15] Theory is one thing, practice another, and Beecher has said that it is impossible to combine the two. He ought to know.[16]

1. Cure House, the spa hotel where King Wilhelm I of Prussia (1797–1888) stayed on vacation.

2. On 5 August 1871 the *Tribune* had published an article on "Transatlantic Steamships" by Smalley, contrasting the German ship *Main* and its gentle captain with the Cunard ship *Russia* and its brutal captain—the same Captain Cook who had been indifferent to KF's dying mother and KF's grief. Adding to his own evidence, Smalley quoted a portion of KF's letter to Reid on 28 May 1871 and cited Bailey, Jerome, and Sheridan.

3. A takeoff on Byron's line in *Childe Harold's Pilgrimage* (canto 4, stanza 178): "I love not man the less, but Nature more."

4. Delivered by KF at the Haymarket Theatre, 23 July 1871.

5. Kate Willcox, KF's New Orleans cousin.

6. Dickens's former manager (d. 1900).

7. From *Réflexions ou sentences et maximes morales* by Rochefoucauld (1613–80).

8. They were debating the proper grounds for divorce. For Greeley, the only ground was adultery; for James, the death of love.

9. Pen name of Mary Abigail Dodge (1833–96), an opponent of women's suffrage.

10. Hamilton charged that Dickens had shown a "coarse and shameless selfishness" in discarding his wife Catherine and continuing, nevertheless, to live with Georgina, Catherine's sister. "England," she wrote, "is beating her obstinate head against marriage with a deceased wife's sister; but here it is the living wife's sister superseding the living wife. [Now] by his last will and testament he [Dickens] has even stretched his dead hand out of the grave to injure his discarded wife [again]" (*Tribune*, 17 June 1871). (Dickens had bequeathed Georgina eight thousand pounds unencumbered, but his wife only the interest on a like amount, in effect more than halving Catherine's income from the amount stipulated in their separation agreement.)

11. An account (published in 1870) of Hamilton's quarrel with publishers over royalties.

12. Pen name of Cincinnatus Hiner (or Heine) Miller (1841?–1913); called by the English "The Byron of Oregon."

13. "Myrrh" appeared in Miller's *Songs of the Sierra* (1871).

14. In addition to including himself among the princely few, Miller hailed himself as "The Lion of the North," "The Poet of the Sierras," and "The Byron of the Rockies."

15. Tilton, now editor of the *Golden Age*, had in its pages taken issue with Greeley about divorce and women's suffrage. See n. 8 to this letter.

16. A venerated preacher who drew thousands to his Plymouth Church (also known as "Beecher's Theatre"), Beecher was regularly cheered and applauded during his sermons. When Beecher asked a friend why he never came to hear him preach, the man answered: "I make it a rule never to go to places of amusement on the Sabbath Day." Stories about Beecher's seduction of women parishioners had been rife for years. It was said that he preached to at least twenty of his mistresses of a Sunday. Beginning in 1868 he had an affair with Mrs. Tilton. In 1870 Tilton's wife, to heal her "wounded spirit," confessed her adultery with Beecher; and Tilton, in discussion with a man whose own wife had also been seduced by Beecher, revealed his wife's secret (Altina L. Waller, *Reverend Beecher and Mrs. Tilton: Sex and Class in Victorian America* [Amherst: University of Massachusetts Press, 1982], 8–9, 17, 76).

To Mary Aurelia Anthony (HC)
Sept. 26. 1871.   Vevey. Switzerland

Dear friend;—

. . . Yes, I have done what was best in remaining abroad. There was nothing else for me. How it will all turn out or what will happen next, God only knows. I live from day to day, try to act out my best judgment, and trust to Providence. When health breaks down a human being becomes worse than useless, he becomes a burden to others; and as there is no place in the world for me without physiques,[1] my plain duty is to take care of myself, and that under the circumstances can only be done on this side of the water. America is no place for invalides. Ems has done me good. I was there six weeks, occupying the Kaiser's apartment. I drank twenty-six gallons of tepid water, took seventeen baths, walked up and down an alley of trees, saw a great many unsympathetic Germans, took a dislike to most of them, made adoring friends of several (among them my clever doctor who wanted me to remain during the Winter and study German with him), watched the gamblers, played several times (*with a view to an article of course*), went to bed at nine o'clock, got into the way of sleeping occasionally, acquired an appetite, gained flesh and blood, and left lighter in pocket and spirits. From there I went to Heidelberg, thence to Strasbourg where I saw the cathedral and examined the ruins, after to Basle where there are some fine Holbeins, then to Freyburg where I had a concert on the magnificent organ all to myself and paid seven dollars for it, and wound up at Geneva, the abiding place of my old chum Lina Warren. I remained with her and her sister ten days. Yesterday I came here—Vevey—at the other end of the lake, as Geneva is detestable, while this little place, besides being surrounded by vineyards, is exquisitely situated in the midst of the Alps. At this moment the Great St. Bernard is looking in at my window. I am here alone for the grape cure, which means I am to eat four pounds of delicious white sweet grapes every day for three weeks. At the end of that time I'm to return to London—stopping a few days in Paris—and obtain a verdict from my physicians. If they say I can go to work, I'll remain in England. If they counsel differently, I'll sadly pack my trunks once more and depart for Italy. [Elihu] Vedder wants me to join him and his wife in Rome, and if the worst happens, I know that I shall find a devoted friend in Carrie Vedder, to say nothing of the artistic pleasure I find in the society of your husband's aversion, otherwise E. V. himself. But I hope for the best. I do want to study singing with Garcia. He is a great maestro and has taken a fancy to me, and it would be of immense advantage in many ways to receive instruction from him. His sister (Madame Viardot)[2] and George Eliot are the only women I want to know. The latter has sent me very kind messages and I shall meet her when I return to London. She was in the country during the Summer. The former I'll be sure to know if I study with her brother whom she adores.

Alas! I must give up all idea of having my aunt abroad. Uncle Milton has decided to send a stable to New Orleans this Winter which means that he goes too, taking with him his wife. I am extremely sorry for Aunt Corda is far from well and needs medical care as well as relaxation and change. I wish that Uncle Milton could see this and feel too that helping me this Winter would be greater satisfaction than winning—or losing—a few horse-races—but nature is nature, and there is no use expecting even our best friends (and he *is* one of my best friends) to act in opposition to it.

Tell your husband that if he were here we'd have charming rows on Lake Geneva, rowing to Chillon and seeing the dungeon made famous by Byron.[3] It is only seven miles distant.

... Is Joaquin Miller to supplant Bret Harte? I like a man who [in "Myrrh"] sets his wife's disgrace to music and talks about himself as among "the princely few." Poetry seems to kill the man,—at least when there is not a vast deal of moral backbone. Miller was a rabid Southerner in London. Has he turned his coat in the North? And what does Harriet [Prescott] Spofford[4] mean by going on so about him, and what is the matter with the women that they gush at such a rate? I can't help being disgusted.

My regards to Mr. Anthony, Mr. Osgood and kisses to the children. Ask Mr. O. to find out (quietly) whether it is true that Dolby is to be Olive Logan's agent in London next Spring. I have read the report.

Write when the spirit moves.

1. French for *physics*; e.g., remedies, especially cathartics or purgatives.
2. Pauline Viardot (née Garcia, 1821–1910), sister of Maria Malibran and, like her, one of the greatest singers and stage presences the world has known. Retired from the stage, she became a distinguished singing teacher.
3. By his poem "The Prisoner of Chillon."
4. New England author (1835–1921).

To Whitelaw Reid (MU)
Oct. 16. 1871.   Vevey. Switzerland

Dear W.R.;—

... The news about Chicago[1] made me feel very badly. I fear the Brosses are ruined. It will appear a century before details come to hand. Not knowing what fate may have done to Jessie Bross,[2] I enclose a note for you to address.

Is Theodore Tilton mad? He is well-rebuked by that Chicago writer. His biography of Mrs. Woodhull[3] (thanks to *The Tribune*, do you advertise her gratuitously?) has penetrated to the Alps and may be read at the foot of the Pyramids of Egypt for aught I know....

1. The Chicago Fire of 8–9 October 1871, in which some three hundred people were incinerated, one hundred thousand left homeless, and property losses estimated to be between two hundred and four hundred million dollars.
2. Daughter of William Bross, former lieutenant governor of Illinois.
3. *Victoria C. Woodhull: A Biographical Sketch* (1871), a 35-page tract. In 1872 the Equal Rights Party nominated Woodhull for the presidency of the United States and Frederick Douglass (1817–95) for the vice presidency.

To Milton H. Sanford (LW)
[Nov. 1871]   [17 Half Moon Street, London]

Five months only since I left home, and already I have drawn the amount I started with, $2000. When I next call for money, it will probably be on your letter of credit. I am sorry, but I've undertaken to regain my health and in doing this I am obliged to spend a great deal—for me. At this rate, I shall expend the remaining $2000 by next February or March; consequently it behooves me to consider the future. I am going to try to lecture here, and if I succeed, I need give myself no concern about money. But if I do not, I must sell out some of my stock. What shall I sell? N.Y.C. Scrip or the Louisville and Nashville R.R. bonds? Please answer this question. [The] Chicago [Fire] may have killed stocks of all kinds, for aught I know, but as I need not sell before February, everything may revive before then.

To Whitelaw Reid (MU)
Dec. 9. 1871.   [17 Half Moon St.] London

Dear W.R.;—
   ... The English edition of my Pen Photographs of Dickens's Readings is exhausted. Don't you want to say so in The Tribune and copy the notice I send, taken from today's [*London*] *Graphic*? Not a person has used influence for me, the book has not even been advertised, and Chapman & Hall tried to prevent my publishing it at all, Forster[1] not wishing to have anybody but himself write about Dickens. This is entre nous.

   1. Dickens's official biographer, who was writing a three-volume *Life of Charles Dickens* to be published by Chapman & Hall (1872-74).

To Whitelaw Reid (MU)
Dec. 25. 1871.   *Private.* [17 Half Moon St.] London

Dear W.R.;—
   I have seen Mitchell's great nephew—Mitchell is the agent here and Queen's bookseller—with regard to lecturing and he thinks very favorably of it. He says, as I say, that it all depends upon whether I am clever or not. I have no notices with me and of course can obtain none. Mitchell himself is ill and will not be in town for a month but ill or well it is not advisable for me to appear out of the season. The nephew suggests my presenting to the great uncle letters of intro-

duction from prominent American editors as (between ourselves) kissing goes by favor.[1] Will you send me such a letter stating who I am and how I am esteemed publicly and privately? And please ask Major [Jonas Mills] Bundy[2] to send one also. I don't know anybody else well enough in New York to ask the favor. I have written to Boston....

    1. English proverb. As Thomas Fuller put it in *The Appeal of Injured Innocence* (1659): "But 'kissing goes by favour,' as the saying is; and therefore let him favour whom he pleases, and kiss where he favoureth."
    2. Bundy (1835–91) was part owner and editor-in-chief of the *New York Evening Mail.*

To Whitelaw Reid (MU)
Feb. 2. 1872. [17 Half Moon St.] London

    ... "Is London pleasant?" How can you ask me such a question? Nothing is pleasant to me. I have been interested in nothing, and, if anything, I become more and more indifferent. I have been to see no sights. I can't make up my mind to exert myself. I've not been to the tower even. I read the papers with ineffable disgust except when republican meetings are reported,[1] and I heartily despise the English government. It is rotten and that leader on Odger in *The Tribune* the other day was unworthy of a paper that upholds Dilke. You take a report from the *Pall Mall,* one of the most conservative papers here![2] I was to have written a series of papers for it, but its tone is so mean regarding America that I won't. The hypocrisy of this Press is enough to turn righteous hairs gray. Even the Standard people are liberal *privately* while they lie publicly. To breathe this air another year would make me a pétroleuse.[3] But why am I here? Because I am less wretched here than I should be elsewhere on account of being able to form friendships with clever people, to carry out two or three designs, to study singing with dear old Garcia who may go to America next Summer to stay. If he does, The Tribune must support him. America will have me to thank for this gain.

    And why don't I return home? I hope to do so before long, but I want to be better before crossing that dreadful Atlantic. I have two physicians, one for my throat and the other for nervous dyspepsia. The first is delighted with my progress and thinks that by April I'll be all right. The second has harder work but henceforth I'm to ride (on horseback) an hour and to walk several miles daily. This with regular diet and new medicine—I've just changed this doctor—ought to help me.

    I dined with Browning the other evening. George Eliot is polite to me. Lady Morgan's[4] niece [Mrs. Inwood Jones] has been very civil and I see much of Charles Dilke who was married this week [to Katherine Sheil] and (between ourselves) has made a mistake. The letter he wrote to me immediately after the ceremony at which no friends were present, is strange enough. I wish *he'd* waited until I had left the country, as I shan't like the wife and our republican seances will be at an end. *This is private.*

Gen. [Robert Cumming] Schenck is polite. He presented me with a copy of the *Alabama Case*[5] the other day, and last Sunday he, Gen. [Adam] Badeau[6] and Gen. [Maxwell Van Zandt] Woodhull[7] met by accident in my little salon which is very pretty, for lodgings. We had a regular American talkee talkee and decided that "we could lick all creation." Which our language is plain,[8] *but we can.*

... English people may abuse us as much as they like but I find that English men are ready enough to adore American women. They come to me and tell me how inane English girls are and how much freer and better our social system is. (I thought it bad enough until I came here.)

I dine out a good deal to get rid of myself and find that barbaric America is far more attractive than conventional London. And London delights in the change. "Dixie," that I sing with words of my own, makes a sensation. Classical, aren't they? And for myself, I go about without receiving any sensation whatever. The other evening some people became quite wild with delight when at their request I sang *The Black Brigade*[9] and "patted juba."[10]

Thanks for the letter of recommendation and for inserting notices of my book [*Pen Photographs*] in *The Tribune*....

(My leader on *Free Speech*[11] was copied into North of England papers.) ...

---

1. The Republican movement, led by Sir Charles Dilke, reached a climax when the trade unions combined in 1871 to protest Gladstone's attempt to destroy them. Gladstone objected to the unions' demands for raises, enfranchisement, new factory and mine legislation, and national education.

2. The *Tribune* (8 Oct. 1870) had reported that George Odger (1820–77), a trade unionist who had made a speech at Reading, had been almost killed by an organized mob of three hundred thugs. Just when he thought he had found refuge in the railway station, a railway official pushed him back into the pursuing crowd. The article concluded: "That official ought to have his salary doubled at once."

3. A female arsonist who uses petrol, as during the 1871 uprising of the Paris Commune.

4. Popular novelist (d. 1859).

5. As U.S. minister to Britain, Schenck (1809–90) made claims against the British government for damage done against U.S. shipping by the *Alabama* and other raiders built in England during the Civil War. An international tribunal settled the case in September 1872 by awarding the United States $15,500,000.

6. Badeau (1831–95) was Consul General of the U.S. legation in London.

7. Woodhull (1843–1921) was a member of the U.S. legation in London.

8. A take-off on Bret Harte's line in "Plain Language from Truthful James" (1870): "Which I wish to remark, / And my language is plain."

9. Words and music (c. 1863) by Dan D. Emmett (1815–1904), composer of such blackface minstrel standards as "Old Dan Tucker," "The Blue Tail Fly," and, most famously, "Dixie."

10. An African dance, brought to the New World, whose rhythm is marked by clapping of the hands.

11. Unfound.

To Whitelaw Reid (MU)
Feb. 20. 1872.   17 Half Moon Street [London]

Dear W.R.;—

What I went through yesterday can't be gone through often—thank Heaven. I had two admissions to the Commons, took Miss Schenck with me, met by two M. P.'s, shown the House, waited two hours in horrid ladies' Gallery (gallery horrid not the ladies) for great Collier debate. Left at six—dined with [the] Dilkes, went with them to hear Sir Charles [Dilke] address his constituents—great demonstration—I taken for Lady D. and cheered tremendously—meeting over after eleven—then driven by the other Chelsea member, Sir Henry Hoare, back to House of Commons where my place had been reserved, in time for Gladstone's speech (*lame*), drove Mrs. [Frank] Hill (wife of [editor of] Daily News) to her home, got to bed after three.

... Dilke's speech was admirable. He is remarkably clear-headed. A marvel in an Englishman. Hoare was groaned down and hardly allowed to open his mouth. It was very exciting.

To Whitelaw Reid (MU)
Feb. 29. [1872]   [17 Half Moon Street, London]

Dear W.R.;—

Heard the working-men denounce the Thanksgiving.[1] Will send account by next steamer. St. Paul's stupid.

1. The Thanksgiving service (also called the theatrical exhibition) was held on 27 February at St. Paul's Cathedral to celebrate the recovery from typhoid fever of Queen Victoria's eldest son, Albert Edward. Workers denounced the service largely because it cost thirteen thousand pounds, for which they—who were given only fifty-eight tickets—would be taxed. Moreover, it was said, "If prayers had restored the Prince of Wales, why had not prayers restored Blogg, his groom?"

To Whitelaw Reid (MU)
April 6. 1872.   [17 Half Moon Street] London

Dear W.R.;—

A friend of mine, Franz Hüffer,[1] a very clever young German, who is Wagner's exponent in England, who first introduced Rossetti to German readers, who is the musical critic of *The Academy* and writes for the *Fortnightly* [*Review*], has recently composed some very pretty songs that he wants to have published in America. I send them by this same post. Two are being published here but the other two are written for me and are for America only. One is John Hay's "Through the long days and years." Now I want you and Col. Hay to see what you can do with Schirmer or some [other] leading music dealer. The songs are very nice and are meeting with great success here in private. . . .

   1. Hüffer (1845-89), a German Ph.D. who took the name of Francis Hueffer, was a voluminous author, editor, literary critic, translator, music reviewer for the *Times*, and sometime playwright (his *Colomba: A Lyrical Drama in Four Acts*, with music by A. C. Mackenzie, was copyrighted by Charles Dickens Jr. and his partner Frederick Evans, a printer). Despite KF's efforts, he seems never to have published a musical note.

To Thomas Wentworth Higginson (HC)
May 14. 1872.   17 Half Moon Street [London]

Dear Colonel;—

Mr. [Henry] Fawcett[1] is in Scotland but Mrs. [Millicent Garrett] F[awcett].[2] will come on Tuesday at 2 to lunch, also Mrs. [Augusta] Webster,[3] another of the Suffrage women. Miss Beedy[4] will join us after. I'll ask Mrs. [Eliza Lynn] Linton,[5] Mrs. [Julia Ward] Howe,[6] and William Allingham.[7] More will be impossible in my little room.

As I have an engagement on Thursday at quarter before 3, I hope your breakfast will be as brief as wit.[8]

   1. English economist, Cambridge professor, and MP (1833-84); author of *Pauperism: Its Causes and Remedies* (1871).
   2. Noted English feminist (1847-1929); leader of the nonmilitant suffragists.
   3. English poet and translator (1837-94); her essays in the *London Examiner* on the question of suffrage were reprinted as leaflets by the Women's Suffrage Society.
   4. Unidentified.
   5. English journalist and novelist (1822-98).
   6. Poet and lecturer on social reforms (1819-1910); most famous for her "Battle Hymn of the Republic" (1862).

7. English poet (1824–89); friend of Carlyle, Rossetti, and Tennyson, among others.
8. Echo from *Hamlet* (II.ii.90): "Brevity is the soul of wit."

To Thomas Wentworth Higginson (HC)
May 23. [1872]   17 Half Moon Street [London]

Dear Colonel;—
   Mrs. [George Henry] Lewes [George Eliot] returns sincere thanks for the [autumn] leaves and says if you will kindly send them to 21 North Bank (The Priory) Regent's Park. N.W. she will enjoy them in the autumn.
   Mrs. [Clementia] Taylor returns on Saturday. She writes "Of course I am anxious to see Col. Higginson and delighted that he wants to see me—only how awfully disappointed he'll be. I'm growing too old to care about anything."
   Hoping that you have not seen everything in London,

To Whitelaw Reid (MU)
[May 1872]   [17 Half Moon Street, London]

   Received with tremendous applause and pronounced *the* speech of the evening.[1] I never heard people go on as they did. Many gentleman told me that I had converted them. Lord Clarendon—a young man—was absolutely enthusiastic. So much for conservative, staid England.
   If you do not care to copy it, will you send it to Mr. Bowles?
   Thanks for sending money to [my cousin in] N[ew]. O[rleans]. I sail [for the States] Aug. 6th, Mr. Smalley advising me not take the earlier steamers.

   1. Unfound.

To Whitelaw Reid (MU)
June 12. 1872.   [Ems, Germany]

Dear W.R.;—
   ... I hate presidential elections.[1] I wish the office of president were abolished. It is a base imitation of one-man power and upsets America every four years, to say nothing of rendering newspapers unendurable for a year and killing their editors with work. I'd like to see that photograph of the holy trinity, Greeley, his publisher[2] and managing editor [Reid]. Will you send it to me, together with *Scribner* for June? Of course you won't.
   ... If you see letters from me in the *American Register* (Paris) it is because

the editor has begged me to help him and I am always too weak-minded to refuse. . . .

May the best man walk into the White House.

1. On 1 May 1872 Greeley had been nominated by both the Democratic Party and the Liberal Republican Party (a split-off from the Republican Party that Greeley helped to found) to run against the Republican Ulysses S. Grant. Reid had been instrumental in securing the nomination of Greeley and was now plumping for him.

2. Samuel Sinclair; he succeeded Thomas L. McElrath (1807-88), the former publisher, who retired from the *Tribune* in 1857.

To Milton H. Sanford (LW)
[Summer 1872] [London]

To solemnly declare that I will never appear in public is beyond my power. I would make no such promise to any human being, not even to my dear father and mother, were they alive,—but they would not ask it. If I have the gift of speaking; if I can move people by so doing, and if in addition I can make money,—I think it my duty to use all the faculties given me.

You offer to put aside for my use the interest on $10,000, provided I will give up at least $10,000 a year! Don't you see how impossible this is? I want money for others as well as for myself. I want to help the Willcoxes;[1] I want if I live to do a thousand things. It is useless to cramp me. If I am deprived by health of an active life, then I must be resigned to fate, and accept poverty if necessary, but until then I want freedom to work in whatever direction I feel called.

I don't want your money, Uncle Milt,—I want health and independence; but to prove I am not mercenary, I will compromise. Withdraw your offer of $600 a year,—for I suppose that is the amount,—and I will consider Aunt Corda's health in all that I may do publicly, lecturing comparatively little and making every effort not to go great distances. Next winter (D.V.) I have no desire to lecture extensively; but I shall have something to say, if I live, about the low-down people of England, and I want to say it in New York, Boston, and other cities.

1. KF's widowed cousin and her five children.

To Whitelaw Reid (MU)
Sept. 11. 1872. Newport [R. I.]

Dear W.R.;—
Private
I see that The Tribune has begun to praise Emily Faithfull.[1] I don't like to

see The Trib. on the wrong scent and so I hope to be forgiven for saying of another woman that everybody I met in London warned me against Miss F. as a philanthropic adventurer, thoroughly untrustworthy and not *comme il faut*, one who manages to advertise herself by writing letters to journals and getting up subscriptions for herself, and who sometimes succeeds in taking in the unsuspecting—vide—Mrs. Bullard. She tried to inveigle me but I wouldn't be inveigled. As a speaker she is nothing, as a writer she is less, as a woman she's a fraud. Mrs. Howe has warned Mrs. Botta who has already been fooled by another foreigner, Mrs. [Anna Harriette] Leonowens.[2] I hope the American Press will let Miss F. alone and not puff her as though she were a great woman at home.

[Edmund] Yates[3] too is coming [to the States to lecture]. The best newspaper men call him "a howling cad." He has the jaw of a prizefighter. Will the Lotos Club treat him with distinction? If so, I hope the President [Reid] will not make him a speech. "*Black Sheep*" would be a good text.[4] It afflicts me to be honest but in the account sent me I was not charged with $8 paid on a second trunk sent to New Orleans.

Is the enclosed mss. of any use? A paragraph just read in Eng. paper suggested it. If you don't want letter on [Henry Morton] Stanley[5] & [Andrew Gregg] Curtin,[6] let me have it.

My aunt is in a very wretched state of health and I am very, very anxious. Writing is my only distraction. I see that [George] Bancroft[7] abuses Greeley. If you want me to write out what I know about Bancroft as a snob, I'll do it with effusion.

The elections look ominous.

---

1. Faithfull (1835-95), an English lecturer, was editor of *Victoria Magazine*, intended as a mouthpiece for the women's movement.

2. Leonowens (1834-1914) was the Anna of Margaret Landon's *Anna and the King of Siam* (1944). For five years (until 1867) she tutored the royal children in English, wrote books (*The English Governess at the Siamese Court* in 1870 and *The Romance of the Harem* in 1872), and lectured about her experience. In general, she was considered a fantasist, if not a fraud, in that she created a romantic past for herself in her books and lectures.

3. English novelist and journalist (1831-94).

4. Title of a Yates novel (1867).

5. Stanley (1841-1904) had found David Livingstone (1813-73) in Africa in November 1871. KF's interview of Stanley in Paris was published in the *Tribune* (21 Sept. 1872).

6. Curtin (1824-94) was twice governor of Pennsylvania. Though American minister to Russia from 1869 to 1872, he returned to the States, hoping to be nominated for the presidency, but the Liberal Republican Party Convention preferred Greeley.

7. American historian and statesman (1800-1891); he was urging the reelection of Grant in opposition to Greeley.

To Whitelaw Reid (MU)
Oct. 17. 1872.   Everett House. [New York]

Dear W. R.;—

I am tolerably well broken down in nerves. I hope this note will be "coherent."

It is by my uncle's wish that I leave my aunt as soon as possible.[1] I shall move God knows where in a day or two. Early in the season I gave out that I should not lecture. My engagements are few, my lecture not written and I begin life unexpectedly with a few hundred dollars in cash. J. G. Bennett came to see me in Newport. I was not at home and was glad. Today he sends word that he is going out of town for a week, that he wishes me to name a time when he can call, "that we can be of use to each other." Under the present unlooked-for circumstances the temptation is great. I need advice. Do you care to give any? I don't know that I have any right to ask for help from any quarters, I feel so utterly alone and now more than ever realize my dear mother's loss. You said you were tired. I am tired enough to commit suicide.

---

1. Sanford was blaming KF for worrying his wife, whose mental and physical condition was worsening. He wanted KF to be a nurse-companion to his wife and offered to support her. But much as KF loved her aunt, she dreaded losing her independence as well as the opportunities to exercise her talents.

To Whitelaw Reid (MU)
Oct. 18. 1872.   [Everett House, New York]

Dear W.R.;—

I forgot to ask you to have my stray letter mss. sent, after tomorrow a.m., to 161 W. 23d St.

Suppose the editor [Bennett], spoken of yesterday, makes me [a] special proposition but asks me what I am willing to do and suppose I suggest an independent column in Sunday's paper (headed Independent Column and signed Free Lance or something of the sort) in which the week shall be reviewed exactly as *I* please, totally regardless of the regularly expressed opinion of the paper [the *Herald*]?

This is a sensation at least for which the gentleman would be inclined to pay handsomely I fancy; but if you say "no," I won't mention the idea. Silence for 24 hours will give consent.

To Mary Aurelia Anthony (HC)
Nov. 13. 1872.   23 Gramercy Park [New York]

Dear M.A.;—

How thankful I am that you have all escaped injury by that dreadful fire![1] How rejoiced I am that Mr. Osgood is not among the sufferers. Please say so to him, and that I do not write him a letter of congratulation because he wouldn't have time to read it. Of course you are in a state of excitement and confusion, but when you return to your normal condition, let me know how much is left of everybody and whether *your* trade[2] will be affected seriously by the terrible catastrophe. There seems to be nothing left now for sensation but a tidal wave. I dare say it is lying in wait for all of us.

I've moved. I went up so many stairs that I nearly died of them. Now I've a parlor floor in a nice house well kept and my aunt is to have the floor above, which will be nice as I don't like to be away from her. . . . I've had a fine offer here [from the *Herald*] and have accepted it (for writing) and postpone lecturing until the universe is in a listening mood. . . .

1. The Boston Fire of 9 November, which raged for twenty-four hours and burned out Boston's business center at an estimated damage of a hundred million dollars.

2. Anthony's husband was art director for J. R. Osgood & Co. and for Fields and Osgood's magazine *Every Saturday*.

To Whitelaw Reid (MU)
Nov. 18. 1872.   [23 Gramercy Park, New York]

Dear W.R.;—

Will you accept the enclosed?[1] I wrote it to please Uncle Milton who was tickled muchly at my desiring to do so. It is sound from the turf point.

If you reject [the enclosed], my address is 23 Gramercy Park (as I appear to be hated in The Tribune). Please return [the enclosed] tomorrow morning.

I was sorry to miss you on Friday. Will you dine with me on Thursday, Saturday, or Sunday? Not publicly; I mean in my cosy parlor.

1. KF's article "The Turf: Racing in America During 1872" (*Tribune*, 29 Nov. 1872). The article was a reply to a card on the racing season by Colonel McDaniel, whose horses had been the winningest.

To Whitelaw Reid (MU)
Nov. 30. [1872]   23 Gramercy Park [New York]

Dear W.R.;—

I have read today's sad news [about Horace Greeley's death][1] with grief. God help those orphan girls [Greeley's two daughters].

If Tribune contributors are to testify their respect in any special way, at the funeral or elsewhere, kindly let me know.

I know you must feel badly. If you are obliged to dine in public today or tomorrow, and had rather be alone, come to my rooms and dine.

I shall lay my offering on the great man's grave tomorrow morning—if they are generous enough to publish it.[2]

With sympathy

1. Greeley had been exhausted by his strenuous campaign for the presidency, branded as a crackpot and traitor by his adversaries (he afterward said that he did not know if had run for the presidency or the penitentiary), shocked by his wife's death a few days before the election returns, and overwhelmingly defeated at the polls. His mind became unhinged, and he died insane on 29 November 1872.

2. The *Tribune* (30 Nov. and 2 Dec.) published tributes to Greeley, but they were all unsigned.

To Whitelaw Reid (MU)
Dec. 3. [1872]   23 Gramercy Park [New York]

Dear W.R.;—

I'm ill, but I'll go as you request [to Greeley's funeral], and hope a special Providence will help me not to take more cold.

Will you dine with me on Saturday? Mrs. Moulton and Mrs. Bullard are coming,—and I want you.

My tempters[1] urge and urge again my going to Washington and say I need not sign my name and need not remain more than two weeks. I don't wish to go, and yet being "despised and rejected"[2] where my heart is enlisted, I am in a quandary. What do you think? . . .

Remember that I am always glad to have you dine with me when you feel like coming. I need only a few hours notice—except tomorrow night.

You are very tired and *must* rest.

1. Those at the *Herald* who wanted KF to report on the electoral college. Greeley had died before his sixty-six electoral votes were cast, and they had to be redistributed.

2. From Isaiah 53:3.

To Whitelaw Reid (MU)
Dec. 4. [1872] 5-1/2 p.m.   23 Gramercy Park [New York]

Dear W.R.;—

It was all dreadful to me today, because it was so hard. I did so long to have people's hearts softened. But to the point, I decided to go to the cemetery because Mrs. Runkle and Mrs. Moulton didn't. We got as far as one block this side of the ferry when the coachman, much to my astonishment, turned off and then had the impudence to ask us whether we wished to go on! When we got [back] into the line [leading to the ferry] we were at the end. In the evening, it was late, nearly 4 p.m., the two Brooklyn ladies evidently expected to be driven home and I knew I had not strength to endure the fatigue. So I said I would go home, so did Nelly Hutchinson,[1] and we two took an omnibus, leaving the other women in possession of the carriage.

I write all this that you may know why I failed at the eleventh hour—if you wish to know.

Who is Mrs. Hull?[2]

1. Ellen Mackay Hutchinson, a *Tribune* reporter.
2. Mrs. G. H. S. Hull; listed among the mourners of the *Tribune* staff who attended Greeley's funeral on 5 December 1872.

To Whitelaw Reid (MU)
Dec. 8. 1872.   23 Gramercy Park [New York]

Dear W.R.;—

Today's *Herald* publishes my note in which I contribute $50 to Greeley Fund. Now I must write another, saying that the money can be given for a statue. But don't you think a Greeley scholarship for farming at Cornell University would be better than a statue? Or if a [page missing]

I hope you have not taken more cold. I'm housed with my cough. Drop in when the spirit moves.

To Whitelaw Reid (MU)
Dec. 26. 1872.   23 Gramercy Park [New York]

Dear W.R.;—

... Will *The Tribune* make any suggestions about the position of Mr. Greeley's statue?

It is not necessary for me to say what I think about the Tribune revolution.[1]

1. Almost a month after Greeley's death, just before Christmas 1872, Reid became editor-in-chief of the *Tribune*, though not without a bitter struggle that involved the *Tribune*'s stockholders.

To Whitelaw Reid (MU)
Dec. 28. 1872.   [23 Gramercy Park, New York]

To W.R.[1]
We've heard, e'en since the world began,
That "He who runs may read,"
And now we find *The Tribune* takes
This motto for its creed.

A goodly motto 'tis, and true,
For turn it as you may,
You'll find that he who runs may read
The Tribune ev'ry day.

And further, strange though it appear,
I really tell no fib
When I declare, upon my oath,
'Tis *Reid* who runs *The Trib*.

Reid runs it, though by friend betrayed,
By one whose name is Sinclair,[2]
So *clair* a case of *sin* was his
As made creation's eyes stare.

He runs it gallantly and well,
And now, by this same token,
The Tribune Staff lean on a *Reid*
They swear can ne'er be broken!

K.F.

1. Written to be read at the banquet held at Delmonico's to celebrate Reid's becoming the *Tribune*'s editor-in-chief.
2. Samuel Sinclair; started on the *Tribune* as a clerk, advanced to business manager, then publisher; became the largest single stockholder in the Tribune Association. He opposed Reid in favor of Schuyler

Colfax (1823–85), who was serving his last months as vice president of the United States. After a bitter struggle, the stockholders forced Sinclair out as publisher and made Reid editor-in-chief and publisher as well. The upshot was that at age thirty-five Reid was in absolute control of a newspaper that had become the most influential daily in the United States.

To Cordelia Riddle Sanford (LW)
[Sept. 29, 1873] [Bayonne, France]

I am safely through the Carlist lines,[1] and in two days I shall be in Paris.

1. The Royalist Don Carlos (1848–1909) was leading an insurrection against Emilio Castelar (1832–99), president of the first Spanish Republic. KF was returning from an interview with Castelar and had to brave the Carlists (followers of Don Carlos). KF's book containing the interview—*Ten Days in Spain* (1875)—proved one of her most popular.

Part Five: 1874–1879

Becomes Playwright and Actress
Promotes Bell's Telephone
Helps Establish Shakespeare Memorial Theatre

To William Winter (FL)
Feb. 12. 1874.   [23 Gramercy Park] New York

Dear Mr. Winter;—

I've been asked by Sir Charles Dilke to write 8 letters a year (4 columns each) for the London Athenaeum.[1] I shan't accept it if I succeed in finding a competent person to take my place. If I wrote, it would be anonymously and *on trial*; to stop if I were not liked by English country gentlemen. Now, are you willing to *try* for the correspondence, sending say three letters as samples (to be paid for of course)? Dilke wants English letters after the manner of Edmond About's[2] French correspondence, in order to be copied into *The Times*—books, art, drama, music, everything but politics.

The least you would be paid would be £1 per column. Their columns are short and if you "took" you could double your price. What do you say? Let me know as soon as possible.

    1. Dilke had inherited not only his father's baronetcy but the *Gardener's Chronicle, Notes and Queries,* and the *Athenaeum.*
    2. Voluminous French author (1828-85); his *Dernierès lettres d'une bon jeune homme à sa cousine Madeleine* (1863) was the work to which Dilke had referred.

To Annie Adams Fields (HL)
April 2. 1874.   23 Gramercy Park. New York

Dear Mrs. Fields;—

Have you forgotten me? I write for help. Can you tell me about the success of your Holly Tree Inns?[1] Can you give me any statistics, expense &c? I want to agitate the subject here. The women are making such big fools of themselves in this temperance crusade that it seems a pity not to tell them how they really can help real temperance.

Won't you send me your card when you come to town?

   1. Actually, Holly-Tree Coffee Rooms (a name derived from a Dickens Christmas story, "The Holly-Tree Inn"). These coffee rooms were intended to attract Boston workmen away from saloons.

To Edmund Clarence Stedman (CU)
   Stedman (1833–1900) was a poet, critic, and broker in a Wall Street firm. He became one of KF's closest friends.
May 24. [1874]   [237 Madison Avenue, New York]

The plot thickens. I *must* go to Boston on Tuesday for Wednesday p.m.'s recitation,[1] and I've just had a note from Daly. I may appear here in Peg [Woffington]. Between them all I am quite crazy. . . .

Pray for me on Wednesday at 4 P.M.

   1. On 27 May KF recited Thomas Hood's "Bridge of Sighs" at the Boston Theatre in a benefit held for Henry A. McGlenen, the business manager of the theatre. The *Tribune* of 28 May 1874 reported that KF "acquitted herself splendidly."

To Edmund Clarence Stedman (CU)
July 17. 1874.   237 Madison Avenue [New York]

Dear Poet;—

Do you think I care nothing for woods and deer and guns and roughing? Why have I not a gun, and have I not shot a deer (if you don't believe me, ask Osgood to show you the head that adorns his office) and am I not the best sort of fellow at camping out? Would I not be wearing the shortest sort of skirts, the highest sort of boots, and the biggest sort of hat this very moment if I were free

Edmund Clarence Stedman, poet, critic, and Wall Street broker. (From Laura Stedman and George M. Gould, *Life and Letters of Edmund Clarence Stedman* [New York: Moffat, Yard, 1910], 2:314.)

to choose my life? You don't know me. I'm here because Fate (with a very big *F*) glues me to the spot....

I don't regret Central Park reading a bit.[1] My enemies have had a chance to say their worst (which they have done with effusion). My friends have not the remotest idea of me in consequence, but I tested my nerve and [Theodore] Thomas[2] was satisfied and we'll do it in Steinway Hall next Winter. No glory can ever come of it, for the poem ["The Bridge of Sighs"] is ineffective, but we'll do it, and be heard. I've nothing left in me but dogged perseverance. The more I am blamed and abused, the sicker I get of existence and the more determined I am to disappoint my loving relatives and mean-spirited foes.

    1. The event was not covered by the *Tribune* or *New York Times*.
    2. Thomas (1835–1905) was a conductor of his own touring orchestra. He brought symphonic music to areas in the United States where it had never been heard. From 1868 to 1875 he gave summer programs in Central Park.

To Edmund Clarence Stedman (CU)
Nov. 17. 1874. 145 East 21st St. [New York]

Dear, good, best of friends;—

How can I ever repay you for all you have done and are doing? At the theatre they are perfectly satisfied with me.[1] The success they say was genuine. The talk about the applause coming from friends they utterly repudiate. They told me that the critics on going out said "Well, now we've got Miss Field at our mercy and we are going to pitch in." They all went to see me fail and not doing so made them mad. If Whitelaw Reid does not let me have justice in *The Tribune*, he is not my friend. I shall not write to him. If you choose to tell him, I am willing. Do you write your response to *The Tribune*, and get some one of influence to protest in *The [Evening] Post*. If I see [William] Wheatley[2] I'll ask him to write a line. The more talk the better for the next performance. The house was not papered.[3] There was $1000 in money and I made several hundred.

I shall send you 4 seats for Saturday.

I know Mrs. [Elizabeth C.] Winter.[4] She pulled me all to pieces and informed people I was *42*!

1. At age thirty-six KF tried to fulfill a childhood ambition: to become an actress in the family tradition, though her mother had debuted at fourteen. Thus, at Booth's Theatre, to a crowded house, she mounted the stage in the role of Peg Woffington in Charles Reade's *Masks and Faces*.

2. Wheatley (1816–76) was the director of *Masks and Faces*.

3. Theatre talk: to fill the house by giving away free tickets.

4. Journalist and author (1841–92); sometimes published under the pen name Isabella Castelar.

To Edmund Clarence Stedman (CU)
Nov. 17. 1874. [145 East 21st St., New York]

God bless you, Edmund Stedman.[1] The management are pleased.[2] The stage manager said I did much to be commended but did not do nearly as well as at rehearsal. This I knew. But I'm afraid now. The animus of the Press is such that my strength is taken away from me, and I feel ill. The article in *The Tribune* almost killed me. I expected more generous treatment. Is Whitelaw Reid in sympathy with it? If so, what did his note to me mean?[3]

Ah, noble friend, the world is hard and I want to be out of it more than ever. I hoped to get away from myself in acting, but these attacks make me desire to bury myself.

What a mistake that I was ever born!

How thankful I am for your existence. Tell your wife how grateful I am.

Kate Field on stage. (From Lilian Whiting, *Kate Field: A Record* [Boston: Little, Brown, 1899], 468.)

1. Stedman had praised KF's stage debut and defended her against the "severe sentence pronounced [on her performance] in a few of the newspapers" (*Tribune*, 18 Nov. 1874). The *New York Times* of 15 November, for instance, had written: "It is difficult to imagine anything more unsympathethic than Miss Field's presence and delivery.... Unhappily, Miss Kate Field is neither young nor handsome; her voice is inexpressive and the frailty of her physique makes the acquisition of power in the future at least improbable." Even the *Tribune*, for which KF was writing, had little forbearance for her performance. On 16 November, *Tribune* reporter Elizabeth C. Winter had declared KF unsuitable for the title role.

2. Henry C. Jarrett (1828-1903) and Albert Marshman Palmer (1838-1905) were comanagers of Booth's Theatre.

3. Reid had written KF on 15 November, the morning after KF's debut: "I congratulate you with all my heart. You can never appear before a more severe audience than that of last night . . . and you did not fail" (LW, 326).

To Edmund Clarence Stedman (CU)
[Nov. 19, 1874]   145 East 21st St. [New York]

Best of friends;—

I am so sorry to have missed you today. I want to take you by both hands and tell you with a heart full of gratitude what I think of your noble article in *The Tribune* and your note in *The Graphic* [defending my theatrical debut]. I absolutely ache to break a lance in your defence. I want somebody to say something against you in my presence. I want to leave you a large fortune. I want to do a thousand impossible things.

I enclose four seats—the best I could get. Almost all the parquet[1] is always sent to the hotels. Also I send admissions to the gallery. I have only given away 20 tickets. Jarrett & Palmer hate to make presents of this sort. Their company get nothing and come begging to me for tickets.

I feel better. I was awfully down but the devil in me is up again. Stage manager, management and leader of orchestra say I was a success and laugh at the attacks. I hope the house will be tolerable. But if it isn't it shan't affect me. My fright is of the stage not of an audience.

1. The section of seats near the orchestra pit.

To Mary Mapes Dodge (PUL-D)
Nov. 28. [1874]   145 East 21st St. [New York]

Dear Dodgie;—

I think your *Rhymes & Jingles* charming. If it is not simultaneously published in England send me a copy to review in *Athenaenum*.

I was interviewed in last night's *Graphic*.[1] If you want to know my sentiments, get it.

1. Concerning KF's reaction to the criticism of her performance in *Masks and Faces*.

To Edmund Clarence Stedman (CU)
Aug. 7. 1875.   New York Tribune Offices.
                                                                        13 Pall Mall. London

(*Private*)
Dear friend;—

... How I wish I could make you well[1] and rich! Ah, what a curse life is when you can neither help yourself nor those you most care for. Sometimes it seems as though I should go mad.

But I'm not mad, dear friend. I look better than on leaving America and I weigh seven pounds more. The climate has something to do with this. It is not so excitable. Then I am out of a hotel. The hole I lived in had grown hateful to me and I could not eat the food. In England you go into apartments, order what you want to eat and do not come in contact with unpleasant people. For this quiet too you pay less money than for one room in a boarding house....

That bosh of the Marquis of Lorne's has had a great run—first edition exhausted.[2] Only be a lord and you are a success. Such is life—even in America.

I hope you are better—in spite of Lord Houghton.[3]

1. Stedman kept a journal of his afflictions; the most recurrent were headaches, rheumatism, nervous exhaustion, neuralgia, constipation, and diarrhea.
2. The "bosh," written by the Duke of Argyll, was *Guido and Lita: A Tale of the Riviera* in verse, which ran through three editions in 1875.
3. Formerly, Richard Monckton Milnes (1809-85); poet, critic, biographer, and friend of Tennyson, Thackeray, Swinburne, and Browning, among others. He was currently in the States and was being escorted by Stedman.

To Edmund Clarence Stedman (CU)
Sept. 10. 1875.   New York Tribune Offices.
                                                                        13 Pall Mall. London

Dear B.P. (Blameless Prince)[1]

... Why is it that a certain set of American writers don't want to admit that I am a woman, with a woman's feelings and a woman's manners? It is disgusting, and if I live long enough I'll have a noble revenge.

I've just heard from Henry Watterson.[2] . . . He engages me on very good terms to write whenever I please on whatever I please—preferring music and the drama. I've written three letters already, and I suppose they've appeared. So far, I've not succeeded in impressing on Watterson's mind the fact that I want to see myself in print. Let us cultivate a sublime patience.

Confidential

Now I know you're anxious to know what I'm dying to tell you, yet I'm afraid lest my secret get into print. Nothing is a secret which more than one person knows and so many must become acquainted with my movements that I almost despair of preserving an incognita;[3] still I shall endeavor to do so and you are not to talk about me dramatically. . . . I want to keep out of the papers until I get ready to go into them, which will not be for some time. . . .

When I came here it was with the intention of sinking K.F. and becoming somebody else so as to be judged impartially on my merits. I had had enough of disgraceful jealousy and unfair criticism. So on the 30th of August I went to Liverpool, the second town in Great Britain, and appeared in a new musical burlesque under an assumed name. No one knew that the new actress was K.F. The people to whom I took letters received me cordially in private. The United States Consul Gen'l [Charles S.] Fairchild, who was very polite, had not the faintest idea of my movements. I made my début as an utterly unknown, friendless person. All that the critics knew was that report stated me to be American. I had a cordial reception, was heartily applauded and the papers the next day gave me cordial praise. The stage manager complimented me on my dresses and appearance before I went on the stage. "Half the battle is won already" he said. "She is up to Dick!" was the verdict of Americans present, meaning that I was all right. The editor of the [*Liverpool Daily*] *Post* (leading paper) wrote me a most complimentary note in addition to a criticism, which the editor of *The Era* here (*the* dramatic paper which circulates all over the world) says I don't value half enough. "Praise from Mr. [Edward R.] Russell" he says "means everything." The critic of the *Porcupine* (satirical weekly) called and congratulated me and wrote at once to managers in my behalf. Mr. Russell also wrote to the leading manager at Manchester with whom I am now in correspondence.

A manager at once engaged me to produce the burletta [farce] at Middlesborough (near Newcastle-on-Tyne). I star there for a fortnight beginning October 4th, and the manager of the Newcastle Theatre Royal wants to engage me for the principal part in pantomime (singing). You know that in England the pantomime begins at Christmas, lasts eight weeks and swallows up everything else, so, as I sing, I've an opportunity of acting when others are obliged to do nothing. This, dear friend, is what has come from acting one week in Liverpool! I shall keep out of London for some time. Charles Reade[4] applauds my plan. I dined with him last night. First he complimented me on my way of speaking

English, which he said was wonderfully pure, and then, asking me to sing, was warm in his praise. After I had sung him something comic he exclaimed "Sing with that same expression of face on the stage and you'll do. You've humor." Old [James Robinson] Planche, the dramatist, was talking about writing a play for me the other day, and when I went out of the room said to my friend Mrs. Inwood Jones (Lady Morgan's niece), "I'll take the *Field* against the favorite!"

So far so good. Of course I shall have a tug. I expect it; but if my health is preserved and my money holds out until I can command my own terms, I'll not complain. I can live on my salary and my letter writing but of course if I buy plays and dress well I must draw on my very small capital which can't last very long. However, I've made a beginning, have succeeded and am in a fair way to get the experience I want in as easy a way as possible, without any compromise of dignity or position. The editor of *The Era* knows my secret and seems very much interested. He has asked me to call on him early next week, which Miss Ward[5] says is a special attention. What he wants I don't know.... All I ask is opportunity.

I'm all alone in a friend's house, the family having gone to the continent. I pay $5 (five *dollars*, not pounds remember) for my lodging and provide for myself, the servant cooking for me and doing it so well that when I don't dine out I have a friend in. Today Ashton Dilke will come. His brother Charles went to America two weeks ago. Life is a deal easier here than at home, I'm sorry to say. The Smalleys are at Broadstairs. Col. [John Wien] Forney[6] has just returned from the continent and I expect to see him on Sunday à propos of the [American] Centennial. I have the Hills (Editor Daily News), Mrs. Inwood Jones, Charles Reade and the Dilkes for near neighbors, so although everybody is supposed to be out of town, I am not without friends. Then Geneviève Ward is here and we go to the theatres together. I want an advance copy of your *Victorian Poets*. Remember. If I can help you, I'll do so with all my heart. Unfortunately I'm not likely to be in London when it comes out. Still, I'll try to do something....

I'm glad you are better.

1. A reference to Stedman's *The Blameless Prince and Other Poems* (1869).

2. Watterson (1840-1921) was editor of the Louisville *Courier-Journal*, an influential Kentucky newspaper.

3. KF's incognita—Mary Keemle—consisted of two of her four names, Mary Katherine Keemle Field.

4. English playwright, theatre manager, and novelist (1814-84).

5. Geneviève Ward (1838-1922), opera singer who sang under the name Madame Ginevra Guerrabella. She married and separated from Constantine de Guerbel, a Russian count whom she met in Italy. Her singing voice failing, she mounted the dramatic stage. Retired in England, Ward was made a Dame of the Order of the British Empire, the first time the DBE was conferred on an American actress.

6. Forney (1817-81) was editor of the *Philadelphia Press*.

To Edmund Clarence Stedman (CU)
[1875] [Middlesbrough, England]

They only publish evening papers here so I have only had the theatre verdict this morning [on my *Folie Musicale*]¹ and that of two critics who were there. One, a young man, told my landlady that he was delighted with me. The other, the leading physician and amateur musician, said he did not think much of the play (neither do I) but that I was "first class—a beautiful singer, very handsome, very young and sure to take!" Perhaps you'll send this to *The Sun* or *The Times*. I've learned how to make myself up, which is just doing as little as possible with my face and wearing a blonde wig. My dresses (two) are very handsome. They are short and make me look like a little girl.—Later—Papers are all right—say nothing could be better.

Ask Jennie [Jeannette] Gilder² to take up my ideas of a [national] conservatory of the drama and of a Centennial Benefit.³ She can help a great deal if she will. *Don't forget, please.*

How far away I seem from everybody. In London I have a feeling of home but out of it I am lost in a barren wilderness.

    1. Written by KF and performed at Middlesbrough for a week.

    2. Journalist and critic (1849-1916); her obituary tribute to KF appeared in the *New York Critic* (6 June 1896), a magazine she cofounded with her brother Joseph.

    3. That U.S. theatres help in raising funds to celebrate the Centennial of American Independence.

To Edmund Clarence Stedman (CU)
Dec. 4. 1875. London

Dear friend;—

... Don't you think you were a little hard on a body? W[illiam]. J[ermyn]. Florence¹ wrote me that he would do all he could to advance the idea. It is a good one—would reflect immense credit on the theatre if carried out, and *ought to be carried out*²—so, too, ought the second idea of all trades and professions contributing to the Centennial. I don't say anything will be done. I only say it ought to be done and I'm not ashamed of having given birth to a good idea. Next year we celebrate our 100th anniversary and all Europe is told that it is a national undertaking. So far, it is a Pennsylvania undertaking. $1,500,000 are still needed to meet expenses. ...

Don't scold me for thinking about things that don't concern my own interests. I always have; I always shall. I don't think an artist is the bigger for having but one idea. In olden times the big men were *big all round.* They could paint and sculp, and write, and build churches, and engineer, and act as diplomats. I don't neglect my special work because I write for the newspapers. And if I write, I must evolve opinions that are sure to offend somebody. I'm quite reconciled to the situation. If I had my way everybody should either like or love me, but that is impossible, so I've made up my mind to be hated. . . .

So you saw Watterson. . . . Not a paper or a dollar have I got from him yet, and he owes me $400, enough to keep me alive four months. I know that my letters are printed because I see extracts from them in other papers and the *Journal* is sent to *The Tribune* office. "Evil is wrought by want of thought as well as want of heart," as Hood says.[3] Fortunately I go to work next week and so need not draw further on my letter of credit which means selling out the little remaining stocks I possess.

Now about your book.[4] You've seen the mean reviews in *The Athenaeum* and *Examiner*. Expect nothing better except from those who know you. The *Newcastle Chronicle* will have a notice written by the U.S. Consul. I enclose [John] Fraser's[5] letters. I sent my *Athenaeum* article to the *Courier-Journal* before receiving his first letter, so will write another for the *Westminster*. Smalley spoke of your book with praise. Today Hermann Vezin[6] came in en route to Robert Buchanan[7] with whom he was to dine. I asked Vezin to call Buchanan's attention to V[ictorian]. P[oets]. and [to] ask him whether he would not review it, if he liked it. Vezin promised to do so. I may know Buchanan when I go north. Vezin believes he is the coming man for the drama, says he has written some plays of great promise.

I start for the north two days hence. [Dion] Boucicault[8] says when I return the middle of February, he'll get me an opening here. I'm gradually meeting managers and actors and find them all friendly. Marie Wilton's husband, [Sir Squire] Bancroft,[9] was quite effusive the other night because of my Dickens [Pen] Photographs which he said had delighted him. Only actors know the value of that little book. No, there are others. A short time ago I had a letter from the Principal of a Deaf & Dumb Asylum in Kansas, à propos of this same book.

I see that you are still dining Silenus[10]—otherwise Lord Houghton. He's a clever man and an amiable to Americans but he's as arrant a coward as ever sat in the House of Lords. Politically, of course, he amounts to nothing. When Swinburne first reared his head, Houghton took him up tremendously and urged his publishing Songs & Ballads. Then when the cry of indignant virtue rent the air, my lord told Swinburne that there must be an end to the acquaintance! Lord Houghton has himself the largest collection of erotic literature in England! . . .

Love to your wife and the boys and a Merry Christmas to you.

1. A leading American comedian (1831–91).
2. See *To Edmund Clarence Stedman*, [1875], n. 3.

3. Thomas Hood, in his poem "The Lady's Dream."
4. *Victorian Poets*, an anthology (1875).
5. Editor of the *Glasgow News*.
6. English actor (1829-1910).
7. English dramatist (1841-1901).
8. Boucicault (1822-90) was an Irish-born actor and dramatist who worked in London.
9. Wilton (1839-1921) and Bancroft (1841-1926) were English actors and theatre managers.
10. Chief of the satyrs.

To Edmund Clarence Stedman (CU)
March 25. 1876. [15 New Cavendish St.] London

Dear friend;—
 . . . So you are going to have a shingle of your own![1] May it be an irresistible magnet, attracting all manner of flies to your net. Shouldn't I like to give you a big order to start with? . . .

Well, I'm settled comfortably in an admirable American Hotel, kept by an admirable American young woman, daughter of [Frederick William] Herring, the N.Y. artist. When you have friends coming over, send them here—good house, capital situation, good food, pleasant people—15 New Cavendish St. Portland Place. W. near the Langham Hotel. I never lived for so little money but then I am favored—as usual. Miss Herring wants me, and I bring fish to her pond. I've two rooms and make them look cosy, though I've not a picture on the walls. I stick photographs about and throw newspapers on the chairs and tables. Here I propose to stick, though I get offers to go into the country which some say I ought to accept. I don't think so.

Now as to writing. I want to write for a New York paper. I'm not content to be read only in the South-West and through the medium of paragraphs extracted. I wish you'd find out how often *The Tribune* would care to hear from me, whether if I wrote twice a month my letters would be welcome. I naturally incline to *The Tribune* but if I'm not wanted there, tell me what you'd do in my place. I may write to Bennett about Bayreuth[2] but must be sure first that I can go. . . .

Will you do me a favor? [Moncure Daniel] Conway[3] has got back. His church gives him a reception tonight. He has decided to remain here. Wise—Boston would find him out. He is superficial.

I'm glad Bayard Taylor[4] has gone on *The Tribune*. The Ed. page needs strengthening and so does the reviewing. Please remember me to him and his wife. Buchanan is in town. Vezin who is great friends with him wants me to meet him. Perhaps I shall. I want to meet Swinburne but one of his intimates advises me to abstain as he is horrible when drunk and no one can ever say when he'll present himself sober.

Is business improving? What say people about [Jay] Gould now? I am disgusted with the way the two parties are going to work to pull wires not for the good of the country but for their own aggrandizement.[5] As for Washington! I'm not in the least surprised—"Worse remains behind"[6]—I'm sure. Love to all. . . .

1. In March Stedman had borrowed ten thousand dollars at 7 percent from his uncle William Dodge and opened his own brokerage office at No. 80 Broadway.

2. German town near Nuremburg where Wagner (1813-83) settled at about age sixty and made it a festival center for the performance of his operas. KF wanted to report the opening of the Festspielhaus at which the entire *Der Ring des Nibelungen* was performed in August 1876.

3. A Massachusetts-born clergyman (1832-1907); wrote more than seventy books, including biographies of Hawthorne, Emerson, and Carlyle. In 1864 he accepted the pastorate of South Place Chapel, Finsbury, London, a position he held until 1884.

4. Author and lecturer (1825-78).

5. Refers to the machinations of Gould (1836-92) in the deadlocked election involving Rutherford B. Hayes (1822-93), the Republican candidate, and Samuel J. Tilden (1814-86), the Democratic candidate. Democrats charged that Gould controlled the House of Representatives, which broke the deadlock. Tilden also ascribed his defeat to Gould.

6. From *Hamlet* (III.iv.179): "Thus bad begins and worse remains behind."

To Edmund Clarence Stedman (CU)
May 1. 1876.   [15 New Cavendish St.] London

Dear E.C.S.;—

Yesterday morning you read all about it. I did my best to keep the matter quiet. I told very few, made the American correspondents promise not to divulge my name and all would have been well had not Saturday's *Era* broken faith. Then it was out and of course the *N.Y. Herald* was only too glad to be first *in the field*. I'm awfully sorry for I'm not ready to be talked about, and I'd like you to make people understand that it isn't my fault if I don't quietly pursue my dramatic career until the right play gets written.

Ever since my return to town I've intended to make my début quietly in The Honeymoon at *The Gaiety*, playing *Volante* to Miss Ward's *Juliana*. I said nothing to nobody, told no critics and appeared with only two rehearsals. My second was an hour before the performance when I taught *Roland* his "business" in the forest scene with myself—I having invented the business the night before. I was as nervous as a witch and dressed with Miss Ward to have her keep up my spirits. She was as good as she could be, helped me to dress and was the first to say "You are a great success! Didn't I tell you so? I'm never wrong in such matters." My first dress was lovely—white silk and roses. It was new. I couldn't afford two new dresses, so the second costume wouldn't compare with no. 1, but it was good enough for an afternoon performance. I was warmly applauded and felt that the audience, made up for the most part of strangers, was drawn to me. At the end of second act Hermann Vezin came behind and shook me warmly by the hand. Then I knew that I was all right as he is a severe and honest critic. The stage manager said "very good," the dresser said "wonderful for a first time," and the stage carpenters crowded the wings and led the applause. I had three lovely bouquets from recent acquaintances. After the performance, people came behind and congratulated me. Conway was among them and said he was surprised and pleased.[1] I enclose a few extracts from letters and Press....

[John] Hollingshead[2] has heard me sing and now wants to bring me out in light opera. Nothing is decided at present. I've made one move and succeeded. That's enough for the present.

Thanks for getting my article in *Graphic*.[3]...

Love to all. (Mary Keemle is my own name.) ...

Letters & Press Notices [follow, copied in KF's hand].

Dear Miss Field;—

"I found you charming, extremely natural, gestures very good and not overdone which is a great virtue." Marie Taglioni—the great danseuse.

"I was charmed with Volante yesterday.... Lord Campbell was delighted." P. Girard. *N.Y. World* & [London] *Graphic*.

"You have what most actresses lack—a head. You were very natural and altogether a great success." J. P. Jackson. *N.Y. Herald*.

"I was very much pleased with your performance. Not a bit of a novice. You were as easy and graceful as could be desired and were quite at home. Your wig was wonderfully becoming. I hope you were satisfied. I am sure the public was." Laura Seymour—Chas. Reade's great friend—an old actress and acknowledged critic.

"I cannot tell you how pleased and surprised we were with your acting and appearance. You will do." Mrs. Inwood Jones (Lady Morgan's niece) & Mrs. Chatfield (Dilke's grandmother).

"I took two Englishmen to see you act. One was brother of Sir John Gilbert.[4] They were both quite charmed and enthusiastic. For myself, I must say frankly I was taken by surprise. Tho' I had already a firm faith in your dramatic talent, I was quite unprepared for the perfection of art which your acting showed. Spontaneous, refined and natural. Nothing was overdone and nothing fell short of the requirements of the part—no coldness—no effort—no shade of stage conventionality, and the rare quality of ladyhood enveloped you like a glory and detached you in more eyes than mine from the other 'ladies.' Added to all these qualities, you looked most lovely." W. J. Hennessy, artist.

"Excessively pretty—intelligent and piquante." *Globe.*

"You are all right—in appearance and acting. You are a success." Hermann Vezin.

"First rate and you looked splendidly." Gen. Geo. B. Williams.

"Her performance evinced a genuine feeling for comedy." *Athenaeum.*

"In the part of Volante Miss Mary Keemle, a young actress of distinct power and remarkable intelligence, made her first appearance on the London stage. Her performance was bright and vivacious and showed great aptitude for comedy." *Times.*

I'm told there will be a strong article in *The Hornet.* I didn't invite the critics. They never go to a morning performance. The few who were present were there out of curiosity to see a new person. They were surprised and I'm told the other critics are sorry they were not present.

1. The *New York Graphic* (22 May 1876) printed Conway's letter on Mary Keemle's performance, which declared that "her first appearance in London was a success . . . [and] that the young American will be heard of in the future as winning such favor as her unquestionable talent and patient studies merit."

2. Hollingshead (1827-1904) managed the Gaiety, where KF made her London debut.

3. Printed in the *New York Graphic* (8 Apr. 1876) under the title "A Letter from Kate Field." The article dealt with a recent Knowles lecture on *Macbeth* and with Vezin's recent portrayal of the Thane of Cawdor.

4. Royal Academician (1817-97).

To Edmund Clarence Stedman (CU)

Aug. 25. 1876.   15 New Cavendish St. [London]

Dear E.C.S.;—

The bill of exchange for ten pounds, nineteen shillings has come to hand and as even small favors are gratefully received, accept my thanks for your good offices. What *The Herald* means by its goings-on in underpaying and keeping my letters back, I don't understand. After a month, my Boucicault interview was published July 26, so that I had my second labor for my pains[1] and you will quietly tear up what I sent you for *The Graphic.* At the same time, I want to come to an understanding with *The Herald* about such of my letters as they do not print. It never occurred to me that my weekly letter would not be printed. I won't ride a high horse and say that unless everything I send is printed I won't write, because I can't at present afford to do Dignity. But I do want it distinctly understood that whenever a letter is not published by *The Herald*, it is to be sent at once to you who will (like an angel) offer it to *The Graphic* at as good a price as you can get. I'm sure *The Herald* does not intend to use my letters on *Les*

Danicheff (dated July 10) and on *Women and the Legation* (dated July 22). Won't you ask for them and if they are given to you please alter one or two sentences in the beginning of each—to make them fresh—and put my initials to them. Mr. Bennett does not object to my using a signature, so I shall return to *Free Lance*. For *The Graphic* K.F. must be substituted.

I've just returned from Edinburgh where Louise [Moulton] and I passed a delightful week with Laurence Hutton and his mother. They return in September. I've given Hutton a letter to you. Shake hands with him and he'll tell you just how we behaved and how I did the statues of Livingstone and Albert the Confounded Nuisance.[2] He will also present to you in my name a small whiskey cup which you will cherish as the *apple of your rye*! Edinburgh gave me a genuine sensation. Never was a town more beautifully situated and never was there finer weather. A bright blue sky and warm air made me think of Italy. You'd have knocked off a better poem than New Jersey and Jews could inspire.[3] Perhaps the enclosed blue-bells and heather may excite a poetical emotion. Still, as I'm not a Jewess and never likely to become one, the flowers may fall on sterile ground.

... In Edinburgh I didn't hesitate to tell people what I thought about the slight put upon Bennett & Stanley[4] at the Livingstone unveiling. I used much stronger language than I wrote. ...

1. In revising it for magazine publication.

2. The Prince Consort had begged Victoria not to "raise even a single marble image to my name"; nevertheless, the Queen continued, as was said at the time, to litter the country with them (Daphne Bennett, *Albert, Prince Consort of England* [Philadelphia: Lippincott, 1977], 376).

3. Allusion unclear. Stedman published a series of nine "Hebrew Pastorals" in the *New York Independent* (Jan.–Oct. 1870).

4. At the cost of more than four thousand pounds, Bennett had outfitted Stanley, a *Herald* correspondent, to find Livingstone somewhere in the African interior. In November 1871 Stanley and his rescue party found the explorer-missionary. As Livingstone was the only white man in Ujiji (on Lake Tanganyika), Stanley had no problem greeting him with his now famous remark, "Mr. Livingstone, I presume?" Stanley helped the man regain his health, then left for England. There, though he was fêted by the Royal Geographical Society, honored with degrees by Oxford and Cambridge Universities, and finally knighted in 1899 by Queen Victoria, he was socially snubbed. Some believed he had invented the rescue story. Others resented him because they felt that the rescue of Livingstone should have been made by his sponsors and friends, not by a stranger. Still others, like Dilke, found him to be "brutal, bumptious, and untruthful." Thus, Stanley and Bennett were not invited to attend the unveiling of Mrs. D. O. Hill's statue of Livingstone (a Scotsman) in Edinburgh on 16 August 1876.

To Edmund Clarence Stedman (CU)
Oct. 16. 1876.   [15 New Cavendish St., London]

Dear friend;—
   ... The enclosed[1] is very interesting personal recollection which I should like to have offered to *Scribner*. If Dr. [Josiah Gilbert] Holland[2] refuses it, do what you think best, always giving *The Herald* the preference over other dailies. ...
   I could send a picture of Benedict to be enlarged.

   1. KF's "A Morning with Sir Julius Benedict," published in *Scribner's Monthly* (Feb. 1877). Benedict (1804–85) was a composer and conductor.
   2. Holland (1819–81) was editor of *Scribner's Monthly*.

To Edmund Clarence Stedman (CU)
Oct. 28. 1876.   15 New Cavendish St. London

Dear friend;—
   Rec'd Fred's[1] line telling me about *Graphic*. Please deposit the $14 with Mr. [Joseph A.] Jameson,[2] also the money for enclosed article. It is the Christmas sketch for *Graphic*—Price $25 (twenty-five dollars). That is as little as they have ever paid me and I won't take less. If Mr. [David Goodman] Croly[3] doesn't want it, see if the *Gazette* will take it. If not, the *Herald* may want it for Christmas morning. If it doesn't, Sam Bowles may print it for nothing [in his *Springfield Republican*].
   A few nights ago I had a great success at the [Royal] Aquarium [Theatre] concert. I sang there for the first time and made a hit. I'm told I was dressed perfectly and never looked so well. . . . I had an offer for the stage the next day but shall not appear yet. There was but one verdict on the occasion, that I belonged to the stage. I think if you heard me now, you would open your eyes. I've [vocal] power enough for any place. The Aquarium is enormous. Please send to Croly at once.

   1. Stedman's son.
   2. Of Jameson, Smith & Cotting, KF's brokers.
   3. Croly (1829–89) was editor of the *New York Graphic*; his wife, Jane Cunningham Croly (1829–1901), wrote feature articles under the pen name Jenny June for New York newspapers.

To Laurence Hutton (PUL-H)
[late Nov. 1876]   15 New Cavendish St. [London]

    Both letters rec'd, dear Mr. Hutton. Here's a row. A copy of enclosed sent to Chicago Tribune. Please take enclosed to D. G. Croly of *N.Y. Graphic* and if you can back me, do it. Did *you* not print the kid glove story first?[1] And *isn't* the Arab called a snob and *wasn't* I told what I repeated? I want Mr. Croly to preface my communication with a few feeling remarks and if you'll sail in too, the Rev. Boyd will wish he had never been born.
    I won't be called a liar with impunity.

    1. Andrew Kennedy Boyd (1825–99), minister of St. Andrews, Scotland, who liked to sign his numerous books "Country Parson," had accused KF of "malicious lies." These were that "he had been seen to preach in white kid gloves" and "had acted snobbishly towards a Scots nobleman," the Duke of Argyll. KF's reply, with confirmatory letter from Hutton, was published in the *Graphic* (5 Dec. 1876).

To Edmund Clarence Stedman (CU)
Dec. 15. 1876.   15 New Cavendish St. [London]

Dear Brother Stedy;—
    ... Is anybody in love with me? I'm not prepared to answer this question but I'll own up to two offers of a matrimonial nature which I gratefully declined. One [from Albert Baldwin] would have made me awfully rich. It isn't my first chance at splendid luxury, which no one appreciates more than I, but I love other things better. Probably there never lived a more romantic woman than I. From my childhood my mother has been "all for love." And up to the present moment I've been, right or wrong—"true to the dreams of my youth" as Goethe puts it. I've endured misery and may yet endure bitter poverty in consequence, but I hope to die true to myself, whatever opinion others may have of me, even he who wrote "Hypatia" and little understood me in his concluding verses.[1]
    I wish I could send you a ship freighted with gold, happiness and the elixir of life. Accept at least my love and believe me / Ever faithfully, / Kate Field

    1. "Hypatia" was a poem written by Stedman on hearing KF lecture in "a prairie-town." The concluding verses urged her to choose marriage, a "rarer joy" than that of lecturing. Hypatia of Alexandria (370?–415), also unmarried, was a woman of legendary beauty, virtue, and knowledge.

1874-1879 127

To Edmund Clarence Stedman (CU)
[Dec. 1876]   [15 New Cavendish St., London]

Do you know Mr. MacGinness of your board [of directors] well enough to ask him for a letter of introduction for me to Mr. Walter of the London *Times*? They are very intimate and I'd like to know Mr. W. Don't ask if you're not sure of your man.

The weather is intensely gloomy and suicidal.

Christmas I dine with Anthony Trollope. In the afternoon I go to a large Christmas tree at Morell Mackenzie's.[1] So I'll worry through the dreadful day tolerably well.

I've done the [Luigi Palma] di Cesnola[2] collection. It is very valuable. . . .

    1. Harley Street physician (1837-92).

    2. Archaeologist (1832-1904); as famous in his time as Heinrich (later Henry) Schliemann (1822-90).

To Laurence Hutton (PUL-H)
Jan. 2. 1876. [1877]   15 New Cavendish St. [London]

Dear Mr. Hutton;—

A thousand thanks for coming to my rescue in the Boyd matter.[1] Perhaps I ought to have remained silent but the impertinence of that clerical puppy was too much for my endurance. I don't see the *Chicago Tribune* so I'm ignorant of their action. If they didn't copy my letter and yours, they've behaved shabbily. "Them's my sentiments and I don't care who knows 'em."[2]

Thank heaven the holidays are over. On Christmas I dined with Anthony Trollope and yesterday I received visits as well as made one upon our minister and his wife, the [Edwards] Pierreponts,[3] who received at their house in Cavendish Square. Mrs. P. is rather stylish in dress and ladylike in manner. He is good-natured. They don't disgrace us. . . .

I've been singing here with success. The German Reeds[4] want me to go to them when Mrs. Reed retires, which will be soon I believe, and I've been asked to go starring in the provinces. This last proposition I've declined. It would do me no good in America and would take me away from my work here where I'm entering wedges. I've plays on hand and I've just been asked to join *The Examiner* staff—best literary weekly here. [William] Black begins his new novel in it and the price goes up to 6d. The editor, [William] Minto, a hardheaded Scotchman, says that he sits at my feet and is absolutely warm in praise of a review I've written for him. *The Hornet* has just got an article from me and [its] editor has gone out of his way to praise a blank verse poem of mine[5] that he has seen—my first venture. As all this news is good you are at liberty to repeat it....

I'm writing for the *Herald* and think that my articles will be signed hereafter. I saw that my initials were appended to letter on Cesnola collection....

    1. See *To Laurence Hutton*, [late Nov. 1876], n. 1.
    2. From Thackeray's *Vanity Fair* (chap. 21).
    3. Pierrepont (1817–92) was U.S. minister to the Court of St. James.
    4. Thomas German Reed (1817–88) and Priscilla Horton Reed (1818–95) had formed Mr. and Mrs. German Reed's Entertainment, which produced operettas with great success.
    5. "Forty to Twenty: A Drawing-Room Drama." The editor saw only a manuscript copy of the poem, as it was not published until June 1877 (see *To Edmund Clarence Stedman*, [Mar. 1877], n. 5).

To Edmund Clarence Stedman (CU)
Feb. 3. 1877. [15 New Cavendish St.] London

Dear friend;—

Your kind letter enclosing the introduction to Mr. Walter has just arrived. I need not tell you that I thank you very much and I need not add that I shall express my obligation to Mrs. McGinness.... I'll write tomorrow to Mr. Walter asking when he is seeable. Next week Parliament opens when he'll be additionally busy. I'm going to the opening, Mr. Pierrepont having got me the only ticket asked for America outside of the Legation. I'm going as a Peeress and shall wear an ermine cloak and long trail and look the part better I hope than the Peeresses *I've* seen. Of course I go as a chiel[1] and I hope the notes will be worth taking. The Queen and Lord Beaconsfield[2] ought to make the occasion interesting.

I've sent you recently an article on W[illiam].S[chwenck]. Gilbert[3] for a magazine and still more recently a book for [your son] Fred and a blank verse thing, asking also to have reclaimed from The Herald certain letters mentioned. Bennett is now in Europe.[4] I shall endeavor to see him when he returns from Paris and either get put on a regular salary or be paid promptly for everything I write. The Herald now owes me $300 for unpublished matter. That with Watterson's $350 makes the neat sum of $650! In these times this is a fortune.

I was much interested in your Greek article [on Schliemann's discoveries].[5] Did you see my Cesnola letter in Herald? Cesnola returns home in March. He is a good fellow—one of the few Italians who can be generous. If you meet him, shake hands with him cordially. He will tell you things about Schliemann which are not very creditable. I'm afraid the man's a Jew as well as a German and an American citizen....[6]

Jameson & Co. have sent me my account and I find that I owe them $63.49. According to this account, on Jan. 12 you paid in $61.29 Is this right? I thought Scribner was to pay $50, Graphic $15 and Independent $15. Please let me know if they've not kept their word. Whatever you get for [my article on] Gilbert if you get anything, please hand over to Jameson. I must get the account balanced. I wrote to *The Examiner* asking to review your book on Frothingham and F[rothingham]'s Child's Book of Religion,[7] but have had no answer yet. Perhaps as The Examiner has now six articles[8] of mine to print, the editor thinks I might give him time to breathe. Still he told me whenever I saw any books rec'd by the *Ex* that I wanted to review, to write and I should have them if not already pounced upon by others of the staff. Anthony Trollope has an essay of mine ["Woman in the Lyceum"] which an artist [Hennessy] who has read it says is "worthy of the best magazine" and Mrs. John Wood[9] has a comedietta which a fine actor pronounces "charming." But what I want is the money for the first and an appearance in the second. Ah E.C.S. when we go to another world, have no bills to pay and all eternity to mature in, we'll do something *worth* doing. I'm quite sure I never shall be a butterfly until I exchange my mortal coil for a pair of wings.

With this I send an article for *Independent*. If not wanted there, please turn over to Graphic and be sure that Fred has a percentage for the time and trouble of my business. It is but fair.

The weather is something infernal—rain perpetual. People are in a state about small-pox and scarlet fever. I never saw R[ichard]. G[rant]. White[10] and don't know anything about him—nor do I wish to.

Lou[ise] Moulton is in Paris "and still she is not happy!" Who is, I'd like to know, that has brains enough to think?

1. Used by Robert Burns in "On the Late Captain Grose's Peregrinations Thro' Scotland": "A chield's amang you takin notes, / And faith he'll prent it." *Chiel*, a variant of *child*, generally means "good fellow," but here "reporter."

2. Born Benjamin Disraeli (1804–81); the prime minister at the time.

3. English dramatist (1836–1911); at times collaborator with the composer Arthur Sullivan (1842–1900). KF's article on Gilbert was published in *Scribner's Monthly* (Sept. 1879).

4. On 3 January 1877 Dr. Frederick May cowhided Bennett in front of the Union League Club for having insulted his daughter. Bennett challenged May to a duel with pistols at Slaughter's Gap. Neither party was shot: May deliberately missed and Bennett was too nervous to shoot straight. Given the contempt heaped on Bennett, the episode ended Bennett's life in America. Except for rare visits, he conducted the *Herald* from Paris, where he also founded the *Paris Herald* in 1887.

5. "Treasure-Tombs at Mykenae," *Tribune*, 13 Jan. 1877.

6. Cesnola was resentful of being overshadowed by Schliemann, who had discovered Troy and Mycenae. To regain the limelight, Cesnola proceeded to fake findings. The pieces that comprised the so-called Treasure of Curium, which, he said, "will throw forever into shade those [discoveries] of Schlie-

mann," were not dug up in vaults in Curium, as he claimed—indeed, no such vaults ever existed there—but had been bought from native diggers, or found in isolated tombs, or gathered from the bazaars of the ancient land of Cyprus. Schliemann, a German whose father was a Lutheran clergyman, became a U.S. citizen.

    7. Neither book was reviewed in the *Examiner*.

    8. One was a review of George Wilkes's *Shakespeare from an American Point of View* (*Examiner*, 1 Dec. 1877). Unless one finds a clue, KF's reviews in the *Examiner* cannot be identified, because with rare exceptions contributors were unnamed.

    9. Manager of St. James Theatre.

    10. New York critic (1821–85).

To Palgrave Simpson (ISEA)
English novelist, actor, and voluminous producer of comediettas (1807–87).
March 10. 1877. 15 New Cavendish St. [London]

Dear Mr. Palgrave Simpson;—

It isn't Christian to return evil for good, yet perhaps I'm doing that same in asking you to go next Wednesday evening at 7:30 precisely and see me and my baby of a play [*Extremes Meet*]. The thing isn't an adaptation because I've put the French bones together differently and the clothes are mine. If you go, please tell me whether such a production admits me to your [Dramatic Authors'] Society.

I was much pleased with your performance at the Opéra Comique[1] and thank you heartily for my ticket. I sat behind the husband of Mrs. M. and as I watched him lead the applause, I thought of the [late] lamented [Hezekiah Linthicum] Bateman.[2]

My baby is only 40 minutes long, so it doesn't bore forever.

    1. In the comedy *Partners for Life* by Henry James Byron (1835–84).

    2. American actor (1812–75); had managed the London Lyceum Theatre when Irving debuted there.

To Edmund Clarence Stedman (CU)
[Mar. 1877] N.Y. Herald Office. 46 Fleet St. [London]

Dear friend;—

. . . Did I tell you I was writing for *The Truth*?[1] I've made a hit there. Am to do Boat Race for them.

I hope *Galaxy* will print [my] Gilbert article.² Your verdict is more favorable than I expected on the blank verse ["Forty to Twenty"].³ It's my worry first and I think I get off easily. I'll remember your criticism.

I shan't worry any more about *N.Y. Herald* for the good reason that Bennett has paid up like a man. . . .

If [Oliver Bell] Bunce⁴ *does* accept Forty to Twenty please strike out "Drawing Room Drama."⁵ Call it a Fragment if you think best.

. . . Gilbert, Palgrave Simpson and the papers are all of one opinion which is in the highest degree satisfactory and every night I am called out by strangers. Every dog has his day my friend. Let us hope.

    1. London weekly specializing in society gossip, witty reviews, political satire, and financial advice. See *To Edmund Clarence Stedman*, 14 May 1877, n. 1.

    2. Rejected by *Galaxy*; printed in *Scribner's Monthly* (Sept. 1879).

    3. "In this poem," wrote Stedman, "there is much of your characteristic original strength and vigor. Your very lack of poetic study keeps your mind clear of old or hackneyed phrases" (LW, 300).

    4. New York playwright (1828–90); from 1872 to 1881 he coedited *Appletons' Journal*.

    5. This semi-autobiographical poem about KF's love affair with Baldwin was published with its original subtitle in *Appletons' Journal* (June 1877). KF (a woman of forty in the poem and in fact) is trying to comfort her twenty-year-old cousin, whose heart is broken by her lover, as KF's was by Baldwin when she was in her twenties.

To Laurence Hutton (PUL-H)
April 7. 1877.   15 New Cavendish St. London

Dear Mr. Hutton;—

Can you help me to some law? I want to know what are the legal disabilities of women in the United States—where they have less liberty than men—how married women fare as to carrying on business &c. In fact I want to show the Britishers that we're a great deal better than they, and as I'm hazy as to facts, my article hangs fire. I'd like to know too how the laws of one state differ from those of another. Is this asking too much? . . .

My piece [*Extremes Meet*] goes on successfully. . . . Other notices have appeared, a few of which I send you to publish if you can. Arthur Sullivan the composer was the last to see me. He came behind the scenes last night, said he was charmed and would trust any musical piece of his to me.

I wish you'd get Brentano¹ to take the London *Truth* for which I write. It's just the sort of weekly to sell in New York.

[The following reviews are copied in KF's hand.]

The World. "Miss Kate Field, a sparkling writer and great favorite in society, has written a sketch in which she herself acts the heroine. Miss Field plays with ease and grace, and gives the bright dialogue and a pretty song with point and animation."

Figaro. "Miss Field is as bright on the boards as she is on paper."

Dublin Newsletter. "Miss Kate Field has an engaging manner, a sympathetic voice, and an easy and graceful carriage. It is difficult to say whether her singing is better than her acting for Dublin should remember that Miss Field is as versatile as she is fascinating."

Sporting & Dramatic News. " 'Extremes Meet' is charming. As the Fascinating visitor [in the play] Miss Field acts with infinite grace, point and perfect naturalness."

1. Well-known bookstore named after its owner.

To Edmund Clarence Stedman (CU)
May 14. 1877.   15 New Cavendish St. [London]

Dear E.C.S.;—

First business: I've just drawn on Mr. Jameson for £15 so please pay over to him whatever money comes in. Can't Appleton pay up at once [for my "Forty to Twenty"]? Please ask him [Bunce]—and—*The Graphic* if it has not done so already. I send dates of *Graphic* letters. How about *The Independent* and *can't The Galaxy* be made to say something? I'm sorry I sent that Gilbert article [to the *Galaxy*] as I could have had it printed here. If they don't want it, please return it at once. I didn't copy the thing—like an idiot.

Appleton	$25
Graphic ought to be	40
Independent	15
	$80

... My piece [*Extremes Meet*] goes on and I get praise from all quarters. I've improved on it very much and Vezin says I do it as well as it can be done. I began March 12 and the season terminates May 26—eleven weeks—and I'm sick to death of the thing. My song is nightly encored. Now I want something bigger. Both Gilbert and Sullivan are partially engaged to write me parts but I believe nothing that is not in black and white. I've made a hit in *Truth* by my *Intercepted Letters*[1] which will probably be in every week. The clubs are talking about them which is a good sign and the editor says he wants me to be his mainstay. I wish Brentano would take in *Truth*. It's just the paper for America. My last scalp is Schliemann who has sat to me for his [pen] photograph, coming at 7 o'clock in the morning and being the death of me. He calls himself my "admirer." My article was intended for *The Herald* but being too long I shall try to publish it in an Eng. and American magazine simultaneously if possible.² . . .

 1. These were letters from "Puss" addressed to an imaginary correspondent (a Miss Ella Graham). KF published sixty-three such letters in *Truth* from 1877 to 1880.

 2. "Henry Schliemann: Letter from Miss Kate Field" was published in nearly five columns in the *Tribune* (30 June 1877). In his autobiographical sketch (printed in his *Memoirs*, edited by Leo Deuel), Schliemann borrowed liberally from this article.

To Laurence Hutton (PUL-H)
May 22. 1877.   15 New Cavendish St. [London]

Dear Mr. Hutton;—
Many thanks for your information about women and for your kindly offices in my behalf.¹ The idea of *The Arcadian* publishing anything in my praise is miraculous, and *The Times* too!² Are all my foes dead or merely sleeping?

I've had more than enough of my comedietta [*Extremes Meet*]. The season at the St. James's closes in a week and I shall be glad. I want a heavier gun to fire off. Tomorrow I do the solo singing witch in *Macbeth* at a complimentary benefit given to [William] Creswick³ before his departure for Australia [on an acting tour]. At least I'll have on a picturesque dress and give the audience a few high notes they are not used to in witches.

Talking of plays—to go back to your letter—Stanley McKenna⁴ has a very strong one—*Dead To The World*—that I've adapted from the French. I'd like to have you read it . . .

Mr. [Frederick Barkham] Warde⁵ spoke to me before I left America of wanting *Gabrielle*.⁶ I shall never touch the piece [again]. It is out of my genre, but I send it to you to hold in case Mr. Warde still entertains the idea of playing a part well suited to him. He can have the piece for $100 down and $5 per night for every performance after the first 25. That's cheap enough, heaven knows. Tell me what Mr. Warde says. . . .

Coming over? Then I shall hope to see you.

 1. See *To Laurence Hutton*, 7 Apr. 1877.

 2. The *Arcadian* was notorious for its severe criticisms. The *New York Times* (8 Apr. 1887) reported that the comedietta "has been exceedingly well received."

 3. English actor (1813–88).

 4. Theatrical agent. Years later KF published her adaptation of his "Dead to the World" in *KF's Washington* (30 Sept. 1891).

5. American actor (1851–1935).

6. Her father's adaptation of a play by Dumas *père*. KF had reworked the piece many times.

To Laurence Hutton (PUL-H)
July 11. 1877.   15 New Cavendish St. [London]

Dear Mr. Hutton;—
  ... You've probably seen my Schliemann article in *The Tribune* for June 30th. It appeared here in July *Belgravia*[1] and it amuses me to find people waking up as to who I am. An American is forced to win his spurs on this side. It makes no earthly difference what he is at home. The English neither know nor care. I don't set any value on the Schliemann article, but I'm hearing about it in all directions. Funny world.
  As to [my] piano. It can be seen at 237 Madison Avenue, Chickering maker. Will sell for $200.
  Will you have *Dead To The World* copyrighted for me?
  Dead To The World / Drama / By / Kate Field
  Charge to me. $1.50 will do it. I want you to read the piece. Mrs. Bullard has it....
  As to Summer I know nothing. I'm invited to pass several *months* near Trouville[2] and I'd go tomorrow if I dared, but what with telegrams to *Herald*, articles for *Truth* and managers standing first on one leg and then on another I may be detained indefinitely and get nowhere. I make excursions whenever I can, but it would be a luxury to loaf and invite my soul.[3]...

  1. *Belgravia: An Illustrated London Magazine*; published Twain, Harte, Thomas Trollope, Wilkie Collins (1824–89), and Swinburne, among others.

  2. With her friends the Hennessys, who had leased an old manor house that had twenty spare rooms for guests.

  3. A play on line 4 of Whitman's *Song of Myself*.

To Laurence Hutton (PUL-H)
[1877]   [15 New Cavendish St., London]

  ... Mrs. Bullard has read *Dead To The World* & will turn it over to you. Lydia Foote[1] here thinks it fine and wants to act it. Please see Harry Wall[2] and ask him how plays can be introduced, whether he is [an] agent. Ask too if my comedietta [*Extremes Meet*] can find a theatre after [Samuel] French publishes it.[3] Mrs. [Clara Erskine] Clement[4] will tell you about my Landor album[5] that I want to sell en gros or separately, sketches from $200 to $500.

Have been made member of Dramatic Authors' Society.

    1. English actress (1844-92).

    2. American theatrical manager.

    3. Publisher of plays, with offices in London and New York. KF published five other plays. Ten more of her plays, titled and untitled, short and long, adapted and original, completed and uncompleted, are in BPL. Four additional KF plays are unlocated. See appendix B.

    4. American art critic and art historian (1834-1916).

    5. In her Florentine days, KF had admired an album owned by Landor. It is said to have included 140 sketches and paintings, among which were "heads by Raphael, flowers by . . . da Vinci, . . . sixteen sketches by Turner, a number by Gainsborough . . . Claude Lorraine, Poussin," etc. When KF was preparing to leave Florence, Landor forced the album upon her so that she would "think of the foolish old creature sometimes" (LW, 380-82). In her will (filed at the Probate Division, Superior Court of the District of Columbia), KF bequeathed to "S[tephen]. V[an Cullen]. White of Brooklyn, New York, the Walter Savage Landor Album in his possession for a loan of $500." (White was a member of the New York Stock Exchange.) It is more than likely that KF in hard times had sold some of the sketches.

To Edmund Clarence Stedman (CU)
Sept. 3. 1877.
                                Le Manoir de Pennedepie
                                [near Trouville, France]

Dear Poet;—

    . . . At the present moment, and I've been here three weeks, I'm visiting the Hennessys who are kindness itself. They reside in an old manor house, six miles from the fashionable watering place of Trouville (where J. G. Bennett and Big Bonanza Mackay[1] have villas) and directly opposite Havre that I see whenever I look out of my window. I came here because I knew I'd be out of temptation and could do as I pleased. Nobody crosses the threshold of the door, consequently there's no dressing. I wear as little as the law allows and find that a tooth brush and a waterproof are the only absolute necessities. The waterproof is in lieu of the blanket of the noble Red man. I scorn hair pins and let my hair roll in a fine frenzy[2] down my back. I bathe in the sea and have an appetite that would do credit to a boa-constrictor. The amount of bread and milk I consume is appalling. Cows run when they see me approach and bakers gaze upon me as a special Providence. This wild dissipation has caused me to amass four pounds of flesh with an upward tendency. I aspire to fifteen pounds and shall try at the end of a fortnight to go to Paris and eat grapes for three weeks before returning to dirty London and general worry. I don't know that I shall, but as it costs no more to live in Paris than London and as I've business in Paris, I shall make an effort. People who have no money can live as well in one place as in another. Can't they?

Though supposed to be taking a vacation I'm writing, as usual. I appear weekly in *Truth* and have just sent off a letter about [Le] Havre to *N.Y. Herald* at Bennett's request. I shall also do Trouville for *The Herald*. My last dramatic work is an original comedietta called "Two Fighting Cousins" written for the Kendals (Madge Robertson).[3] They like it so much that they've bought the sole copyright. Won't you put this into a paragraph? "Extremes Meet" will soon be published by [Samuel] French. He writes that the proofs are now ready.

Winter will tell you something about me. He discovered I wasn't the sort of woman he's been taking me for. His poems are to be published by Tinsley this month.[4]

I've just read [Horace Howard] Furness's [*A New Variorum of*] *Hamlet* and [William Rounseville] Alger's *Life of* [*Edwin*] *Forrest*. Furness quotes my article on Hamlet[5]—the very passages I wanted to revise and correct! What a dreadful style Alger has and what a lot of bosh he has put into his work! I'm glad to note that he acknowledges Forrest's very great obligations to my grandmother [Mary Lapsley] Riddle to whom he owed all of the art education he got in early years. Alger tries to make Forrest a better man than he was. He was an Indian in his hate, mean with his money, and coarse in his passions—a genius gone wrong. He hated my father because he espoused Mrs. Forrest's cause.[6] . . .

    1. John William Mackay (1831–1902), who with his partners discovered the "Big Bonanza" silver deposits in Virginia City, Nevada, in 1873. He invested in Western railroads and real estate and with Bennett, his neighbor, organized the Commercial Cable Co., which competed successfully with what had been Jay Gould's Western Union monopoly.

    2. Echo from *A Midsummer Night's Dream* (V.i.12): "The poet's eye, in a fine frenzy rolling. . . ."

    3. William Hunter Kendal (1843–1917), English actor and theater manager; Margaret Robertson Kendal (1848–1935), English comedienne.

    4. In *Thistle-Down: A Book of Lyrics* (1878).

    5. Furness quoted KF's "Fechter as Hamlet" in the appendix volume of his edition of *Hamlet* (1877).

    6. Catherine Forrest was sued for divorce by her famous husband on grounds of adultery, on not unreasonable evidence. In one instance, the actor found his wife with a phrenologist's hands on her person. When Forrest asked for an explanation, Mrs. Forrest replied that the phrenologist had merely been pointing out her phrenological developments. The Forrests' marriage lasted twelve years, their lawsuit sixteen, with a verdict in Mrs. Forrest's favor.

To John Bigelow (UC)
Bigelow (1817–1911) was an American statesman, editor, author, lawyer, and former U.S. minister to France.
Oct. 1. 1877. 78 Rue Neuve des Petits, Champs [Paris]

Dear Mr. Bigelow;—

I believe I'm losing what I am pleased to call my mind. I did not give M. Louis Blanc my address last night[1] and I don't know his! Will you angelically send the enclosed note to him?

I'd give a good deal to see [Léon] Gambetta[2] and I'd dance for joy if I could interview him. Is it possible?

I had a most interesting evening thanks to you and am very glad to have met Mr. Tilden to whom I address a note which I want you to read first and not present unless you approve. . . .

1. Bigelow had invited KF and Blanc (1811–82), a French socialist, to a small dinner party at his hotel. Though now New York secretary of state, Bigelow had taken a three-month leave of absence to tour Europe with Tilden, who had recently lost his electoral battle with Hayes. In extending his invitation to KF in person, Bigelow noted in his journal: "She has now put on the exactiveness of the journalist in place of that of the coquette, her age and plainness rendering the change a necessity. But for that, she would be very agreeable, for her manners are otherwise good, her wit ready, and intelligence more than common."

2. French statesman (1838–82), a founder of the Third Republic.

To Edmund Clarence Stedman (CU)
Nov. 28. 1877. 15 New Cavendish St. London

Dear E.C.S.;—

. . . From their [the Hennessys'] house I went to Paris for five weeks and never in my life got so much for so little money. I've reduced Paris to a science and old residents came to get my addresses for dressmakers &c. I made [Charles Frederick] Worth's[1] acquaintance and he feasted me at his wonderful country house. He calls me "une femme adorable" and when I sang Spanish and English songs to him I thought he'd never stop exclaiming about my versatility. It seems to knock people down that a writer can do anything but write. They forget how *all round* the mediaevals were.

Victor Hugo was very nice to me giving me *Histoire d'un Crime* [1877] with "Hommage de l'auteur" in it. I saw Louis Blanc several times and interviewed him as you know. Thanks for *The Graphic.* You are the only person that ever dreams of sending me papers.

...I have my hands full. *N.Y. Herald, Truth, Whitehall Review, Liverpool Post* and last but not least *The Times* if you please. I enclose you the article with which I have made my début.² It has excited very great attention, called forth warm praise from the editor and Bell, inventor of the telephone, says it is the best article that has ever been written on the subject. It inspired a leader in *The Times* [19 Dec. 1877] soon after and has been of great advantage to the telephone in which there is a great fortune. The sub-editor of *The Times* is a friend of mine. Walter has had nothing to do with this. A fair field and no favor! I shall probably have an article before long in "19th Century."³

The dramatic side is also getting on. The stage manager of Princess's Theatre has just accepted my third comedietta which he says is "charming" and I've finished a fourth, equally good, which I shall keep for myself. I was to have appeared in it ere this but the management wasn't what it ought to be and I'm advised not to be in a hurry. I shall probably produce 4 of my own pieces together after Christmas. With money my friend I'd have a theatre and show the English several things. My ship is bound to come in. [John] Westland Marston⁴ has written a powerful drama for me and I'll do it when the right time comes. My very last success is my Dickens lecture⁵ given here for the first time and with the greatest possible effect. I never addressed so sympathetic an audience. I played upon them as though they were an instrument. The applause was great, despite the sabbath and I'd no sooner left the stage than the committee made me promise to lecture again for them this season. They *never* had had so crowded a house or a lecture that had taken so well. They have since heard me read my Adirondack lecture and want it. Next Sunday evening I'm to repeat *Dickens* at Sadler's Wells Theatre where they say I'll have an audience of 3000. The American eagle is beginning to hold up his head.

Smalley may abuse the "Boulevard Weeklies.". . . It doesn't hurt *Truth* which, although not a year old, is a paying property and I have myself heard Smalley say he read it through weekly as it is so clever! So does his wife!! *Truth* succeeds because it is the cleverest weekly published and [my] Puss's letters are said to be the best things in it. So let Smalley scold. When I want to be serious I can write for *The Times.* Is there anything to attain in journalism beyond this?

Louise Moulton is right again though not strong. She wrote at my request the notice of your poems in *The Tatler.* I did the one in *Whitehall* and will try to get something into *Examiner* and *Theatre. Truth* won't let me praise my friends *because they are my friends*! I do hope the New Year will bring grist to your mill. You deserve it.

I'm going to send you my comedietta of *Extremes Meet.* Can't you get the Frothingham actors⁶ to do it? The play is copyrighted in America and I want $5 *whenever it is produced for money.* See what can be done.

Give to somebody the notices of my lecture and any other items you think will do me good but don't put into print what I tell you about *The Times,* saving, if you like, that the telephone article is by me. Tell Mr. McGinnis with my regards. . . .

    1. An Englishman (1826–95); considered the founder of the haute couture industry. His Maison Worth in Paris was without rival for fifty years.
    2. "The Telephone," London *Times*, 16 Nov. 1877, the first of her series of articles for the *Times* on Bell's new invention. Also, at Bell's request, KF demonstrated the telephone by singing three songs and reciting a poem into Queen Victoria's ear. For her work in promoting his invention, Bell gave KF stock in his company, which soon amounted to a small fortune.
    3. No KF article appeared in *The Nineteenth Century*, an English monthly.
    4. English dramatist (1819–90); father of the blind poet Philip Marston (1850–87).
    5. KF's first public lecture in London, given on 18 November 1877. She had tested the lecture privately on invited London critics in 1871 and 1872.
    6. Troupe formed by George Frothingham, who had achieved fame in *The Black Crook*, a musical extravaganza, with book by Charles M. Barras and music by Giuseppe Operti. One of its sensational features was that the chorines wore flesh-colored costumes to create the illusion of nudity. Celebrities like Dickens watched the musical from the wings.

To Laurence Hutton (PUL-H)
Dec. 12. 1877.   15 New Cavendish St. [London]

Dear Mr. Hutton;—
    Since my return from Paris where I enjoyed myself hugely, I've been very busy indeed. I've been admitted to the sacred circle of *The Times* contributors,[1] I keep on regularly with *Truth*, I've had two new comediettas accepted, Westland Marston has written me a splendid drama, I've written two comediettas for myself and I've made a ten strike in my Dickens lecture which I've given several Sunday evenings. I am praised by the finest critics and my last audience numbered 4000![2] Unfortunately that dreadful woman, Mrs. Woodhull, is disgracing my country and sex at St. James's Hall[3] which I had intended to take; so I shall let it alone until she has departed and the place well fumigated. It is too bad!
    Mrs. [Fanny] Stirling[4] is so pleased with me that she says she can teach me nothing. We are to act together.
    Thanks for your efforts in my behalf pianowards.[5] I'll let it alone. I *won't* sell for nothing. Regarding *Dead to The World*, it is a play for three people and ought to be done by a full company. Hear what Mr. Wall has to say and unless he disposes of it, get it from him before you leave New York and give it back to E. C. Stedman. Its time will come, for the drama is very strong. A copy of it is now in two London theatres and if it is done here, America will then want it. America is flunkey in art.

There is nothing going on theatrically to excite enthusiasm. My last craze is the *Telephone*. That *is* wonderful! and there's no end to its utility. I'm making these people understand it and the Government has already taken it up.

Schliemann is back again, comes to me for advice in everything even to getting his son married. I'm to visit his Trojan antiquities tomorrow.

 1. See *To Edmund Clarence Stedman*, 28 Nov. 1877, n. 2.
 2. The number would appear exaggerated except for the fact that three thousand came to hear Victoria Woodhull in Cleveland and five thousand to hear Anna Dickinson in New York.
 3. Woodhull made her London debut with the lecture "The Human Body: The Temple of God."
 4. English actress and drama coach (1815-95).
 5. At KF's request, Hutton had tried to sell her Chickering piano for two hundred dollars.

To Emily Faithfull (BPL)
Jan. 31. 1878.   15 New Cavendish St. [London]

Dear Miss Faithfull;—

Thanks for the compliment but don't you think I'm too new a comer here to be put into a magazine?[1] I'll state my little views when I see you on Sunday.

 1. Faithfull's *Victoria Magazine*. KF's hesitancy to publish was most unusual and may be explained by what she said of Faithfull—that "everybody I met in London warned me against Miss F. as a philanthropic adventurer, thoroughly untrustworthy" (*To Whitelaw Reid*, 11 Sept. 1872).

To Edmund Clarence Stedman (CU)
March 14. 1878.   15 New Cavendish St. [London]

Dear friend;—

What Chatto [of Chatto & Windus] writes I enclose.[1] If I can do more for you, tell me. Tinsley has just sent me Winter's poems [*Thistle-Down*], just out. I've not yet had time to dip into them but the little volume looks well.

Did you get my Telephone book[2] and letter? I dare say you can get no [American] publisher [for it]. If so, never mind. I'll take the will for the deed.

You wrote that you had about $10 belonging to me. Please send $1 (one) to S. Elliott, Graphic Office, in payment for getting *Extremes Meet* copyrighted; and $1.50 to Laurence Hutton, 229 West 34th St. N.Y. for payment of copyright on *Dead To The World*. Then get from Croly payment on my Stanley letter (1 col. &

1/4) in Graphic (Feb. 21 & 22)³ and send all to Mrs. Kate Willcox, Care of T. Fitzwilliam, 76 Camp St. New Orleans. La.
[part of letter missing]
Nothing extraordinary has taken place since I wrote last, saving that Prince Louis Napoleon, Duchess of Westminster & a large party of swells lunched at the Telephone rooms three days ago and we had a grand time singing & experimenting.

    1. A letter consenting to consider Stedman's manuscript "Lyrics and Idylls with Other Poems."
    2. *The History of Bell's Telephone* (1878), a sixty-seven page pamphlet consisting almost entirely of KF's newspaper items about the telephone and including Bell's address before the Society of Arts.
    3. "The Great Public Reception [for Stanley] by the Royal Geographical Society."

To Charles Edward Flower (FL)
    Flower (1830–92), a Stratford-upon-Avon brewer, conceived the idea for the Shakespeare Memorial Theatre. He donated the riverside site in Stratford and much of the money for its construction, despite protests that the theatre should be built in London.
March 16. 1878.   15 New Cavendish St. [London]

Dear Sir;—
If you will kindly write to me at length on the subject of the Shakespeare Memorial,¹ I can give you a definite answer. I ought to be interested, as Nathaniel Field,² one of Shakespeare's company and an early dramatist, was my ancestor.

    1. Flower, on behalf of the Shakespeare Memorial Association, wanted KF to organize a fund-raiser. That moneymaker turned out to be a Shakespeare jamboree rather than a jubilee because 23 April—the bard's traditional birth and death date—fell during Easter week. Held on 22 May at London's Gaiety Theatre, the jamboree involved eighteen distinguished actors such as Ward and Vezin, who performed scenes from various Shakespeare plays. Also, "musical fire" was produced onstage by Geisler tubes (an early form of the neon sign); and, as a climax, Shakespeare airs, played at Stratford on the telephone harp, were conveyed by a telephone transmitter to a receiver at the Gaiety. Unfortunately, the receiver needed repairs, so the music arrived at the theatre only faintly and at the last minute.
    2. Nathan Field (1587-1620). His name, for obvious reasons, is often confused with that of his brother Nathaniel, a stationer, especially as Nathan signed himself Nat. Like his descendants KF and her father, Nathan was a leading actor, playwright, and comedian. His two known comedies are *A Woman is a Weather-cocke* (1612) and *Amends for Ladies* (1618). He also collaborated with other dramatists such as Massinger (1583-1640), Beaumont (1584-1616), and Fletcher (1579-1625).

The Shakespeare Memorial Theatre. (Courtesy Shakespeare Centre Library, Stratford-upon-Avon.)

To Jessie Bross (FL)
March 29. 1878.　　　　　　　　　　　　　　　　　15 New Cavendish St. London

Dear Jessie;—

　　I want to inspire you with enthusiasm for a subject in which I am deeply interested. I've just returned from Stratford-on-Avon where I've seen the Memorial Theatre which will be completed and opened a year hence, when Miss Helen Faucit[1] will appear in a Shakesperian character. I send you all the documents I have at hand and want you to fill the subscription list enclosed with as little or as much as Chicago can afford. 10,000 visitors go to Stratford yearly, three fourths of whom are American, and it seems to me therefore that we ought to take a peculiar interest in a Memorial which only needs $50,000 to complete Theatre, Library, Gallery and all! Dr. Henry Schliemann has just sent me $100 from Paris and I shall get money on this side of the water, but as the Committee have begged me to raise money for them, I appeal to America. It has occurred to me that it would be a splendid idea for Robert Collyer[2] to deliver a memorial sermon on April 22nd the day preceding Shakespeare's Anniversary—birth and death—and

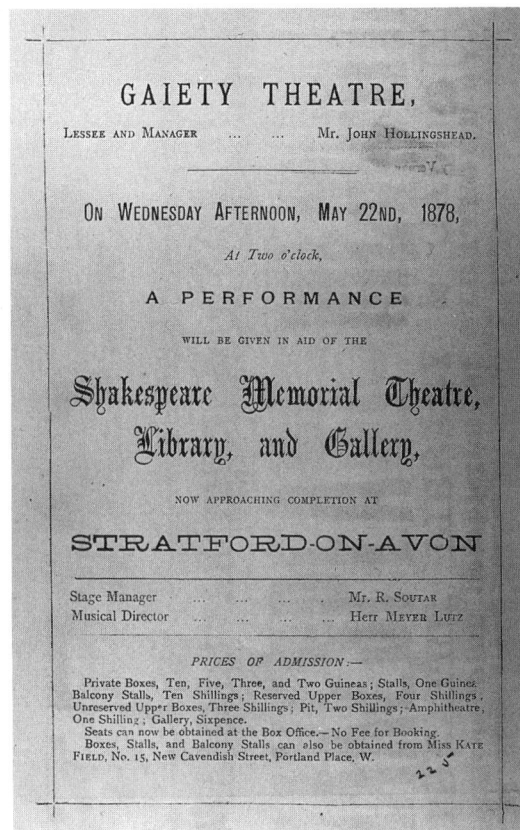

Gaiety Theatre playbill for a performance in aid of the Shakespeare Memorial Theatre, Library, and Gallery. (Courtesy Trustees of the Boston Public Library.)

at the close have a collection taken up for the fund. I wish you'd see Mr. Collyer at once and urge the matter, as you can most eloquently. Mr. Collyer delivered an address at the [McVicker] theatre in Chicago when [James H.] McVicker[3] and Edwin Booth gave a performance for the fund two years ago.

Tell Mr. Collyer that not one penny of that money has yet reached Stratford. Mr. McVicker wrote that he heard the Memorial was a "swindle," and so retained the money at the time. Since then, he has been undeceived and has said that he would send the amount due when times were easier. Don't do anything to anger Mr. McVicker, but if you could gently hint that Mr. Flower and the Stratford Committee hope to hear from him, now that he knows the money will not be diverted to base purposes, you might do much good. Try and interest Mr. Runnion and the able [Chicago] Tribune dramatic critic and, in fact, everybody you can. By all means appeal first to Mr. Collyer and with his support, you may do much. Mr. Collyer's sermon might be reprinted here, given to those who subscribe to the fund, and become a part of the Shakesperian Library. Don't you see? Do what you can, and if you have any money to send me, let it be to the Care of H[enry]. F. Gillig[4] & Co. 449 Strand. London. W.C.

Are you all well? I sent you a [*History of Bell's*] *Telephone* book recently. Did it reach you?

Remember Ce que femme veut Dieu le veut.[5]

1. English Shakespearean actress (1817–98).
2. Minister-at-large to the First Unitarian Church in Chicago.
3. McVicker (1822–96) was an actor and the owner of the McVicker Theatre.
4. Owner of the American Exchange and Reading Rooms at Charing Cross.
5. What woman wants God wants.

To Charles Edward Flower (FL)
April 8. [1878]   [15 New Cavendish St., London]

Dear Mr. Flower;—

I'm glad I'm to receive more printed matter, as I've none left. All given or sent away. You may be very sure that no actor will appear who does not wish to do so. Mr. [Henry] Irving[1] today, after I had argued with him an hour and a half said that he sympathized with the cause but not in a memorial at Stratford. For my sake he would give £21 and get friends to buy tickets. Mr. Irving has promised to keep his opinions to himself.

Mrs. [Marie] Bancroft had never *heard* of the Memorial and when I explained it to her yesterday she was interested. Edmund Yates will support Benefit in *The World*. Hermann Vezin has given £10.10.

As the 23d comes in Easter week when everybody is away, the performance [at the Gaiety] must be postponed.

Surely if you come to town you can come to see me. I'll be at home whenever you say. This matter I'm putting energy into because I never can do things by halves. I expect rebuffs but for Shakespeare I'll do it.

1. English actor (1838–1905) famed for his Shakespearean roles. Like many others, he preferred to have the Shakespeare Memorial Theatre in London, not Stratford.

To J. H. McClure (LW)
   An administrator in Bell's Telephone Co.
April 17. 1878.   15 New Cavendish St. London

Dear Mr. McClure;—
   On May 22nd, an afternoon performance will be given at the Gaiety Theatre for the benefit of the Shakespeare Memorial at Stratford-on-Avon which needs but a few thousand pounds to make it complete.[1] Mr. Henry Irving has sent a subscription of £25, not being able to act, while Mr. and Mrs. Kendal, Mr. Hermann Vezin, Miss Geneviève Ward, Miss Ellen Terry,[2] Mr. Arthur Cecil,[3] and the best artists in London have volunteered their services. With the exception of a comedietta [KF's *Eyes Right*] the programme will be entirely Shakespearian, and I have thought that the introduction of the Telephone harp in one or more entr'actes, especially if the harp were played in Shakespeare's house at Stratford, would add greatly to the interest of the occasion. Hoping this suggestion may be approved by the Telephone Company, Limited, and that I may hear from you at an early date.

   1. To raise additional funds, KF solicited subscriptions from the famous, such as Anthony Trollope, Longfellow, and James T. Fields, as well as from the not so famous, such as Mary Anthony, George Riddle, and Mary Anderson.
   2. English actress (1847–1928). In this year she had joined Irving as his leading lady.
   3. Stage name of Arthur Cecil Blunt (1843–96), English actor.

To William Winter (FL)
June 7. 1878.   [15 New Cavendish St.] London

Dear W. W.;—
   ... At the request of the Stratford Memorial Committee I visited Stratford the last of March and became much interested in the Shakespeare Memorial which I saw was destined to be a success because of Mr. Flower's devotion and money. It is always *one* person that carries through any new idea.
   ... I knew that great prejudice against the Memorial existed among many actors and certain papers. *The Hornet, Theatre, Figaro, Era* were opposed on the ground that there should be a Memorial Theatre in London & nowhere else. The editors however for my sake promised either to be quiet or to assist until after the performance. *The Era* helped and is now on our side, *The Theatre* helped and now sees two sides to the medal. It was furiously opposed a year ago. *Figaro* helped and now while praising me doesn't see how the thing is practicable. *The Hornet* alone of reputable theatrical papers has denounced the scheme and as a

specimen of clear, logical writing I send you the criticism. Well, I found that to make the benefit a success I'd be forced to do everything. I attended to the advertising, printing, business of all kinds. I sold all the stalls, private boxes and larger part of the balcony stalls, I got subscriptions, wrote all the letters, and then applied to the Post Office for a wire to Stratford as I wanted to station a Telephone-Harp in Shakespeare's house, 130 miles away [from London]. It would be a great thing to do and so I wanted to do it. The Post Office refused me, coolly saying they intended to oppose the Telephone as long as possible (as they did the penny post) and moreover they knew music could *not* be conveyed such a distance. "That is our business not yours," I replied. Lord Hertford[1] interceded with that old fool Lord John [James Robert] Manners[2] (Let laws & learning, arts & science die &c) but with no success. Determined to beat the Post Office we, as Telephone Company, applied to the Great Western Railway for one of their wires, and with a courtesy unknown to the Post Office, our request was granted. But still we needed a wire from Paddington station to the Gaiety Theatre. This favor the Great Western asked of the P.O. and the officials dared not refuse. In the end the P.O. men turned round and were as polite as they had been brutal. Didn't it do me good to find the big wigs awfully disconcerted at hearing music 130 miles away! Red tape hasn't had such a shock for many a day. I've heard much better music at less distance, but there was the wonderful fact of hearing airs we could distinguish. The idea set Stratford quite upside-down. Then I had to conciliate Mr. Hollingshead, who gave the [Gaiety] theatre. When he heard that Irving (who gave a subscription of £21) could not act, he said the whole thing had better be given up. I didn't see it. To me Irving does *not* embrace the entire London stage. After I'd smoothed Mr. H. on this point, he declared that unless I had one entire play, the matinee would be a failure. Nobody would come to see bits of plays. I didn't agree with him, and after a confab. this point was conceded by Hollingshead who then told me to go ahead, and I went.

One week before Memorial Benefit, the Mellon Benefit came off at Drury Lane. There was a committee as long as your arm, headed by Lord Londesborough.[3] Mrs. [Mary Ann] Keeley[4] and Madame Celeste[5] came from their retirement to act. [Henry James] Byron wrote an address, everybody was in the bill and the total receipts were £200! Six shillings were the receipts of gallery and upper boxes. This news plunged me in melancholy. If my venture did not draw a pit and gallery, I'd be pronounced a meddling Yankee. The possibility made me so ill that on the day of performance I could hardly stand and when the curtain went up and my eyes saw a jammed pit and gallery, the revulsion of feeling was so great that I almost lost my voice. It came back in a few minutes, but the comedietta was half over before I began to be myself. I don't want to go through such agony again. The rest of the performance was very fine. Everybody in the audience seemed delighted. Vezin was splendid in Shylock, Mrs. Kendal admirable in

Rosalind and Miss Ward *very* fine in Queen Katherine's death. My speech, prepared at the last moment, was loudly applauded and after it the United States Minister [Edwards Pierrepont] sent me £5.5 and Geo. Wilkes did the same. Harry Palmer[6] came behind the scenes and said he'd get up a benefit in America.

The pecuniary result of this tour de force was £*450*, double ordinary receipts. The amount of advertising is not calculable. Mr. Flower is delighted, Stratford holds me in affectionate regard, E[dward]. L. Blanchard[7] says [Frederick James] Furnivall[8] the great Shakespeare man is immensely pleased, Rev. Mr. [Hugh Reginald] Haweis[9] ditto and the Rev. Stopford Brooke[10] has today written thus: "I was delighted with what you said. It was just to the point & not too much. I must wait a little for an impulse. The sermon shall come." (He promises to write a sermon on the necessity of a school of acting.) Letters pour in from all sides and the only carpers are the dirty cads of the *Referee* and "sich."

I have written fully to you because I want to enlist your powerful aid. Through you it may be possible to get at John McCullough,[11] [Lawrence] Barrett[12] and Joe Jefferson.[13] All three might give benefits next season. All three ought to be governors of the theatre, as [Edwin] Booth is already. I want America to give its support to the theatre and set an example of appreciation to England. Do you feel like doing your best in this matter? I hope so. It would be grand if next April 23d several leading theatres at home gave benefits for the Memorial. It would be fine if the Lotos[14] or Century Club[15] or both became governors by subscribing £100. Think the matter over and let me hear from you anon. I send a few circulars and papers for enlightenment. Keep them for reference. I send too a lithograph of the Memorial [Theatre]. I shall confide to Miss Ward, who goes to New York soon, a fine proof engraving of [Gainsborough's] David Garrick,[16] which I shall ask you to accept as a souvenir of Stratford, the original painting belonging to the town. [Lester] Wallack[17] ought to be interested and the English actors. If you can do anything, I'm sure you will. *The Herald* leader assumed that I went in for nightly performances at Stratford! How people *will* get things wrong. My little speech tells the story. I am not an unmitigated fool.

. . . The end of this month I am going to France, first Paris—then Normandy with the Hennessys. He (Hennessy) has painted two capital pictures for the [Royal] Academy and Grosvenor Gallery. . . .

1. The Lord Chamberlain whose duties included regulating the royal theatres and licensing all plays staged in England.

2. Seventh Duke of Rutland (1818–1906), the unobliging postmaster general, whose poem "England's Trust" contained the lines: "Let wealth and commerce, laws and learning die, / But leave us still our old nobility."

3. Albert Denison (1835–1903), first Baron of Londesborough.

4. English actress (1806–99); retired in 1869 after the death of her actor-husband.
5. Parisian actress (1814–82); retired in 1874.
6. Proprietor of Niblo's Garden (a theatre) and co-owner of the Westminster Hotel in New York.
7. English dramatist (1820–89).
8. English scholar (1825–1910); founded the New Shakespeare Society in 1873.
9. Prolific Irish-born literary critic (1838–1901).
10. English belletrist (1832–1916).
11. American actor (1832–85).
12. American actor (1838–91).
13. American comic actor (1829–1905).
14. Club founded in 1870 to promote exchanges among journalists, authors, and artists; the first New York club to allow women to attend designated receptions; it even instituted a "Ladies' Day."
15. Club founded in 1847 by Samuel Jones, chief justice of New York Superior Court, and his associates. Its members were chiefly men of fortune.
16. Garrick (1717–79) was the premier actor at the first Shakespeare Jubilee held at Stratford in 1769.
17. Wallack (1820–88) was an American actor, a dramatist, and the manager of Wallack's Theatre in New York.

To William Winter (FL)
June 27. 1878.

Permanent Address. American Exchange.
449 Strand. London

Dear W. W.;—

... Just had a letter from Gladstone[1] & Pigott[2] (dramatic censor) about [Shakespeare] Memorial. The latter says, "Had you been one of the original 12 apostles you would have taken the bread out of the mouths of all the parsons and lawyers that have followed them, for you would have converted the whole world right off the reel, & have left nothing for the churches to fish for! Flattery is not my forte but I assure you in all sincerity that your *Few Words* seemed to me the gem of the performance. Nothing could be better in taste, feeling or expression; nothing kindlier or more winning." That from the Censor is praise indeed. ...

1. William Ewart Gladstone (1809–98); temporarily out of office as prime minister of England.
2. Edward Pigott had passed, as well as admired, KF's comedietta *Eyes Right*, performed at the Gaiety for the Shakespeare Memorial Benefit.

To Laurence and Eleanor Hutton (PUL-H)
June 28. 1878.   Hotel des Trois Princes
                                                       78 Rue Neuve des Petits Champs. Paris

Dear People;—

I've done it. I've struck a bargain. You can have two fine large rooms on first floor and a little sitting room for 25 francs a day. You can't do better if you go from one end of the town to the other. It is at the corner of my street a few doors from my hotel and rooms belong to my landlady. Say you'll take the rooms at once as they are in great demand and for more money than you give. I've beaten the parlez-vous[1] down.

   1. Slang for *French people.*

To Mary Aurelia Anthony (HC)
Aug. 19. 1878.   St. Moritz

Dear M. A.;—

   ... I left London late in June, quite tired out with a nine months' campaign.[1] Going to Paris,[2] I passed three weeks in perpetual whirl. The Exposition and friends combined gave me no time to sleep, so in desperation I came here with Madame Ristori and her daughter. I've risen at six o'clock, imbibed iron water, bathed in it, sat in the sun, walked, made my début on glaciers, driven to magnificent views, talked French and Italian, had princes and "sich" for breakfast, dinner, and supper, gone to bed at 9 o'clock, been half frozen and half drowned, owing to the exceptional season, had an excellent appetite, gained flesh, and now I'm ready to lie on Hennessy's best stone wall and wallow in the sea. The U.S. Consul at Havre has invited me to make him a visit later, and I'll wind up my holiday in Paris where it pours friends.

   I enclose a few Shakespeare Memorial papers and want you to be interested in the matter. If Mary Anderson[3] gives a benefit, be sure and make all your friends turn out. I send some flowers from Anne Hathaway's cottage and specimens of the famous Alpine Edelweiss....

   If anybody wants to subscribe to Shakespeare Memorial, Geo. Riddle[4] has a subscription list.

   1. In promoting the telephone and the Shakespeare Memorial Theatre.
   2. KF spent three weeks in Paris covering the Paris Exposition for the *Tribune.*
   3. American actress (1859-1940).

4. KF's cousin George, a Harvard instructor in elocution, who was also a professional reader of Shakespeare.

To Cordelia Riddle Sanford (LW)
[Aug. 1878]   [St. Moritz]

Among other things, it rains principessas, duchessas, contessas, and marchesas. Man in Switzerland begins with Baron. Republican as I am, I saw myself in the Fremdenblatt (which is German for Visitor's List) as a Countessa until I expostulated and declared that America soared above titles. Women abound, apparently having packed up their husbands and male kind for the summer, and one soon learns on the promenade who is who.

Madame Ristori, [the] Marchesa del Grillo, is always the centre of a gay circle at the wells. Beauty, wit, intelligence gather around the tragic queen as naturally as though she were the Elizabeth, the Mary Stuart, the Marie Antoinette she so marvellously represents. Her passion for the stage is undiminished, and in October she will begin a three months' professional tour in Spain and Portugal....

To Laurence Hutton (PUL-H)
Jan. 20. 1879.   8 Devonshire St. [London]

Dear Mr. Hutton;—
... Dec. 16th I came over here, went into lodgings, became disgusted and now I'm very comfortably housed. Several of us Americans have taken a large furnished house and go shares in expenses, I having the management. I've developed a capacity for housekeeping of which none of you believe me capable, and more than one declares that I can keep an hotel which is the greatest compliment ever paid me, for if a body can keep an hotel he can keep anything. I've a capital cook and we eat like pigs. I sent to Newcastle for a housekeeper who is fidelity itself....

How about the Shakespeare Memorial? Can nothing be done in N.Y.? The [Shakespeare Memorial] Theatre will be opened April 23d with Helen Faucit as Beatrice in [*Much Ado About Nothing*], and on the 24th Irving takes his Hamlet to Stratford. So the wise people who cried "failure" had better be quiet....

To Laurence Hutton (PUL-H)
April 8. 1879.   12 George St. Manchester Square. London

Dear Mr. Hutton;—

... Houghton & Co. have just notified me that I am to receive one of your books.[1] Very many thanks. If I can get in a paragraph about it, I will. Remember however that my steady address is H[enry]. F. Gillig & Co. The book will go to Devonshire St. from which I've just moved. I found 5 stories, servants with delirium tremens and six people to feed, too much work for a busy person like myself, so I gave notice and my flock is scattered, much to its regret.[2]

I go to Stratford April 21st to remain throughout the [weeklong] Festival. My work will be to entertain the mayor's friends, to deliver Dr. Marston's address (which he would only write on condition I recited it), and to sing at the concert[3] which Sir Julius Benedict is supposed to manage but of which I've really done all the work. [Sir Charles] Santley[4] sings and Arabella Goddard[5] plays, and *Wm. Shakespeare*,[6] a charming tenor, pipes on this occasion. Mrs. [Emma Aline] Osgood[7] and Antoinette Sterling[8] are engaged—all the women singers are American.

So you don't come over this year. There's nothing to come for, and I'm beginning to think of returning to my native land.

   1. Hutton and Clara Erskine Clement's *Artists of the Nineteenth Century and Their Works* (1879).
   2. See *To Laurence Hutton*, 20 Jan. 1879.
   3. KF sang three songs from Shakespeare's plays: "I Know a Bank" (from *A Midsummer Night's Dream*), "Where the Bee Sucks" (from *The Tempest*), and "Should He Upbraid" (from *The Two Gentlemen of Verona*).
   4. Composer and baritone (1834–1922).
   5. Composer and pianist (1836–1922).
   6. Shakespeare (1849–1931), a professor of singing at the Royal Academy of Music, was one of KF's voice teachers.
   7. Soprano (1849–1911); a favorite with the English.
   8. Contralto (1850–1904); Sullivan composed songs for her.

To Edmund Clarence Stedman (CU)
May 28. 1879.   American Exchange.
                                                                 449 Strand. London

Dear friend;—

... I enclose a short article on W. S. Gilbert who expects to go to America in the Autumn. I think it is just suited to the present market, and I hope to have

Sullivan sit to me as Gilbert has done.[1] Please send it at once to Dr. Holland [of *Scribner's*] and get his verdict. If he won't have it, try Harper's. *Don't try Atlantic.*
. . .

I went to Lord Houghton's Fancy Ball the other night. There were very pretty costumes. Mine is said to have been prominent. I went as the Star Spangled Banner. Short white satin skirt over which the stars and stripes were draped. A blue low bodice (starred) with a splendid metal cuirass on which the eagle perched wings wide spread. White silk stockings, blue satin boots—jewelry—necklace and bracelets to imitate gold dollars. A tiara of 13 stars—original states—in my hair. I've received letters of congratulation, so the Eagle is safe.

I hear that M. H. Sanford says he is fond of me. My aunt writes (at last) that her love for me is unchanged and unchangeable. She is very happy at the Providence Asylum[2] and the Doctor says she is better than she has been for a long time. There are strong hopes of her recovery.

Love to all. I expect to see *you.*

1. Articles on both men (titled "W. S. Gilbert" and "Arthur Sullivan") appeared in *Scribner's Monthly* 18 (Sept. and Oct. 1879).

2. Mrs. Sanford, having suffered a nervous breakdown, had been temporarily institutionalized at the Butler Asylum in Rhode Island.

To Edmund Clarence Stedman (CU)
Aug. 27. 1879.

The Establishment.
Great Malvern [England]

Dear E.C.S.;—

I came here as intended—Aug 6th—just three weeks ago and do not regret the change, although the weather is often disgusting, today being the worst on record. The treatment suits me, the air, water, walks, drives, scenery are good—and only man is vile.[1] A stupider set of fifty beings [at this hotel] never was before collected. I am the sole redeeming feature (modest but true). I do the singing in the evening—even going so far as to astound the crowd with negro melodies—do the talking at table—have introduced games of Bean Bags on the lawn and have sent to London for a manual of *Poker*! If I can corrupt the morals of this place I will.

At present I'm cross. I've a boil on my left arm and rheumatics in my left knee—caught cold yesterday, sitting out and making believe there was a sun. Today I'm to perspire myself to pieces and am trying to make a fire burn. O ye Gods! *what* a climate! Most of the country is under water. I am to return in the

Autumn but I don't think I'll be ready for your steamer. A month later suits me better.

Are you rested? Love to your wife.

I remain here three more weeks and perhaps longer.

Please tell Reid not to send me *The Tribune.*

1. " ... Every prospect pleases, / And only man is vile." From the "Missionary Hymn" ("From Greenland's Icy Mountains"), stanza 2, by Bishop Reginald Heber (1783-1826). This stanza is omitted in certain hymnals such as *The Methodist Hymnal.*

To Edmund Clarence Stedman (CU)
Sept. 15. 1879.   The Establishment.
                                                                                        Great Malvern [England]

Dear E.C.S.;—

I got back all right after sitting up half the night with my agent Pond and his wife who settled the title for me—*Eyes and Ears in London.*[1] I hope you do not object to it.

The next morning I had Archibald Forbes[2] for an hour or so at the hotel and we got on immensely. He is a conceited cad but is very amusing. He said my Intercepted Letters in *Truth* had been his solace in Zululand.

Well, I rushed from the hotel and Forbes to Geo. Grossmith who has written an excessively clever scene for me, "Italian Opera in Five Minutes." I think it will be a very taking bit of the monologue, a syllabus of which I'll send you in a day or two. Now I enclose a photograph which is good, it seems to me. At least, it's the best I have to offer. I also send a something I knocked off yesterday. Please tell me whether it is worth anything.

I went to Sullivan's *Light Of The World* at Hereford Festival and was much pleased with music. The effect in a cathedral is fine. Met Sullivan there. He sails [for the States] Oct. 24. I may not go before Nov 1. Pond says I need not hurry. . . .

If you go on 22nd you'll be on steamer with my agent Pond.

1. A musical monologue burlesque in which KF sang and danced. KF wrote the libretto and George Grossmith (1847-1912), an Englishman, composed the music.

2. Forbes (1838-1900) was a *London Daily News* war correspondent; KF wrote on him for *Scribner's Monthly* 21 (Dec. 1880).

To Edmund Clarence Stedman (CU)
Oct. 22. 1879.   London

Dear E.C.S.;—
 ... Major Pond wanted to engage me for something and I invented the monologue. However, I've my doubts (*entre nous*) about Pond. He has not yet written me the final arrangements and I don't think I'll stir until I get them, as I'm valuably employed here and am so improving in my singing that Shakespeare (my teacher and the finest musician in England) sighs at my going at all. He wants me to wait six months longer. If Pond doesn't show the enterprise that he promised, I must get another agent, which will mean bother and delay. I see the papers are noticing my coming and I hope they'll keep on.
 Don't do anything for Gilbert or Sullivan. I've no opinion of either as men, though both are clever. I *do* hope the Lotos [Club] won't make fools of themselves over these two Englishmen. Don't use my name, but you can say to whom it concerns that Sullivan is a selfish snob, and Gilbert a quarrelsome whoppist. ...

To Laurence Hutton (PUL-H)
Nov. 11. 1879.   London

Dear Mr. Hutton;—
 ... I expect to sail [on 27 November] in the *Britannia* for New York. ... My primary reason in crossing is to change climate, see friends—my aunt who is comparatively sane now—and to renew my acquaintance with republican institutions which I swear *by* and hope I'll not swear *at*. Then, when I see the proper time, I've a musical monologue [*Eyes and Ears in London*] to launch, and as people are now going in for sprightly music, I think if I get a good agent I can make money. If you're in the way of inquiry, do look out for me. I don't believe in Lyceum Bureaus for this sort of thing, though Hathaway and Pond engaged me two months ago. I want to be my own mistress. Of course this entails possibility of loss, but I've discovered in this world that nothing ventured nothing gained.
 ... I suppose you are "doing" Gilbert and Sullivan. They are both clever, but really I wish Americans made less fuss over foreigners. It's sickening to hear that vulgar Lady [Mary Anne] Hardy[1] has been taken up and made much of. She's a dreadful creature in point of manners and her brains are third rate. ...

 1. Novelist (1825–91). After her husband's death in 1878, she came with her daughter to the States, where she collected material for two travel books.

Part Six: 1879-1883

 Founder of Ladies' Co-operative Dress Association

To Mary Aurelia Anthony (BPL)
Dec. 24. 1879. [New York]

Dear M.A.;—

It's very good of you but I can't go to Boston now. I leave today for Providence, expect to be with my aunt at Butler Asylum until Monday or Tuesday and then return to begin study, as my show [*Eyes and Ears in London*] opens in Utica Jan. 21. Probably I'll be in Boston in February as I hold forth at Salem Feb. 11th.

I haven't got my bearings yet, but think I shall like it on this side [of the Atlantic]. . . .

To Henry Wadsworth Longfellow (HC)
March 8. 1880. Parker House [Boston]

Dear Mr. Longfellow;—

When I first gave my lecture on *Dickens*, you kindly came. I wonder whether you will come to my musical monologue [*Eyes and Ears in London*] next Wednesday evening, at Horticultural Hall. I should feel honored. I venture to enclose tickets which at least you can give away.

In England the American known and honored by all is yourself. In fact, on one occasion a John Bull actually persisted in claiming you as an Englishman, and we almost came to blows.

Hoping you are younger than ever, believe me / Faithfully yours, / Kate Field

To Henry Wadsworth Longfellow (HC)
March 11. 1880.   Parker House [Boston]

Dear Mr. Longfellow;—
  I shall feel very much honored if you accept the enclosed tickets for next Saturday's matinée. They are the best I can offer you.

To Henry Wadsworth Longfellow (HC)
March 13. 1880.   Parker House [Boston]

Dear Mr. Longfellow;—
  I only wish I could accept your kind invitation for tomorrow, but alas! I am up to my eyes in engagements. Perhaps you will let me come when I next visit Boston, which I trust will be soon.
  Sorry you are ill, believe me / Faithfully yours, / Kate Field

To [?] (MHS-T)
March 19. [1880]   Parker House [Boston]

My dear;—
  ... I've made a success, and I've made money, but I have *not* had a good time. Work and play don't go together. ...
  I go to Providence Easter week. For ten days I shall be straightening out Ladies Dress Ass.[1] Don't you envy me? ...

  1. KF was founding the Ladies' Co-operative Dress Association to provide excellent garments at reasonable prices and thus emancipate women from the exploitation of couturières with their inflated prices.

To [?] (BU)
April 20. 1880.   The Ladies' Co-operative Dress Association
                                                      112 Fifth Avenue. New York

Dear Sir;—
  We are now taking subscriptions rapidly and should be pleased to have you

pay for the shares (four) Mr. Stedman has placed in your name. Owing to want of facilities Mr. Stedman has resigned in favor of James Drake & Co.

To Lucy Ware Webb Hayes (RBH)
    Lucy Hayes (1831–89) was the wife of the sitting president of the United States, Rutherford B. Hayes.
April 28. 1880.   Riggs House [Washington, D.C.]

Dear Madam;—
    I present my letter of introduction and my cause as a token of respect, but having heard of your bereavement[1] I refrain from intrusion.
    With sincere sympathy, I am / Faithfully yours, / Kate Field

    1. The death of Mrs. Hayes's brother, Dr. Joseph T. Webb, who died on 27 April 1880 of an apoplectic stroke.

To John Hay (LW)
    Hay, who had been with the *Tribune* for four years, was now assistant secretary of state.
May 9. 1880.   Hotel Victoria. New York

Dear Colonel Hay;—
    Mr. [Charles Spencer] Francis ("Troy Times") and I have just been talking over Dr. Schliemann and the propriety of making him our Consul at Athens. Two years ago I did what I could to stir up the powers but produced no effect, and now Mr. Francis says he has been pouring Schliemann into your not unwilling ear. Having mentioned that I had the pleasure of knowing you, Mr. Francis urged me to write a good word for the learned champion. Will it do one particle of good?
    Why should Schliemann be Consul at Athens? Because he is so proud of being an American citizen that on the frontispiece of his books is printed "Citizen of the United States." Because, in his way, he is a great man and would reflect honor on the country. Because he would, in gratitude for the compliment, bequeath America many of his treasures and would assist in stocking our Museums.
    Because he would give his services gratuitously. Because he has a beautiful palace in Athens and would entertain finely. Because having made a large fortune as a merchant, he possesses an order of intelligence that would benefit American

commerce. Because he has a knowledge of the East and speaks Greek. Because his wife is extremely nice and is Greek. Finally, because he longs to be Consul.

Are these reasons enough? It seems to me that our Consular service needs a good deal of overhauling, and to ignore a man like Schliemann is throwing away an excellent opportunity of getting a good deal for nothing. Am I right or wrong? Now don't make a pretty speech, but say exactly what you mean and oblige....[1]

1. KF's appeal on Schliemann's behalf proved useless.

To Laurence Hutton (PUL-H)
Aug. 5. [1880]   Paris

Dear L.H.;—
... The weather is splendid, and I haunt the cafes chantants[1]—got some ideas already. As Worth is out of town, I think I'll go to Baden tomorrow night....

1. Cafes where concerts take place.

To Edmund and Laura Stedman (CU)
Nov. 8. 1880.   Hotel Vendome. Boston

Dear friends;—
I can not accept your [Moncure] Conway invitation because I expect to be in Boston for the next two weeks. My agent H. J. Sargent, with whom I had a contract for six months from Nov. 1st, has gone to pieces during my absence, losing all his prestige, and I am trying to find a substitute. I had a splendid house at the Music Hall on election night [for *Eyes and Ears in London*] but it is extremely annoying—to say nothing of the pecuniary loss—to be losing valuable time through no fault of my own. Such is life. Moral—Trust no one.

To Laurence Hutton (PUL-H)
Nov. 16. 1880.   Hotel Vendome. Boston

Dear L.H.;—
Forgive silence, but I've been waiting to name date of my return [to New

York]; however, will defer no longer. I expect to be back some time next week—am remaining to try and repair damage done by Sargent [my theatrical agent].

Osgood told me to certainly make a volume on Fechter.[1] I'll see Jennie Gilder if you prefer.[2] An interview is better than a letter. I fancy that Price woman has nothing of special value; however, no stone should be unturned.

About other subjects we'll talk anon. I'm reading Rachel[3] now in the evening and have written half of my French show.

I'm at Mrs. Clement's & she says you're a good fellow. Amen.

1. As Hutton had been employed by Osgood to edit all six volumes in the American Actor series, he was assigned to oversee KF's book as well. On the flyleaves of the *Fechter* that KF presented to Hutton, she wrote in part: "If all editors let authors as effectually alone as you have let me, what an earthly Paradise Literature would be!" (*Laurence and Eleanor Hutton: Their Books of Association*, compiled by M. E. Wood [New York: privately printed, 1905]).

2. KF sent Gilder to interview Lizzie Price, the Philadelphia actress Fechter had bigamously married in 1874.

3. *Memoirs of Rachel* (1858) by Madame de Berrera.

To Laurence Hutton (PUL-H)
Nov. 27. [1880]   Hotel Victoria [New York]

Dear L.H.;—

The Fechter scare amounts to nothing.[1] I've seen Miss Gilder who went all the way to Phil*a* to find the valuable data. One unimportant Dickens letter was the "dem total." Good for us.

I've just arrived and am in the depths of despair. I must move, and *where* I know not. Can you tell me of a place?

1. The scare was that KF might have overlooked important material for her Fechter biography.

To Laurence Hutton (PUL-H)
Nov. 30. [1880]   [Hotel] Victoria [New York]

Dear L.H.;—

I *don't* move, since matters [have been] arranged here, and I remain in my present rooms until others are found. Thank heaven!

To Laurence Hutton (PUL-H)
Jan. 29. [1881]   Hotel Victoria [New York]

Dear L.H.;—
   ... Edmund Yates has sent a small contribution to [my] Fechter [biography]. Vezin promises one. No news yet from [Wilkie] Collins.[1]
   Go to Mrs. [John D.] Townsend's tonight and meet [Anthony] Pulbrook,[2] Dress Ass'n man. I can't go. Engaged on business. Love to the mother.

   1. The recollections of Fechter by Yates, Vezin, and Collins were included in KF's *Charles Albert Fechter*, chap. 6.
   2. Englishman experienced in operating cooperatives in London.

To Olivia Langdon Clemens (UCB-M)
   Olivia Clemens (1845–1904) was the wife of Samuel Langhorne Clemens.
March 5. 1881.   Hotel Victoria. New York

Dear Mrs. Clemens;—
   I've just paid in your cheque to the Secretary [of the Dress Association] who will send you a receipt. The prospects are very bright and I hope you'll spread the news among your friends. I enclose a form of application for shares in case anyone may want to subscribe. Regards to Mr. Clemens.
   Frank Millet[1] has painted a fine portrait of me. It will be in The Academy.[2]

   1. Francis Davis Millet (1846–1912), American painter and *New York Herald* war correspondent during the Russo-Turkish War (1877–78).
   2. The National Academy of Design (which held an annual exhibition of painting and sculpture) was New York's answer to the official salons of London and Paris. KF's will bequeathed the portrait to the St. Louis Museum of Fine Arts (not to be confused with the City Art Museum in Forest Park). On the museum's dissolution, the portrait was reportedly given to Washington University in St. Louis. As Washington University, however, has neither the portrait nor any record of having received it, the location of the portrait remains a mystery.

To William Warland Clapp (HC)
March 5. 1881.   Hotel Victoria. New York

Dear Mr. Clapp;—
   Thanks for sending me more Rachel[1] matter.

Now I write to call your attention to a Dress Ass'n advertisement which we have just sent to your [Boston] Journal.² Won't you give us a notice? Please. The prospects are very brilliant. Read enclosed prospectus carefully and see what a good thing it is.

I've had a bad cold and have been tied to New York.

---

1. KF had asked Clapp for information about Rachel for her biography of Fechter, since Fechter had acted with the famous French actress. When Fechter was only nineteen, Rachel said to him: "You must act in my pieces; I will play with nobody else" (KF, *Charles Albert Fechter*, 24).

2. Clapp had sold his *Boston Saturday Evening Gazette* in 1865 to edit the *Boston Journal.*

To William Warland Clapp (HC)
May 2. 1881.   Hotel Victoria [New York]

Dear Mr. Clapp;—

This circular to our patrons tells the story of our Dress Ass'n. We've many subscribers in Boston. Can you give us a *pp* [paragraph]?

The Board of Directors have just elected me President. I ought (for health's sake) to have sailed [to England] a week ago but I can't get away until the Association matters are all settled.

. . . I'm tired out and wish we were all in Heaven where Dress Ass'ns will be in vain.

To Edmund Clarence Stedman (CU)
May 21. 1881.   Co-operative Dress Association, Ltd.
                                       Temporary Offices, 112 Fifth Avenue, New York

Dear E.C.S.;—

I will lay your letter before the Board of Directors. If you knew as much about this matter as they and I do, you would take a very different view of the situation.

My suit against Mr. Pulbrook¹ would not have been brought, had he not done all in his power to injure the Association. It is in the interest of the Association, as I will explain to you when we meet. The money, if ever recovered, will not go into my pocket.

A cablegram received from a trustee of the old "Ladies Dress Association," now in London, reads thus, "Pulbrook's record bad; get rid of him."

I wish that you would send to me, or to the Secretary, [the names of] any shareholders who desire information on this subject.

For myself, I had infinitely rather be in London, where I ought to be, for my own interest, at this present moment, than remain here and work like a dog from ten in the morning until ten at night in the interest of the Association, from which I receive no salary, and which has cost me in time and professional loss $25,000.00. If you know of any man who is willing to make such sacrifices for this business, or any other, please let me know him, and we will vote him into our Board at once, to take Mr. Pulbrook's place. I will gladly give him mine, if the Board will allow me to resign.

All the old stock holders will receive an equal number of shares in the new [Association], so give yourself no more concern in the matter. The ex-organizing secretary made false statements to you and others for the purpose of ruining what he could not control for his own benefit. Allotments are coming in well.

1. KF had persuaded Pulbrook to incorporate the Dress Association and negotiate its stock, for which he received fifteen thousand dollars. He was made a director and organizing secretary, but he wanted to be president and general manager and to have the Cooperative buy largely through his London association. Unaccommodated in these demands, Pulbrook abruptly resigned. KF brought a suit against him to recover $2,567 for services she had rendered him, which sum she intended to return to the corporation. KF won the suit (*Tribune*, 15 and 23 May 1881).

To Edmund Clarence Stedman (CU)
June 10. 1881. [New York]

Dear E.C.S.;—

Unless you want to give me brain fever you will kindly assume that the counsel of the ass'n is investigating the old company's affairs[1] and doing all in his power to settle matters. To be attacked by *The Graphic*[2] is bad enough. To have an old friend threaten legal action which is unnecessary, is more than I can bear.

1. The "old company" had been formed by Pulbrook. After his resignation, the company had to be re-formed and a new board of directors elected. As stockbroker for the original company, Stedman wanted to be sure that all legalities had been scrupulously observed so that his company would not become liable.
2. The *New York Graphic* (18 May 1881) charged KF with having indemnified herself in the event that the Dress Association failed, and it maintained that her motive in forming the Association was greed rather than concern for women.

To William Warland Clapp (HC)
July 22. 1881.   Co-operative Dress Association, Ltd.
                                        Temporary Offices, 112 Fifth Avenue, New York

Dear Mr. Clapp;—
"Here we are again," as we say in the circus. I haven't gone to Europe, haven't gone anywhere, don't expect to go anywhere until our Association is fairly launched under the management of Mr. John Wales, who must be well known to you as belonging to the [dry goods] firm of Spalding, Wales & Co. of Boston.
If you can give us a paragraph [in your *Boston Journal*], I shall be obliged. I enclose the materials for the same. If you do notice us, please send me the paper. . . .

To Laurence Hutton (PUL-H)
July 29. 1881.   Co-operative Dress Association, Ltd.
                                        Temporary Offices, 112 Fifth Avenue, New York

Dear L.H.;—
We have been through purgatory and the hotter place since I saw you, and, in the language of the ring, "have come up smiling." Your precious mother probably received a Pulbrook circular denouncing all of us Directors as imps of Satan, or words to that effect. That circular was the immaculate conception of Townsend & Weed, counsel for the immaculate Pulbrook. I do not think many stockholders have been fools enough to sign those cast-iron powers of attorney,[1]—certainly the mother has not, and I enclose her a proxy which she can make out in my favor. "In time of peace prepare for war," as George Washington remarks.[2]
. . . The Dress Association is getting on exceedingly well, you will be happy to hear. Tomorrow, we move into our splendid new building, Nos. 31 & 33 West 23rd St., opposite Stern's. Our rent does not begin until September, when we shall open the store. We have secured as manager Mr. John Wales, a well known dry goods merchant of Boston. He is the best available man in the market and has a high reputation.
All the certificates of stock are signed. If you will send on your allotment paper and receipts, and Lawrence Barrett's, we will see that you get your certificates. . . .

    1. Instigated by Pulbrook to vote KF out of office.
    2. Washington's uncondensed statement (in his first State-of-the-Union address) was "To be prepared for war is one of the most effectual means of preserving peace."

To Edmund Clarence Stedman (CU)
Jan. 7. 1882.   Co-operative Dress Association, Ltd.
                                                31 and 33 West 23d St., New York

Dear E.C.S.;—

Oscar Wilde will lunch with me at Co-operative Dress Ass'n. on Wednesday next 2 p.m.[1] He wants to meet you whom he calls a charming critic. Will Lady Laura and you join a small party?[2] I shall only ask Vedder and the Millets. Wilde is clever and wants to meet artists only.

If you can, reply tomorrow at Victoria [Hotel]. I should like it.

    1. Wilde (1854-1900), Irish author and wit, was on a lecture tour of the United States.

    2. Stedman refused the invitation. "This Philistine town," he said, "is making a fool of itself over Oscar Wilde. Pah!" (Laura Stedman and George M. Gould, *Life and Letters of Edmund Clarence Stedman* [New York: Moffat, Yard, 1910], 2:32).

To Joseph Marshall Stoddart (HC)
    Philadelphia publisher (1845-1921).
Jan. 19. 1882.   Co-operative Dress Association, Ltd.
                                                31 and 33 West 23d St., New York

Dear Mr. Stoddart;—

Thank you exceedingly for the Murdoch book[1] which I shall read with interest.

Happy to have made your acquaintance believe me,

    1. James E. Murdoch's memoirs, *The Stage; or, Recollections of Actors and Acting from an Experience of Fifty Years*, published by J. M. Stoddart & Co. (1880). Page 124 contains remarks on KF's mother ("one of the most beautiful and accomplished actresses of the American stage"), KF's father (an "eccentric comedian and the witty editor of one of the popular papers of St. Louis"), and KF ("our talented young countrywoman").

To William Warland Clapp (HC)
Jan. 27. 1882.   Co-operative Dress Association, Ltd.[1]
                                                31 and 33 West 23d St., New York

Dear Mr. Clapp;—

If you care to publish enclosed [in your *Boston Journal*], it is at your disposal, but don't put my name to it. I am disgusted not at [Oscar] Wilde but at the goings-on of people and Press [about him].[2]

1. To promote the Co-operative, KF briefly (from 15 February to 26 April 1882) edited a two-column department titled "Art of Adornment" for the Philadelphia weekly *Our Continent*.
2. The goings-on were circusy. D'Oyly Carte (1844–1901), the producer of *Patience* (Gilbert and Sullivan's burlesque of Wilde), persuaded Wilde to make an extended lecture tour of the United States. It was D'Oyly Carte's way of hyping the comic opera, then playing in New York. Wilde, given his self-destructive streak, played Reginald Bunthorne (the "fleshly poet" in *Patience*) to the life.

To Laurence Hutton (PUL-H)
Feb. 16. 1882. [New York]

Dear L.H.;—
I intend to wind up the book [on Fechter] with accompanying recollections [from Collins, Vezin, and Yates] which I have had copied. For this boon bless me, as Collins's *mss.* would have made you somewhat profane, clear as it is. The erasures and interpolations are many.

Now you've something to begin on. Of course the critics will say that the sole interest of the book lies in the male recollections, but there's nothing mean [ungenerous] about me. I want justice done Fechter, and I want the book to be different from the others. It is its only chance of selling, for who is there to mourn for Fechter? Just one!

[This chapter of recollections] Makes about 28 printed pages.

To Laurence Hutton (PUL-H)
[Apr. 1882] [New York]

Fechter in U.S. Please find out name of second character played by F. in *Duke's Motto*.[1] I've left space.

Please use *paste* in place of my *pins*.

I've said nothing about Fechter's married life as nobody, not even Collins, knows anything. He was married in 1847 and had two children.[2] Perhaps I'd better put this in somewhere. What do you think? I shall not refer to his [bigamous] relations with *Price*.

Please let me have these Reminiscences again as I want to add something. They make Chapter 6th.

I want to see all proofs.

1. Play adapted from the French by John Brougham (1810-80). Fechter played dual roles in the melodrama, namely, Henri de Lagardere and Aesop the Hunchback.

2. Fechter married a Mlle. Roebert of the Comédie Française. His son Paul studied law; his daughter Marie became an operatic singer.

To Laurence Hutton (PUL-H)
April 20. [1882] [New York]

Dear L.H.;—

I've sent off all the proof [for the Fechter biography] so far, including what you left today. I want to know where the plates are going in and how they are to be labelled.

Did you speak to Osgood about payment? I don't object to receiving a check for $225.

I hope you'll get your reward for editing [the biography].[1] Nothing but love compensates me. I expect to be awfully abused—"Wild fanaticism," "utter absence of critical faculty," &c. Show me any criticism where you get the faintest idea of what a great actor does at any given moment. That's what people and artists want to be told. Not eloquent sentences picturing nothing.

1. The payment Hutton received from Osgood for editing KF's *Charles Albert Fechter*—as well as the other five volumes in the American Actor Series—was, in his words, "too insignificant to merit a deposit in the bank" (*Talks in a Library with Laurence Hutton*, recorded by Isabel Moore [New York: G. P. Putnam, 1905], 275).

To Olivia Langdon Clemens (UCB-M)
May 2. 1882. Co-operative Dress Association, Ltd.
31 and 33 West 23d St., New York

Dear Mrs. Clemens;—

I heard recently through the Millets that you had lost your allotment paper and had no means therefore of obtaining your certificate of stock. I have therefore taken the responsibility of issuing the stock and now enclose it. I wish when you are in New York you would visit the Association and see for yourself. It ought to be of great service to members living out of town. I send a catalogue and illustrations of building.

To Laurence Hutton (PUL-H)
May 4. 1882.   Hotel Victoria [New York]

Dear Friend;—
What can I write except that I am stunned and grieved at your unexpected bereavement? One of the dearest, kindliest of souls and best of mothers has left a void that no one can fill. I know how terrible your loneliness must be for I have gone through it all. Heaven give you strength to bear the blow, and when you can bear sympathy believe in the sincerity of / Yours faithfully, / Kate Field
I called today to offer my services. If I can be of the least assistance in matters big or little, remember that I shall esteem it a proof of friendship to be summoned.

To Benjamin Ticknor (MHS-LFM)
Son of the late William Ticknor; had joined Fields, Osgood & Co. in 1870.
May 13. 1882.   Co-operative Dress Association, Ltd.
                                                            31 and 33 West 23d St., New York

Dear Mr. Ticknor;—
When I see proofs [of my Fechter biography] I'll tell you where to place illustrations. Both Mr. Hutton and I think the playbill unnecessary.
I also want to see the Fechter motto on Dedication page.[1]....

1. This page read "To the Memory of Charles Dickens."

To Lilian Whiting (LW)
Journalist and author (1847-1942). Among her many books is *Kate Field: A Record* (1899). She was such a devotee of KF that, at her own request, her ashes were placed beside those of KF in Mount Auburn Cemetery, Cambridge, Massachusetts.
[June] 1882.   [London]

I've dived into art. My soul hungers and thirsts for music—for pictures—for all the things I've had no taste of since I've *been in trade!*[1]
... I'm quite miserable over the paintings I can't buy. There's a fine portrait of Dickens in 1842 for sale for $750. It would fetch double that in America. There's a charming Gainsborough[2] for $150, and another for $125,—a Sir Peter Lely[3] for $300. I go and look at these things and ache at not being able to buy them.

Lilian Whiting, Kate Field's biographer and friend.
(From Lilian Whiting, *The Golden Road* [Boston: Little, Brown, 1918], frontispiece.)

1. Refers to the Dress Association.
2. English portrait painter (1727–88). KF bequeathed to "John E[nnis]. Searles of New York the drawing of Gainsborough in his possession in payment of $1000 invested in Kate Field's Washington" (KF's will, filed at the Probate Division, Superior Court of the District of Columbia). (Searles was president and director of three railroads and five related industries.) The drawing was probably taken from the Landor album (see *To Laurence Hutton*, [1877], n. 5).
3. Dutch portrait painter whose original name, before coming to England in 1643, was Pieter van der Faes (1618–80). During his years as court painter, his subjects were the great figures of the court of Charles I, the Protectorate, and the Restoration.

To Laurence Hutton (PUL-H)
June 28. 1882.   American Exchange. 449 Strand. London

Dear friend;—
I've just arrived in [the steamer] "City of Berlin" after a placid voyage and should much like to know how you are. I'm at the Grand Hotel but shall get out of it as soon as possible and already have the refusal of an apartment in Craven St.
My address is this Exchange. How long I shall remain here I don't know, but after transacting business and seeing the new plays I shall be ready to go to the continent and take care of myself. . . .

To Edmund Clarence Stedman (CU)
July 13. 1882.   London

Dear E.C.S.;—
. . . I'm in London still but in about ten days shall go to Paris. Thence to Mont Dore in Central France where I shall go about with a tumbler of warm water and a brass band daily for three weeks—as a cure. Nothing does me so much good as the regular life and medicinal waters of a healthy Spa. Mont Dore is 3000 ft. above the sea, so I shall have mountain air. You know too that I'm always *getting into hot water* and, strange as it may seem, thrive in it.
I'm seeing few people as I'm doing music, theatres and business, and can't afford to waste any time. I've had a message from Mr. [Richard Henry] Horne[1] who wants to see me, and I go to Wilkie Collins tomorrow. Yates has invited me to his cottage on the Thames. . . .

1. Poet (1802-84); famous for his *Orion*, an epic that he published in 1843 at a mere farthing "to mark," as he put it, "the public contempt into which epic poetry had fallen" (quoted by Ann Blainey, *The Farthing Poet: A Biography of Richard Hengist Horne* [London: Longmans, Green, 1968], 133).

To Lilian Whiting (LW)
[July 1882]   [Paris]

Paris is always interesting until one has heard all the music and seen all the plays and pictures and bought all the new books. Then I want to cross over to England, where people think in an Anglo-Saxon way. . . .
I saw [Sarah] Bernhardt[1] in "Camille"[2] last Wednesday night. She is an ad-

mirable artist who acts from the head down. Still, I prefer Modjeska's conception and rendering of the part, as truer to Dumas's novel.[3]

1. French actress (1844–1923)
2. *La Dame aux camélias* by Dumas *fils.*
3. Dumas's novel (1848) bears the same title as the play.

To Laurence Hutton (PUL-H)
Sept. 28. 1882.   Co-operative Dress Association, Ltd.
                                                     31 and 33 West 23rd St., New York

Dear L.H.;—
Thanks for the slips. They treat the book [my *Fechter*] very fairly and it *may* astonish us by selling. I hope so. Has the author any privileges that the publisher and editor are bound to respect? I've rec'd no copy of "Fechter" and it seems to me I ought to have some copies to give away to Vezin, Collins, Yates and English and American critics who would benefit the book. Let me know whether "Fechter" has been reprinted in England. . . .

To Edmund Clarence Stedman (CU)
Oct. 26. 1882.   Co-operative Dress Association, Ltd.
                                                     31 and 33 West 23rd St., New York

Dear E.C.S.;—
Miss Whiting tells me that Mr. [George Washington] Cable[1] is in town. Won't you please tell him that Miss Genèvieve Ward wants me to know him and *I* want to know him and I'd like you all—including him—to lunch with me tomorrow between 1 and 2 o'clk. and if you can't, why then some day next week after Wednesday, as I'm going to Newport on Saturday for a few days.

1. Southern author (1844–1925).

To Mr. Clarence Clough Buel (MHS-LFM)
Buel (1850–1933) was assistant editor of the *Century Magazine.*
Jan. 8. 1883.   Hotel Victoria [New York]

Dear Mr. Buel;—
Thanks for your note. I should have resigned under any circumstances next

Spring and only remained because my going out would have imperilled the [Dress] Ass'n. But Wales killed it the first six months.

The bad trade of this Autumn prevented our regaining lost ground. No reserved cash settled the matter. I have been cruelly slandered in the Press and I am terribly hurt in consequence and don't know what the consequences to my health would be were it not for my horse who makes me forget for an hour a day. I shall probably lose

Money loaned	$15000
Stock	$3500
Time	Two years

Money not earned in [mean]time.
So much for trusting to the capacity of others.

To Edmund Clarence Stedman (CU)
Jan. 24. 1883. Hotel Victoria [New York]

My dear friend;—

Life is short at the longest, friendship is rare and I would not for worlds have a cloud come between you and me. If I told you nothing about the condition of C.D.A.[1] when failure became inevitable, I did my duty, which was silence. As an officer I should have been guilty of grossly unbusinesslike conduct to have breathed impending failure to a soul.

We expected a good Christmas season which would have made things right. It did not come and the debts contracted by John Wales were too heavy to carry. Had we been a firm we could have put in an assignee, sold off the goods and begun over again. Being a corporation we were helpless against judgment creditors, except through a receiver appointed by the Court. It is all wicked and I shall never forgive the two men [Wales and Pulbrook] who brought this wreck about. I was not permitted to know of or interfere in the merchandise dep't where all the harm was done.

Give yourself no concern about your stock. I own $3500 and disposed of not one share.

Will you dine with me next Monday and let me tell you the story?

1. Co-operative Dress Association.

Part Seven: 1883–1886

Campaign Against the Church of Jesus Christ of Latter-Day Saints

To Lilian Whiting (LW)
July 22. 1883.   Denver, Colorado

Here I am, my dear, feeling very like the traditional cat in a strange garret, yet very much interested, and new things turn up so fast that my head feels as though it would burst. A sister of Julia Dean, the famous actress, has just left me, having called on the strength of knowing my dear mother,[1] and the result is that I'm going to visit her ranch.

People appear here in the most amazing manner and one makes friends inside of five minutes. My journey west was uneventful and perfectly comfortable, thanks to Pullman cars. I stopped over night at Chicago and went with Mr. [George Mortimer] Pullman to his town,[2] which is unique and wonderful and such a monument as does honor to its founder. It is worth a journey west to "Pullman" alone. . . .

I had not been two hours in town [Denver] before a committee of ladies engaged me to give my monologue [*Eyes and Ears in London*] on the 31st. Eugene Field[3] called at once and has been as kind and attentive as though he were a real cousin—kinder. He is very clever. . . .

---

1. Dean (1830–68) had played in Ludlow & Smith's company as a child and would have known KF's parents, if not KF herself.

2. Pullman (1831–97), an inventor, was the builder of the Pullman railway sleeper car. The town of Pullman, now part of Chicago, was built entirely by the Pullman Palace Car Company for the accommodation of its employees.

3. Journalist and poet (1850–95); he liked to call KF "cousin Kate."

To Cordelia Riddle Sanford (LW)
[Aug. 1883]   [Denver]

God bless you and make you brave! I wish I were with you. It seems such an awful distance away when sorrow comes.

Poor Uncle Milton![1] Yet why should I write "poor"? No. He leaves his tired body, and begins life over again with truer insight and higher aspirations, as we all must. You think of this, I know, dearest aunt, and you accept temporary separation with resignation to a will wiser than we can conceive.

   1. KF's uncle died on 3 August 1883.

To Edmund Clarence Stedman (CU)
Oct. 31. 1883.
                                                                Continental Hotel.
                                                                Salt Lake City. Utah

Dear friend;—

It was very good of you to reply so speedily to my letter. . . . What aggravates me is that I can be of no use to you. That you should suffer for no wrong of your own is so horribly unjust.[1]

I learn from Lilian Whiting that you have moved.[2] It is too bad. Why did your rich friends let you?[3] Of what good is money if not to help such as you in the hour of adversity? Do let me know how you are and how Lady Laura bears up.

What is Fred doing and where are his family?

For myself I am repairing the damages done by Co-operation.[4] I can never regain the time and money lost, but I am regaining health. I weigh 12 lbs. more than when I left N.Y. and am studying the West to good advantage, I hope. My public appearances[5] are eminently successful. Now I am investigating Mormonism, & the more I study, the more devilish polygamy and theocracy (one and inseparable) become. The government is an ass. From here I return to Colorado, thence to New Mexico, Arizona and California. No East this Winter. . . .

   1. With the stock market in precipitous decline, with clients failing to meet their obligations, and with his son Fred using company securities for his own secret speculations, Stedman had suspended his brokerage operations and used his personal capital to pay off debts.
   2. His business having failed, Stedman let his beautiful house and gave up his elegant offices.
   3. Reid and Stedman's Uncle Dodge, among others, offered to help him; but Stedman refused on the grounds that the only honest course was to suspend operations.

4. Refers to the Dress Association.
 5. These involved lecturing on Dickens and performing *Eyes and Ears in London*.

To Laurence Hutton (PUL-H)
Nov. 25. 1883.

Continental Hotel.
Salt Lake City. Utah

Dear L.H.;—
 ... I'm in Zion with God's chosen people. ...
 I came here for a week and remained six. I'm not yet ready to leave. I'm trying to get at the "true inwardness" of the worst theocracy in the world today. Result—a book.[1] I've been very successful publicly everywhere. I have no agent. I go where I like and sit down if I think the place good for "material." Then a committee of citizens, or a church or a manager waits upon me and begs me to give my "Dickens" or my monologue [*Eyes and Ears in London*]. I ask sixty, sixty-five and sometimes 75 per cent of gross receipts and have no bother or extra expense. Thus I make money and see the country as I could not possibly, did I rush through professionally. Of course in my way I can not gather a fortune when I spend my profits in lingering, but I gain what is worth more than money. I return to Colorado, thence to New Mexico and Arizona to visit Gen. [George] & Mrs. [Mary Dailey] Crook.[2] ... I enclose Mormon criticism of yours truly.
 Is this true about your club and [Matthew] Arnold?[3] I have *never* gained in a Summer in Europe what I have gained in the West either in knowledge or—avoirdupois!

 1. The book KF wrote on Mormonism was rejected by publishers because of its inflammatory nature.
 2. General Crook (1829–90) was known for his pacification of Native American tribes and for defending them against imputations of bad faith and a proclivity for warfare.
 3. Arnold (1822–88), English poet, critic, and educator, addressed the Authors' Club (of which Hutton was a charter member) when lecturing in the States in 1883.

To Laurence Hutton (PUL-H)
Feb. 8. 1884.

Continental Hotel.
Salt Lake City. Utah

Dear L.H.;—
 ... It will be strange if *The Tribune* does reject an article the sole purpose

of which is to call attention to suffering Southerners who at the risk of their lives have broken away from Mormonism. It will teach me a lesson as to big newspaper[s'] desire to break up this iniquity.

Did you hear the Capel-Pullman-all-together-religious row at Cortlandt Palmer's?[1] It must have been great fun.

Did you hear Geo. Riddle read my comedietta of *Extremes Meet*? Did the Millets? Of course not. 'Twas ever thus &c. . . .

1. On 6 February 1884, the Palmers had opened their parlor to the Nineteenth Century Club for a religious discussion. Monsig. Thomas John Capel defended the Catholic position against the Protestant, Jewish, and agnostic positions (represented by Rev. Dr. Pullman, Rabbi Gottheil, and T. F. Wakeman, respectively).

To Lilian Whiting (LW)
[Feb. 1884]   [Salt Lake City]

It is no matter now that Wendell Phillips has passed away.[1] He had done his great work and needed a radical change of atmosphere to begin anew. *He has now got it!* He did me worlds of good when I was a young girl and helped to make me a radical. My uncle [Milton] was the worst sort of Democrat.

1. Phillips died on 2 February 1884.

To John H. Holmes (MHS-LFM)
    Managing editor of the *Boston Herald.*
April 10. 1884.   Continental Hotel.
                                                                                                                Salt Lake City. Utah

Dear Sir;—

The most important event in Salt Lake—the [Mormons'] Conference—has just taken place. I have given it my strictest attention and report what the Saints really said, which is more than either Mormon or Gentile[1] papers have done. I have boiled down as much as possible, and regret the length which can not be shortened and [still] give a proper idea of this religious farce. In consequence of this length, I shall keep silent for some time.

Please send copies.

1. Among Mormons, any person not a Mormon.

To Edmund Clarence Stedman (CU)
May 19. 1884.
Continental Hotel.
Salt Lake City. Utah

Dear E.C.S.;—

I read recently in *The Boston Traveller* that you are fast regaining your lost fortune,[1] and I heartily rejoice. I only hope that the recent panic has not affected you. It has given me a fright, as all my cash is in the Second National Bank, and it is no thanks to John C. Eno[2] that I'm not seriously embarrassed. I thought a bank in which Wm. W. Phelps[3] is a director could be depended upon.

Sic transit.[4]

I'm still among the Saints. If I'd known what a "big job" Mormonism is, I never should have had the courage to touch it. "H. H."[5] may treat a subject without knowing about it (see May *Century*)[6] but I can't. She's too clever a woman to mislead the public as she has done. I like her and am sorry....

    1. Stedman had been readmitted to the Board of the New York Stock Exchange in December 1883. For the loss of his fortune, see *To Edmund Clarence Stedman*, 31 Oct. 1883, n. 1.

    2. Eno (1848–1914) was president of the Second National Bank of New York until his resignation in May 1884.

    3. Phelps (1839–94), lawyer and businessman, was at the time a U.S. congressman.

    4. "Sic transit gloria mundi": Thus passes the glory of the world. From *De Imitatione Christi* (I.iii.7) c. 1427; attributed to Thomas à Kempis (1380–1471). The words, "Sancte Pater, sic transit gloria mundi," are still recited in the ceremonial for the Pope's coronation.

    5. Initials used by Helen Hunt (1831–85)—at the time, Mrs. William Sharpless Jackson—a popular author.

    6. Helen Hunt's article on Mormonism, "The Women of the Bee-Hive." The beehive was an emblem of the Mormons.

To Thomas Gregg (MHS-T)
    Writer on Mormonism (1808–92).
July 27. 1884.
South Norwalk. Connecticut

Dear Mr. Gregg;—

Your very kind letter with its excellent suggestion reached me yesterday through Col. Hay who happens to be in New York. I wish I had seen Dr. Philastus Hurlbut[1] but he was not at Painesville [Ohio] and I could get no information about him. I *did* see Mr. [Eber D.] Howe,[2] who struck me as honest and who bears an excellent reputation. I will ask a friend to put to him your questions. I heard no good of Clark Braden at Kirtland [Ohio]. People who hate Mormonism declare that he did not argue with [E. L.] Kelley. He scolded like a fishwife. Kelley kept his temper. His book[3] is about to appear I believe.

I've written to Judge Sharp[4] enclosing a check for eight dollars, the price of your History of Jackson County.[5] I had borrowed his copy which now I've concluded to keep, and have requested him to purchase another for himself.

It is about decided that I'm to lecture on Mormonism early next winter. This lecture will be made up largely of anecdotes, as I believe as much in stories as did Abraham Lincoln. Now that narrative of Judge [Stephen S.] Harding[6] is just the sort of stuff to interest an audience. Are you willing to sell it to me? As it does not belong to the main body of your book, I have thought you might be willing to dispose of it. Kindly let me know.

You perceive that I send you "something."

1. Hurlbut had been "disfellowed" from the Mormon Church for having used obscene language.
2. Editor of the *Painesville Telegraph* and author of *Mormonism Unvailed* (1834).
3. *Public Discussion of the Issues Between the Re-Organized Church of Jesus Christ of Latter Day Saints and the Church of Christ Disciples, Held in Kirtland, Ohio, Beginning February 12 and Closing March 8, 1884, Between E. L. Kelley and Clark Braden* (1884).
4. Unidentified.
5. Error for *History of Hancock County* [*Illinois*] (1880).
6. Former governor of the Utah Territory, who, as a boy, had known Joseph Smith (1805–44; American founder of the Mormon Church) in New York. The narrative in question is included in Thomas Gregg's *The Prophet of Palmyra: Mormonism Reviewed and Examined* (1890).

To Thomas Gregg (MHS-T)
Aug. 29. 1884.   South Norwalk. Connecticut

Dear Mr. Gregg;—
Here I am down for a lecture, as you perceive by enclosed circular. Thanks for your kind letter. I'm sorry you don't feel inclined to let me have the Harding story for my lecture.[1] It is just what I want and could not in any way affect the sale of your book. *I* shall very likely use in my lecture what I shall put into my book, and expect to sell more books in consequence. Whatever advertises is good and, besides paying you for the *mss.*, I'd give you credit for it. Reflect on the matter.

I'm reading the Clark Braden-Kelley discussion[2] and hard work it is. What do you think of it? They are both vulgar and abusive.

If the Keokuk [Iowa] paper will notice my lecture, I'd like it.

I do hope you'll be able to bring out your book. If I could help you I would. My publisher will not touch two books on same subject.

Do you want "Tucker"?[3]

1. See *To Thomas Gregg*, 27 July 1884.
2. Ibid., n. 3.
3. John Randolph Tucker's *Polygamy: Speech . . . in the House of Representatives, March 14, 1882.*

To Thomas Gregg (MHS-T)
Sept. 4. 1884.   South Norwalk. Connecticut

Dear Mr. Gregg;—

Your letter has just arrived. It is too bad to throw cold water on your proposition but I do not believe in the serial idea. It is only good for sensational novels and pictorial work. I know that my publisher would not listen to it for a moment, and I have no acquaintance with other publishers.

No, the idea is not feasible. If you put money into it, I'm sure you would lose it. Your only way is to publish in book form. My own stuff is so voluminous that I fear the publisher will want a lot left out as it is.

I hope you will favorably entertain my proposition to sell me the Harding story—I only want that relating to Palmyra—should you be willing to let me have part only. Lectures do not interfere with books.

Hoping you will forgive my frankness and with cordial remembrances to your family. . . .

Thank you for letting me read the poem.

To Thomas Gregg (MHS-T)
Sept. 16. 1884.   South Norwalk. Connecticut

Dear Mr. Gregg;—

I agree to your conditions [for the Harding narrative][1] and enclose a check for thirty dollars. I wish I could make the amount much larger.

The chances are that I shall use very little [of it] for my lecture, but I want to be fortified with all possible proof in case of attack which will probably come.

If ever I get back the money I've spent on Mormonism I shall be lucky.

As soon as I've finished writing my lecture, I'll make a few extracts from "Tucker"[2] and then return the book, which is quite safe.

Nobody knows anything about Mormonism in the East, and I fear that few care. My lecture will be a test of interest or the reverse.
Kindly acknowledge.

1. See *To Thomas Gregg*, 27 July 1884.
2. See *To Thomas Gregg*, 29 Aug. 1884, n. 3.

To Hugh Erichsen (UM)
Erichsen (1860–1944), a physician, was collecting material for his *Methods of Authors* (1894).
Sept. 23. 1884.   South Norwalk. Connecticut

Dear Sir;—
Your inquiry [about my writing habits] has just reached me.
I prefer daytime. The brain is far clearer in the morning than at any other time. I refer of course to a normal brain independent of stimulants. Under pressure, night work on journalism is often more brilliant than any other; but it is exceptional in my opinion.
I make no outline in advance.
I never use stimulants, hot water excepted.
I am not aware of having any particular habit when at work, except the habit of sticking to it.
I have no specified hours for work.
I spend no time at a desk, as I write in my lap. Mrs. Browning did the same. It is far easier for me and prevents round shoulders. It is also better for the lungs.
I *have* forced myself to write at times and do not believe in waiting for ideas "to turn up." Some people think with pen in hand. I am one of them. It seems to be the medium by which thought is conveyed from brain to paper. What "Planchette" was formerly to "mediums," a pen is to / Yours truly, / Kate Field

To Thomas Gregg (MHS-T)
Oct. 9. 1884.   South Norwalk. Connecticut

Dear Mr. Gregg;—
I return to you by registered mail and with many thanks your "Tucker" [book]. Kindly acknowledge receipt. I have received the Harding *mss.* and am very much obliged to you for copying it for me.[1] I do not think I was more than

just in the price paid for it. I doubt however whether I can use more than a few incidents in my lecture—perhaps not these unless I give a special lecture on the Book of Mormon. My "Mormon Monster" as originally written takes *six hours* in delivery. I've cut it down to less than two hours, so you see I can't add anything to this particular lecture. I'm to deliver it experimentally next week in a town near Boston.

No, I don't write for *N.Y. Tribune*, saving very occasionally. That check[2] was for an article on Mormonism and [James G.] Blaine.[3] I've ordered a *Boston Traveller* on same subject to be sent to you and I hope you'll get it.

    1. See *To Thomas Gregg*, 27 July 1884.

    2. The *Tribune* had given KF a check for thirty dollars for her article on "Utah Politics and Morals" (7 Sept. 1874), a check she endorsed to Gregg to pay for his story about Harding's recollections of Joseph Smith.

    3. In 1873 Blaine (1830-93), Speaker of the House of Representatives, told Brigham Young (1801-77), president of the Mormon Church, that Utah would never be allowed into the Union as long as his church permitted polygamy.

To Thomas Bailey and Lilian Woolman Aldrich (HC)
Nov. 12. 1884.   Hotel Vendome [Boston]

Dear Mr. & Mrs. Aldrich;—

Will you serve your country by hearing me next Tuesday and Thursday evenings (Nov. 18 & 20) on *Polygamy* and *Mormon Treason*?

I want to make public opinion and can't if the right minds are not present. If you can come, I'll gladly send you tickets.

I'm here for ten days or more and shall be glad to see you.

To a Theatrical Manager (RC)
Dec. 1. 1884.   South Norwalk. Connecticut

Dear Sir;—

I have just received a note from Mr. Whyte[1] requesting me to send you Press notices of my musical monologue. I think I have already done so, but I send still another circular that was used in N.Y. My monologue was very taking and made money in Boston, N.Y., Washington and Baltimore. It is very fatiguing and requires a first rate accompanist. I can not give it at the same price as a lecture. It takes too much out of me.

The *Mormon Monster* must not be lost sight of. I want to stir up the people on a big subject, but I do not wish to go West until I am sure of good engagements. You must let me know what the prospects are, as there is enough to do in the East, unless the West offers strong inducements. I am averse to long journeys and low fees. Let me have a perfectly honest opinion from you. When people are entirely frank in business, there is no possibility of misunderstanding.

I have just rec'd a letter signed by the Governor of Massachusetts, the Mayor and leading clergy of Boston requesting me to return and give still another lecture on the *Mormon Monster* in Tremont Temple at popular prices, so the poorer people can hear me. I shall do so next week.

Awaiting an early answer.

I send a few lithographs. If liked and needed, a number can be forwarded.

1. Unidentified, but probably the theatrical manager's assistant.

To Laurence Hutton (PUL-H)
Dec. 18. 1884.   South Norwalk. Connecticut

Dear L.H.;—

I heard yesterday that you were on this side of the water and also that you were engaged to Eleanor Mitchell. Accept my congratulations, particularly as to the matrimony. You've been so good a son you ought to make an equally good husband, therefore Miss Mitchell is a lucky woman. I don't know her as well as I do you, but I should think you are a fortunate man. Bless you, my children.

Much to my amazement I'm in the grand moral reform business. My *Mormon Monster* is stirring up New England and about Jan. 20th I expect to appear in N.Y. So please remember and turn out. Everything in N.Y. has failed this season—(few stars excepted)—and if I don't lose money there I shall be lucky. But I've got to be heard in Gotham and the sooner the agony is over the better. I should like my friends to be interested and to give moral support if they can. Will you get your clergyman to promise to be present? I'll send him a ticket. I want all the clergy possible present on the platform. They all turned out last week in Boston and I had an ovation. What is much better, I am producing an effect.

Where are the Stedmans living now? When do the Millets return?

Merry Christmas!

To Hugh McCulloch (IU)

    McCulloch (1808–95), an American banker and financier, had been originally appointed secretary of the treasury by Lincoln and had recently been reappointed to that office by President Cleveland.

Dec. 24. 1884.   South Norwalk. Connecticut

Dear Mr. McCulloch;—

    How I should like to accept Mrs. [Susan Maria] McCulloch's very kind invitation! Perhaps I can later in the season, but on Jan. 19th (D.V.) I start for Chicago, in the vicinity of which I may be orating for some time. The West at present is much more alive to the political meaning of Mormonism than the East, and as the iron is hotter there I shall do a little striking. Until the 19th prox. I endeavor to enlighten New England where I've been asked "Who is Joseph Smith" and "whether Brigham Young is still alive." We needn't talk about English ignorance of this country when the Atlantic Coast knows so little about the Far West.

    Do help to pound a little sense into Republicans anent the tariff. Denunciation now means canonization a few years hence. I really wonder where our boasted intelligence is situated.

    I'll dream of your generous hospitality and if I'm very good, kind fate may render it possible for me to enjoy it.

To Hugh and Susan Maria McCulloch (IU)

Jan. 16. 1885.   South Norwalk. Connecticut

Dear Mr. & Mrs. McCulloch;—

    I *did* receive your kind letters and nothing but travelling and lecturing constantly has prevented me from replying at once, as I should have done.

    It is very good of you to ask me to stay with you so long a time. I'll come as soon after the 27th as I possibly can and will let you know next week on my return from Syracuse the exact day. I've so many managers proposing things that I don't know where I am. It may be that I may remain in Washington after my visit to you in order to accomplish certain results, and if so, I'm sure you can suggest a proper abiding place. In that case I'd like to be present at the Washington Monument celebration.[1] As I am always more or less connected with the Press, I suppose there will be no trouble about securing a good place.

    If I can do anything for either of you in N.Y. before starting for W[ashington]. please let me know.

1. The Monument was dedicated on 21 February 1885, though it was not opened to the public until 9 October 1888.

To Reverend Andrew Preston Peabody (MH)

Peabody (1811–93) was a Unitarian clergyman of Massachusetts and Professor of Christian morals at Harvard.

Jan. 17. 1885.   South Norwalk. Connecticut

Dear Sir;—

I am to lecture on Mormonism next Thursday evening at Cambridgeport and should greatly like you to be present for no other reason than that I think leaders of opinion like yourself should know what Mormonism really means. You doubtless believe that it is a religion and therefore should be let alone. In reality it is a vast business and political machine bent upon undermining our government. Accident acquainted me with "the true inwardness" of the Latter Day Saints' scheming, and duty, rather than inclination, prompts me to tell the tale.

No one should ever lecture unless he has something—I honestly think I *have* something—to say.

To Susan Maria McCulloch (IU)

Feb. 19. [1885]   814 Twelfth St. [Washington, D.C.]

Dear Mrs. McCulloch;—

Will you invite Rev. Mr. [William Andrew] Leonard[1] to my lecture [on Mormonism] for me, and let me know whether he can come? If so, I will send him tickets. Kindly ask him whether he will announce the lecture from his pulpit on Sunday. It will be given in the Universalist Church, corner of L and 13th Sts.

1. Leonard (1848–1930) was Rector of St. John's Church in Washington, D.C.

To Augustus Lowell (LW)

Related to John Lowell (1799–1836), the founder of the Lowell Institute, whose will stipulated that the administrator be a male descendant of his grandfather and bear the Lowell name.

March 19. 1885. [Boston]

Dear Sir;—

Going West for pleasure, I was arrested against my will by the presence in Utah of a hierarchy in the heart of a republic. After months of study I have returned and am doing all in my power to enlighten public opinion in order that Congress may be forced to consider it and take speedy action. The lecture which I am giving to the general public in no way covers the whole ground of Mormonism. I am preparing half a dozen lectures with a view to delivering them to thinking associations, etc., early next autumn. As Lowell Institute is in the habit of giving courses of lectures, I now write to inquire whether such a subject as mine—of vital national importance—commends itself to your consideration. It would be easy for me to obtain letters of introduction to you from Mr. James Russell Lowell and other prominent Americans, but I prefer to let this matter rest entirely upon its merits. Whether I know what I talk about can be told you by Judge [Stephen Johnson] Field[1] of the Supreme Court, Washington, D.C., Judge Arthur MacArthur[2] of the District Court, Washington, D.C., [U.S.] Senator [Henry Laurens] Dawes[3] of Massachusetts, Governor [Eli Huston] Murray of Utah, and many another, if you care for references. As I leave town in a few days, an early answer will oblige.

1. Field (1816-99) was appointed by President Lincoln to a newly created tenth seat on the Supreme Court in 1863.
2. Judge MacArthur (1845-1912) was the father of Gen. Douglas MacArthur (1880-1964).
3. Dawes (1816-1903) performed his most important service as Chairman of the Senate Committee on Indian Affairs and gave his name to the Dawes Act and the Dawes Commission, both relating to Native American matters.

To Augustus Lowell (LW)
March 21. 1885. [Boston]

Dear Sir;—

Many thanks for your prompt reply to my letter of inquiry.[1] Will you kindly answer three questions?

Did the generous donor of the Lowell Institute Fund specify the sex of the lecturer, or does he leave this matter to the discretion of his executors?

Were I a man, would you entertain the idea of lectures on Mormon Treason before the Institute?

Were a man delegated to deliver my lecture, would this arrangement be acceptable?[2]

1. Lowell had rejected KF's offer to lecture on Mormonism at the Lowell Institute.
2. Lowell responded that a literal interpretation of the testator was that lectureships should be confined to men; that an institution devoted to instruction was not a fitting place to put down Mormonism; and that permitting a man to read a woman's lecture would be an innovation he was not prepared to introduce.

To American Publishing Company (BPL)
April 12. 1885.   South Norwalk. Connecticut

Dear Sirs;—

I am writing a book on Mormonism[1]—having lived in Utah a year and having, as you may have read, lectured on the subject with success during the past season.

I already have a publisher if I conclude to appear in the usual way, but the more I think of it, the more I am convinced that my book should be sold by subscription. Do you care to entertain the idea of such a publication? I write to you at the instigation of my friend, C[harles]. D[udley]. Warner.[2] An early answer will oblige / Yours truly, / Kate Field

1. No manuscript for a book on Mormonism by KF has been found.
2. Author (1829-1900); wrote his first novel in collaboration with Mark Twain (*The Gilded Age*, 1873).

To Lilian Whiting (LW)
[Summer 1885]   [Denver, Colo.]

I've been to Colorado Springs, lectured there and visited H[elen]. H[unt].'s grave. It is on Cheyenne Mountain, 2,500 feet above the town, reached by a mountain road good enough for carriage and two horses. The situation of the grave is beautiful, romantic, and appropriate. I walked several rods in a foot of snow to get to the grave, but only a few steps beyond I found bare rock, where I sat in the sun for an hour, and thinking of the unique woman and generous heart that had passed many a day in the same place, I gazed upon the beautiful plain that stretches to the Missouri River. No monument at present marks H. H.'s grave, and it would require a sympathetic genius to create a fitting design.[1] The usual white marble atrocity would desecrate nature and insult the dead. . . .

I liked her very much for her great cleverness and vivacity. It is impossible for me to give an analysis of her character as she appeared to me. . . . As I care for Shakespeare and a few old fellows supremely, perhaps you can understand why the poetry of H. H. does not appeal to me. . . .

You will, of course, use your judgment in publishing scraps that I send. . . . But for yourself, pray don't think it womanly to be too easily disgusted. Whatever a man can read, a woman can read. Whatever a man can write about, a woman can write about.

1. In accordance with her wish, Helen Hunt was buried beneath a cairn on Cheyenne Mountain in Colorado. Since visitors carried the rocks away as souvenirs, her remains were reinterred in Evergreen Cemetery.

To Lilian Whiting (LW)
[Summer 1885]   [Out West]

I started for Alaska, and at the rate of speed with which I was approaching it, I probably would have reached it near the close of the twentieth century. I have been figuring on the subject somewhat, and the seeming fly-tracks you see [sketched] here represent the tangents I pursued while traversing that State. I have delivered my Mormon lecture at Paw Paw, Weeping Water, Lone Mound,— in short, I have elucidated the problem of polygamy at every little cross-roads in Michigan and in Iowa. Last week I began to realize that if I had kept on fly-tracking the intervening territory, I would have reached Alaska in 1970—that is to say, eighty-five years hence. Much as I wish to see Alaska, I really have not the time to devote to this method of accomplishing a realization of that wish. . . .

To Miss Shepherd (MHS-LFM)
    Reporter for an unidentified paper.
Sept. 1. 1885.   [South Norwalk, Connecticut]

Dear Miss Shepherd;—

Had I known last evening that you had written the advance notices of my lecture, I should have thanked you last evening. Pray accept the amende honorable this morning.

One good turn deserves another! If the papers refer to last night's lecture, I should like at least one to get matters straight, so I enclose the only correct outline that has ever been published. If you can get what I say of a national marriage law and legislative commission copied verbatim, I shall be greatly obliged.[1]

Hoping to meet you again.

1. KF wanted to outlaw polygamy (as well as variations in state marriage laws) by passage of a uniform national marriage law. She also wanted to install a federal legislative commission to govern Utah, thereby abolishing the power of the Mormon Church to rule the territory.

To John Bigelow (UC)
Oct. 9. 1885.   Chester. Vermont

Dear Mr. Bigelow;—

I don't suppose you know where I've been or what I've been doing the last two years, so I mark a page of enclosed circular by way of explanation. I went to Utah accidentally for a week en route to the Pacific, and remained a year in spite of myself. The result is that I'm delighted to speak for the Gentiles of Utah and tell the public what they want. I've produced some effect in Massachusetts and on Nov. 21st I'm to appear at Chickering Hall in New York. Will you and Mrs. Bigelow give me the pleasure of your company?

Furthermore, it is thought that public opinion will be more strongly influenced if leading men, regardless of party, sign a call for me to give my lecture on the Social and Political crimes of Utah. Do you feel like giving your name? And do you think it would be possible to get Mr. Tilden's. I am particularly desirous of having Democrats on the call, as I believe that this administration and the new Congress will do more than has been done in twenty years by the Republicans—I mean in settling the "Mormon problem," which is no problem at all. I treat of Mormonism as a political machine of organized treason.[1] Judge Field of the Supreme Court says my argument is sound.

An answer addressed to Victoria Hotel, New York, where I shall be on Sunday will oblige / Yours very truly, / Kate Field

1. The Mormon Church held that its laws took precedence over federal laws.

To Thomas Gregg (MHS-T)
Oct. 17. 1885.   *New address*: Victoria Hotel. New York

Dear Mr. Gregg;—
   . . . Nothing would please me more than to lecture in your vicinity, in which

case I should give you a private séance, did your deafness make it impossible for you to hear me in public. I expect to go West in January, lecturing in Cleveland on the eleventh of that month. If your people want me, all they need do is to address the Redpath Lyceum Bureau, Tribune Building, Chicago.

I'm sorry about your book but I know publishers so well, I'm not surprised. After all, you may be willing to let me look over your *mss.* and see whether your material could be incorporated in my book. I've never yet used the Harding *mss.* I bought from you,[1] but I intend to do so. I've cut it down very much, because as originally written, it is tiresome. The good points are lost in verbosity. . . .

How is Judge Sharp?

1. See *To Thomas Gregg*, 16 Sept. 1884.

To John Augustin Daly (FL)
Dec. 8. 1885.   Victoria Hotel. New York

Dear Mr. Daly;—

Do you remember "when I was a boy"[1] how you, as usual, anticipated your generation by proposing Sunday lectures and how we tried it twice on bad Sunday nights and lost no money while we made no fortunes? Are you in a mood to discuss Sunday nights and matinees of lectures and musical monologues for February and March or during Lent?[2]

The "Mormon Monster" is in the air and I want to make N.Y. understand his meaning. He's not so much a social evil as a political criminal bent on Treason. Moreover, he is very amusing. My lecture at Chickering Hall was a success, and I had no help from any source. The ice therefore is broken. I shall be in town for a week. An early answer will oblige. . . .

1. From Thomas Hood's "I Remember, I Remember": "Now 'tis little joy / To know I'm further off from heaven / Than when I was a boy."
2. At Daly's Theatre, said to be a miraculous transformation of the old Broadway Theatre.

To Grover Cleveland (LW)

Cleveland (1837–1908) was twice elected president of the United States (1885–89 and 1893–97).
[Feb. 1886]   [Boston]

Dear Mr. Cleveland;—

As you say that friends are always sending you unkind remarks about yourself, I venture to enclose an interview extorted from me during my recent visit to Boston. The reporter was very anxious to know what you said.[1] I think I know one woman who can hold her tongue. What I told the reporter I believe.

Àpropos of the Utah U.S. Marshal [E. A. Ireland], if you meet John W. Mackay of Nevada, ask him what he thinks of P. H.[2] . . . There never lived a truer man, a sounder Democrat, a pluckier soul or one who understood so well the requirements of Utah. Several things have occurred recently to prove the weakness of the present incumbent, who is, however, an honest, well-meaning man. Natural limitations are a misfortune, not a fault.

I also enclose some Mormon scraps to be read by you at your leisure. It is said that a good way to influence men is through their wives. If Mormon agitation can be made fashionable, matters can be expedited. . . .

1. KF had interviewed Cleveland on 23 February 1886.
2. Unidentified.

To Samuel Langhorne Clemens (UCB-M)
March 6. 1886.   Victoria Hotel. New York

Dear Mr. Clemens;—

I'm told you have a very poor opinion of me because I have lectured against Mormonism. I think if you had ever heard me you would revise this opinion, as my lectures are against the *treason* of the political machine, called a religion to blind the unwary.[1] However, this is not the cause of my boring you with a letter. You represent a big publishing house. I am writing a history of Mormonism which I think will be entertaining as well as enlightening. Such a book is fit only, it seems to me, to be sold by subscription. Does it appeal to you from a business point of view?[2] I think I know what I am writing about.

An answer will oblige / Yours truly, / Kate Field

1. Twain replied (8 Mar. 1886) that he had the same objections to Mormonism as KF and in any event would not have a "poor opinion" of her even if they differed. But, he added, "considering our complacent cant about this country of ours being the home of liberty of conscience . . . the attitude of our Congress and people toward the Mormon Church is matter for limitless laughter and derision" (LW, 449).

2. Twain, a partner in Charles L. Webster & Co., declined KF's proposal, saying he had a backlog of two to four years and had to pigeonhole his own book indefinitely "to make room for other people's more important books" (LW, 449). Twain's "own book" was apparently *A Connecticut Yankee in King Arthur's Court* (1889).

To Samuel Langhorne Clemens (UCB-M)
March 13. 1886.   Victoria Hotel. New York

Dear Mr. Clemens;—
That "Mark Twain" should wait for anybody's book is absurd enough to print,[1] but *I* won't betray your embarrassment of—riches.

Now, oblige me by reading enclosed pamphlet and then you'll know what I'm aiming at, and don't think I went to Utah to study up for a crusade. The going there was pure accident.

Please ask your wife with my compliments whether there is any charity she is interested in that would care to have me give my Mormon lectures—one or three—for half of the profits. I want to interest you Hartfordians in the cause.

1. See *To Samuel Langhorne Clemens*, 6 Mar. 1886, n. 2.

To Laurence Hutton (PUL-H)
March 17. 1886.   [Victoria Hotel, New York]

Dear L.H.;—
When I wrote you the Fechter article,[1] you told me to call upon you whenever you could help me.

I give two Mormon lectures at Chickering Hall on Friday Mar. 27th: *Vice & Treason of Mormonism.* Saturday Matinée, Mar. 27th: *Polygamy in Utah.*

Lectures in Lent are being done to death and I must make an extra effort. If you can sell tickets for me, you can assist me as my expenses will be $500.

This will be my last Mormon crusade in N.Y. as I leave for Washington. . . .

1. For the fourth volume of Hutton and Brander Matthews's five-volume edition of *Actors and Actresses of Great Britain and the United States* (1886).

To Benjamin Perley Poore (BU)
Poore (1820–87) for three decades reported Washington politics for various Boston newspapers under the signature Perley.
April 19. 1886.   Welcker's Hotel. Washington, D.C.

Dear Sir;—
I should like to make your acquaintance. Will you come and see me?

As you know more about Congress than the oldest Congressman, will you answer several questions?

Did not [Charles Stewart] Parnell, M.P., address the House by invitation, on the subject of Ireland?[1]

Has any rule been made since, prohibiting any outsider from using the House or Senate for similar purposes?

A bet is pending, and you are the likeliest to decide it. Most Congressmen don't seem to know anything beyond their own wants.

1. KF, evidently desiring to bring the Mormon question before Congress, was looking for a precedent. In 1876 Parnell (1846–91) and John O'Connor Power were delegated to present to President Grant an address congratulating the American people on the centenary of the Declaration of Independence. Grant declined to accept the address from the Irish people, as protocol demanded that it be received through the British ambassador. Parnell, who returned to England, left Power to negotiate with congressmen, who finally accepted the address over the head of the president.

To Thomas Gregg (MHS-T)
April 22. 1886.   [Washington, D.C.]

Dear Mr. Gregg;—

... In case I ever finish my own book I don't know now what I'd do with it. There is really no money in a book on Mormonism. My lectures have paid because people are curious to hear me speak, but many come to hear me *in spite of my subject.* ...

I'm temporarily in Washington where the Mormons are working like beavers to kill adverse legislation, and they may succeed. Congress knows nothing about the subject and cares less. People and press may stir them up eventually.

To Lilian Whiting (LW)
Xmas 1886   [The Arlington Hotel, Washington, D.C.]

Why did you? The pretty present with its tender inscription has just come and my eyes have filled with tears in reading the engraved lines. Ah, my dear friend, the Love that is true, for which we all aspire in some form or other, comes, perhaps, hereafter. But there can be honest, helpful friendship, genuine affection in which is no time-serving—and let us thank God for it, "hitching our wagon to a star"[1] meanwhile, and hoping for everything. You remember Lowell's lines [in "Longing"]: "Perhaps the longing to be so Helps make the Soul immortal."

1. From Emerson's "Civilization."

To Lilian Whiting (LW)
[1886]   [The Arlington Hotel, Washington, D.C.]

... The only noble ambition is the desire to be fully one's self, to act out one's whole nature; and if that nature leads one into more than one path, I see no reason to wail. ... I deny that versatility must necessarily be shallow. The trouble is not on account of superficiality, but because of the want of time to carry out many ideas. But what of that? ... Americans are the least tolerant of "versatility" of any people on earth, and it is probably due to the hardness of life in a new world. It requires so much exhausting work to make a living at one thing that half-educated souls can't believe in the soundness of those who turn from one art or profession to another in sympathy with it. And yet Americans contradict themselves by being a doctor one year and a merchant the next; a banker one day and a diplomatist the day after; a soldier for five years and a lawyer forever after, until the speculator supplants both. The trouble with most critics is that they are led by early prejudices and not by reason.

To Eleanor Varnum Mitchell Hutton (PUL-H)
    Laurence Hutton's wife.
Dec. 30. 1886.   The Arlington [Hotel]. Washington, D.C.

Dear Mrs. H.;—
    If then you don't hear to the contrary, I'll leave Newark on next Wednesday at 10.11 o'clock, reaching N.Y. soon after. Please order a coupé to be at ferry and let the man meet me at the landing exactly where the boat touches shore on ladies' side of ferry boat. Let him call out West 34th St. and be on the watch for a single woman in a hat (not bonnet) and a black circular. Said driver can get somebody to watch his horse or can bring some one along for that purpose. I never trust myself in unknown cabs at night. Of course you have a stable you can depend upon.
    Save me some bread & cold meat.
    I must leave afternoon Jan. 6th.

Part Eight: 1887–1889

~ Crosses America to Lecture
Against Prohibition
Promotes Alaska

To Laurence Hutton (PUL-H)
May 7. 1887.   Metropolitan Hotel. Salt Lake City, Utah

Dear Hutton;—

... I'm stopping here for some days to take in the present situation and to try and put my prohibition stuff together.[1] ... I've recently been through Prohibition Kansas and got so angry as to stir up the bile as effectually as though I've been to sea. On arriving in Omaha I took to my bed for a day and, after ridding myself of Kansas, arose a wiser if not a better being. ...

Can you send me C.O.D. [Henry Wood] Elliott's book[2] on Alaska published by Scribner? Send to above address.

From here I go to California ...

1. For her lecture "The Intemperance of Prohibition."
2. *Our Arctic Province: Alaska and the Seal Islands* (1887). KF drew on Elliott's book for her article "Our Ignorance of Alaska" (*North American Review*, July 1889).

To Lilian Whiting (LW)
[May 1887]   [Metropolitan Hotel, Salt Lake City]

Never was a woman more taken by surprise than I was on being presented with a beautiful gold badge set with diamonds.[1] I had been entirely thrown off my guard by being called upon to pay for the regulation badge prior to my initiation. Governor Murray is commander of the corps here and expressed great delight at my becoming a member of his flock.[2]

1. In tribute to KF's crusade against Mormonism.
2. A member of the Women's Relief Corps of the Grand Army of the Republic, an organization of Union veterans of the Civil War.

To Lilian Whiting (LW)
[1887]   [Metropolitan Hotel, Salt Lake City]

I think the "North American [Review]" is too severe on [James Russell] Lowell.[1] He may deserve all that criticism, but I doubt it. The great crime seems to be that he is a *Mugwump*.[2] As I am a Mugwump, I feel differently. Lowell's great trouble is that he has always been self-indulgent and has never liked the people. The people are *not* agreeable at dinner parties, and Lowell likes clean clothes and wit.

1. In a two-part article (published in April and July 1887) by Arthur Richmond.
2. Someone who belongs to no political party or who votes for another party's candidate. Lowell was elected to the Electoral College by a Republican constituency, but he voted for the Democratic candidate—for Cleveland, not Blaine.

To Lilian Whiting (LW)
[1887]   [Port Townsend, Washington Territory]

It rained twelve days out of seventeen and we had fog two more! I wore out a pair of arctics on shore and went about in a riding-habit and a seal-skin. The habit did away with petticoats, and in it I defied mud and ascended the Muir glacier. Alaska is very interesting to me, and I shall probably go to work on a lecture at once. I remain here to consult Judge [James Gilchrist] Swan,[1] an Indian authority, and then go over to the Britishers in Victoria. Here I am the guest of [Henry Ward] Beecher's son.[2] He has a charming little boy named after his grandfather. . . .

1. Voluminous writer on the Northwest Territory and Native Americans (1818-1900); associated with the Smithsonian Institution.
2. Henry Barton Beecher (b. 1841) was a special agent in the Custom House at Port Townsend.

To Houghton Mifflin Co. (HC)
Boston publishing house that reprinted KF's *Ten Days In Spain* (1886).
Aug. 25. 1887. Occidental Hotel. San Francisco

Dear Sirs;—
Please send to me to above address eight copies of *Ten Days In Spain*.
The last [royalty] check sent me was again addressed to South Norwalk [Connecticut] where I have not been for two years. My regular address is Victoria Hotel, New York.

To Eugene Woldemar Hilgard (UCB-H)
Hilgard (1833–1916) was Professor of Agriculture and Director of the Agricultural Experiment Station in Berkeley, California.
Sept. 21. 1887. Occidental Hotel. San Francisco

Dear Prof. Hilgard;—
I've returned from Alaska and have had a glimpse of grapes in Napa Valley. Next week I am going to the Mission San Jose and on my return shall be very glad if you will dine with me and enlighten me on viticulture. Do you have lectures at the University? I mean outside of regular instruction. I shall lecture next month in this state and have wondered whether the University indulged in such things.
I saw a "must" machine[1] in Napa Valley.

1. A recent project in the wine industry was to condense freshly pressed wine juice by means of steam and vacuum until the product (must) was thick as molasses. This method reduced the volume by about one-third. The must, together with its extract, was then shipped to other countries, where the wine was reconstituted. Winegrowers pronounced American must far superior to the must from Spain, France, and Italy. The advantage to winegrowers was that must was admitted free of duty.

To Laurence Hutton (PUL-H)
Dec. 17. 1887. Occidental Hotel. San Francisco

Dear L.H. & Missus;—
... I have written, in addition to my lecture on Alaska, the following articles: 1. *A Trip to Alaska* (a description of the steamer route which can be beautifully illustrated). 2. *Rum In Alaska* (showing the absurdity of Prohibition). 3. *National Ignorance of Alaska* (showing how Congress has neglected a great coun-

try). 4. *Native Races of Alaska* (with legends and anecdotes. Can be illustrated). 5. *The Missionary In Alaska* (showing the right and wrong way to educate the Natives).

Nos. 1 and 4 and 5 are magazine articles. Nos. 2 & 3 are for Reviews. I'm a great distance from the literary market and wonder whether you L.H. would receive these articles and offer them for publication.[1] Mr. [Henry Mills] Alden[2] said he would read No. 1, but I don't like to send it to him by post. I don't mean for you take any responsibility but to act as broker on a commission. It will oblige me if it will not bore you.

Rum in Alaska ought to suit *The Forum* or *North American*.[3]

I always feel like a whipped cur when I offer an article to an editor and wouldn't write a line if I could help it. I rarely do [write] unless a subject forces itself upon me. . . .

1. Hutton agreed to offer his services.
2. Alden (1836–1919) was known as the dean of American magazine editors because of his long tenure as editor of *Harper's Monthly* (1869–1919).
3. Only one of these articles ("Our Ignorance of Alaska") was published (*North American Review*, July 1889).

To Laurence Hutton (PUL-H)
Jan. 1. 1888.   Occidental Hotel. San Francisco

Dear L.H.;—

. . . I shall send on two more articles: *Native Races of Alaska* [and] *Education In Alaska.*[1]

It seems to me I've written a book, but in preparing a lecture I can't help writing the equivalent of a book.[2] From all, I cull what will hold a public for an hour and a half. . . .

1. Unfound.
2. KF's "book" of 177 pages, bearing the title "Despised Alaska," is in BPL.

To Samuel S. McClure (MHS-T)
McClure (1857–1949) was the editor and publisher of the first U.S. newspaper syndicate, founded in 1884.
Jan. 15. 1888.   Occidental Hotel. San Francisco

Dear Sir;—

If I send you a letter from California on a charming valley I have discovered,[1] how many papers can you publish it in, and what are they?

You can have the letter gratis if the papers are good. If they are not, the letter will go unwritten. Please reply speedily to above address.

   1. KF wrote a chapter on the valley ("North of the Golden Gate") for a book by naturalist John Muir (1838-1914), *Picturesque California and the Region West of the Rocky Mountains* (1888).

To Laurence Hutton (PUL-H)
Feb. 5. 1888.   Arlington Hotel. Santa Barbara

Dear L.H.;—
   I've written to John Foord[1] telling him what [that article on] Alaska has cost me and asking him to name a price. I can't because I don't know what Harper will pay.[2] Alaska has cost me $2200 and six months of time, so you see I'll never get back my money except I lecture on the subject. . . .

   1. Foord (1842-1922) was editor of *Harper's Weekly*.
   2. In a letter to Hutton of 25 February 1888 that is in PUL-H, KF wrote, "I've just accepted Mr. Foord's offer"; but no KF article on Alaska has been found either in *Harper's Weekly* or *Harper's Monthly*.

To Laurence Hutton (PUL-H)
March 31. 1888.   Hotel Westminster. Los Angeles

Dear L.H.;—
   . . . I've been in the City of the Angels for two days and, while the scenery outside the town is fine owing to the Sierras, I much prefer San Diego. Nothing can compensate for the lack of water and S.D.'s harbor is beautiful. The people for the most part are uninteresting. Real estate is the topic of conversation and "booms" the rage. If I had invested in Southern California instead of Washington, Kansas and Omaha, I'd be a howling squillionaire. "There's much virtue in an if."[1]
   Gen. and Mrs. Frémont[2] with others lunched with me today. The Frémonts have been given land and a house a few miles out of town and are to live here permanently. They like it better than I could.
   Has the missus received some ostriches—on paper? Is it in your line to notice the San Diego book?[3] It is the best thing of the kind done on the Coast and the author (literally the son of a Gunn) is a very clever journalist, made rich by the rise of property.
   Is it true that Julian Hawthorne has gone into trade?[4]
   If you want the best of California wines I can put you in the way. . . .

1. In *As You Like It* (V.iv.102-3) Touchstone says, "Your If is the only peacemaker; much virtue in If."

2. John Charles (1813-90) and Jessie Benton (1824-1902) Frémont. As a lieutenant in the U.S. Topographical Corps, Frémont oversaw the scientific mapping of the Oregon Trail, the first of many such explorations. Mrs. Frémont was an author whose books included one on California, *A Year of American Travel* (1878).

3. *Picturesque San Diego* (1887) by Douglas Gunn.

4. Nathaniel Hawthorne's son (1846-1934). The rumor was baseless; Julian Hawthorne had been a lyceum lecturer, had worked on the *New York World*, and was a very productive writer. In 1887-88 alone he published eleven books.

To Laurence Hutton (PUL-H)
April 13. 1888.   Hotel Westminster. Los Angeles

Dear L.H.;—
... The thermometer was only 97 here yesterday and in that heat I lectured! Gen. N[elson]. A. Miles[1] introduced me and a fine fellow he is. He is the best officer I've yet met, [William Tecumseh] Sherman[2] excepted.

You would die laughing to see a drawing that has just been sent me. Riverside (nearby) has had an election. Prohibition versus High License,[3] in which the H.L.'s have been beaten by a small majority of 45. I happened to be in the town just before the election and the License people drew me into the contest by interviews &c. Had I remained and rolled up my sleeves—as it were—I'm sure my side would have won. Well, no sooner did the news of defeat arrive than I received a scroll which on opening disclosed an indescribable irate female with oh! such a foot planted upon a prostrate bottle of California brandy. It is now being framed appropriately. The W.C.T.U.'s[4] are as great a pest as phylloxera.[5]

I'm lecturing in these parts and expect to go to S. Francisco on the 24th.

How good [Constant Benoît] Coquelin's article is on Acting and Authors![6] He delights me. Wonderfully clever is that story of *Last Island* in April Harper['s Monthly Magazine].[7] You are a capital reviewer.[8]

1. Leader of campaigns against Native Americans of the West, including the Sioux and Apache (1839-1925).

2. Union general (1820-91); best known for his devastating March to the Sea and his remark "War is hell."

3. High license was intended to raise the cost of a liquor license steeply, the expectation being that higher prices would reduce the consumption of liquor.

4. Woman's Christian Temperance Unionists.

5. Lice that attack grapevines.

6. The article by Coquelin (1841-1909), a French actor, appeared in *Harper's Weekly*, May 1887.

7. "Chita: A Memory of Last Island," by Lafcadio Hearn (1850-1904).

8. Hutton was literary editor of *Harper's Monthly Magazine* from 1886 to 1898 and conducted the department of "Literary Notes."

To [?] (UV-F)
Jan. 7. 1889. Victoria Hotel. New York

Dear Sir;—

Thanks for your offer. The enclosed explains my position and you can use it as an interview if you will. The State of California considers my advocacy of Temperance so valuable to her great industry as to pass a resolution to pay my incidental expenses in five big towns. Here is the foundation of all this idiotic hue and cry which is not worth noticing and I shall do no more denying.[1] If you will take up my suggestion of [serving] only American wines *on March 4th*, you will be doing what I am trying to do—serving my country.

... I'll write an article on Temperance versus Prohibition for ... [page missing]

It is true that I am about to issue a weekly *national* paper—*Kate Field's Washington*—the end of December, if not earlier, a prospectus of which will appear in advance. It will be politically independent, aim for the best society all over the country and warmly support the new states and struggling territories. It will oppose all sumptuary laws and therefore will oppose prohibition, but will treat of so many subjects as not to come under the category of an organ for any specialty. It will be *my* organ, and what I conscientiously believe, of course the paper will advocate. It will avoid vituperation and endeavor to be *temperate* in all things.

I will send you a prospectus when ready. The heading will be very effective.[2]

In the course of a few weeks I expect to make Washington headquarters where my address will be *The Shoreham* [Hotel]. I have taken a pretty apartment in Vice-President [Levi Parsons] Morton's[3] beautiful new building.

1. Prohibitionists were accusing KF of being a "drummer" for a California wine syndicate because she had accepted "incidental expenses" to promote its wines. KF in her "Reply to Her Critics" (*New York Tribune*, 21 July 1889) avowed that her "conscience had never yet been for sale," and if ever it was, it would not be for such a trivial sum. For further charges and countercharges, see Introduction, n. 22.

2. The heading of the prospectus featured an image of the Capitol and the great seal of the United States.

3. Morton (1824-1920) was vice president under Benjamin Harrison (1833-1901).

To John M. Carson, L. Q. Washington, C. M. Ogden, and Many Others (LW)
Members of the Washington Press Corps.
March 15. 1889.   The Arlington [Hotel]. Washington, D.C.

Gentlemen:

That you, who represent the unequalled power of the "Fourth Estate [the Press]," should ask me to speak on a vital topic is a compliment I fully appreciate. My address on "The Intemperance of Prohibition" is about ready for delivery and most cordially I invite you and your confreres to meet me at Grand Army Hall on Friday evening, March 22d, at eight o'clock.

To William Warland Clapp (HC)
March 23. 1889.   The Arlington [Hotel]. Washington, D.C.

Dear Col. Clapp;—

My lecture last night on *The Intemperance of Prohibition* was pronounced a success by a very critical audience. Dr. [William Alexander] Hammond[1] who presided endorsed every word I said. I should much like to give this address in Boston and, as you are on the eve of a fight at the polls,[2] I should think anti-prohibitionists would like to have me. Is there any organized force arrayed against the cranks? Please let me know at once, addressing me [at] *Victoria Hotel*, New York. . . .

---

1. Former Surgeon General of the U.S. Army, professor, and prolific author on a variety of medical disciplines (1828–1900).

2. Over the question of prohibition, raised by a coalition of the National Prohibition Party and the Woman's Christian Temperance Union.

To Elliott Coues (UV-F)
Coues (1842–99) was one of the best-known scientists of the nineteenth century. An extraordinarily accomplished American, he was a surgeon, explorer, naturalist, zoologist, geographer, ornithologist, historian, professor, editor, and voluminous author.
May 10. 1889.   [Victoria Hotel] New York

Dear Dr. Coues;—

I am asked to give the name of a flower that should be used as a national emblem. Can you suggest something? I think a Rocky Mountain or California flower that is indigenous should be selected, don't you?

Regards to your wife.[1]

1. Mary Emily Bates (b. 1835), whom Coues married in 1887, was an accomplished musician, art critic, and linguist.

To Ward Hill Lamon (HL)
Lamon (1828–93), a Lincoln biographer, had been Lincoln's law partner, his friend, and, when "Honest Abe" became president, his bodyguard.
June 30. 1889.   Victoria Hotel. New York

Dear Sir;—

Will you kindly settle a dispute about Lincoln?[1] Lately in Pennsylvania I quoted Lincoln to strengthen my argument against Prohibition and now the W.C.T.U. quote him for the other side. What is the truth? An answer, pro bono public, will greatly oblige.

1. The full story concerning this dispute is told in Carolyn J. Moss, "Lincoln and Temperance: Ward Hill Lamon's Testimonial Letter and Its Draft," *Lincoln Herald* 97 (Winter 1995): 165–68.

To Ward Hill Lamon (HL)
July 11. 1889.   Victoria Hotel. New York

Dear Sir;—

I cannot be too grateful to you for your generous reply to my note of inquiry. May I use publicly the information you have given?[1] And as you are the best of authority on the subject of Abraham Lincoln, can you explain *why* he is quoted on the Prohibition side?

Did he at any time make speeches that could be construed into total abstinence? As you have the manuscripts of several Temperance addresses, perhaps you can help me to a solution. The Prohibitionists are furious because I have quoted Lincoln on *my* side, and you saw by what I enclosed that the W.C.T.U. claims him for their own, by extracts that have puzzled me. Are they spurious?

With renewed thanks. . . .

1. Lamon had reported to KF that Lincoln "was neither . . . a 'drinking man,' a total abstainer nor a Prohibitionist," but he refused her permission to publish his remarks. Only after his death did KF publish his letter (in *KF's Washington*, 12 Dec. 1894).

Part Nine: *1889–1894*

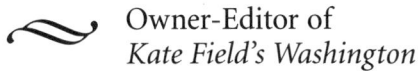 Owner-Editor of
Kate Field's Washington

To Owner of a Printing Plant in Washington, D.C. (BPL)
Oct. 19. 1889.   Victoria Hotel. New York

Dear Sir;—

Your letter has been rec'd. I stated at the close of our conversation in New York that I would go to Washington and if, after consulting counsel and expert, I was advised to buy the paper[1] I would do so. I kept my promise to the letter. It took one week to obtain a decision, which was unfavorable to purchase. My expenses were $65.70. I think it would be as just for me to ask you to pay *my* expenses as for you to ask me to pay yours. I have sent your letter however to Gen. [Reuben Delavan] Mussey[2] to whom I refer you. If he thinks I ought to pay your bills in New York I will do so. I understood that you had a pass on the railroad, and as board at the Victoria is only $4.50 a day and you were here only half a day, how could legitimate expenses amount to $16.00?

I only decided that I did not want newspaper plant after decision about [the Columbian] Gazette had been reached.

---

1. To launch *KF's Washington*, KF had considered buying the *Columbian Gazette*, as well as an existing printing plant, rather than starting from scratch. KF hired two Vassar graduates to serve as managing editor and as business manager, Caroline Gray Lingle and Ella S. Leonard, respectively.

2. KF's lawyer (1833–92).

To Russell Benjamin Harrison (IU)

Russell Harrison (1854–1936) was the son of the sitting U.S. president, Benjamin Harrison, and publisher of the *Daily Journal* in Helena, Montana.

Nov. 5. 1889.   Victoria Hotel. New York

Dear Sir;—

I'm about to issue an independent *weekly—Kate Field's Washington*—in Washington. Will your paper exchange with me? And can you tell me how best to circulate my prospectus outside of American News Co.?[1]

An early answer will oblige. . . .

The paper will be a good friend to the new states and to the territories and of course to Gentiles [non-Mormons]. I want Western subscriptions and advertising. Scope of paper *national.*

1. A wholesale news and book agency in New York.

To Laurence Hutton (PUL-H)

Nov. 20. 1889.   Victoria Hotel. New York

Dear L. H.;—

I'm going to Washington today to make arrangements for opening our office [of *KF's Washington*] &c. and will be back (D.V.) on Saturday or Sunday. My address there is *The Shoreham* [Hotel], prohibitionally known as "Morton's[1] Rum Shop."

I've seen Mr. [Albert M.] Palmer today and he thinks very favorably of the Players' Column[2] and agrees with me that the proper person to appear in first issue is Mr. [Edwin] Booth. Mr. Palmer says you are to have a Directors' meeting tomorrow and that he will speak to Mr. Booth and you, but as his memory is bad I nudge yours and hope you'll get Mr. Booth to say "yes" [to an interview]. Tell him I'll interview him myself at the Club if he prefers and he'll see the copy before it goes to press.

Don't forget that *Growl* for the *Growler.*[3]

How do you like my circular? It pays all its expenses in ads.

1. Vice President Morton owned the Shoreham Hotel.
2. "The Players," a title suggested by Edwin Booth, became a regular theatrical news column of *KF's Washington.*
3. A column in *KF's Washington* containing letters to the editor, which came to be called "The Grumbler's Corner."

To George F. Williams (IU)
  Editor of the *New York Herald*, since Bennett was living as an exile in Paris.
Nov. 30. 1889   Victoria Hotel. New York

Dear Sir;—

I called upon you today to inquire whether *The Herald* would exchange with my Weekly, which will be issued Dec. 20th for the first time. If not the Daily, will you exchange with Semi-Weekly or Weekly? An answer will oblige. . . .

To William Warland Clapp (HC)
Dec. 4. 1889.   Victoria Hotel. New York

Dear Col. Clapp;—

Is enclosed worth a notice? Will you exchange papers [*Boston Journal* for *KF's Washington*]?

Will you insert one ad. of us for one in our paper of Journal? An answer (early) will oblige. . . .

To Maturin Murray Ballou (UV-F)
  Ballou (1820–95) was a Boston magazine publisher.
Dec. 10. 1889.   The Shoreham [Hotel]. Washington, D.C.

Dear Mr. Ballou;—

Many thanks for your subscription [to *KF's Washington*]. I hope the paper will be worth reading.

To Laurence Hutton (PUL-H)
Jan. 1. 1890.   [New York]

Dear L.H.;—

Your *Grumble* [in *KF's Washington*] is a great success and is being copied by all Free Trade papers.[1] Have you rec'd your paper? I shall leave half a dozen at The Brunswick [Hotel] for you with Mrs. Mitchell.[2] What do you think of the first no.?

Send us pps. [paragraphs] whenever in your line. . . .

Kate Field as publisher-editor.
(From the first issue of *Kate Field's Washington*, 1 January 1890.)

1. Hutton's "Grumble," which appeared in the first issue of the paper (1 Jan. 1890), was his objection to the U.S. tariff on imported art and artifacts, a cause that KF came to champion.

2. Hutton's mother-in-law.

To John Augustin Daly (FL)
Jan. 20. 1890.   The Shoreham [Hotel, Washington, D.C.]

Dear Mr. Daly;—
    When last in N.Y. I called at your office and delivered a message to your secretary, leaving No. 1 of my weekly.
    Do you feel inclined to contribute to my column dedicated to The Players? I have begun this series out of compliment to the profession, but can not keep it up without cooperation. I send you what has been done so far and would much like 600 or 1000 words from you about your method of producing Shakespeare or your ideas on anything pertaining to the stage. What answer?
    Can I have a talk from Miss [Ada] Rehan?[1] What about Mrs. George H. Gilbert's experience as a Professional Old Woman?[2]

Nameplate of the first issue of *Kate Field's Washington*.

Please reply at your earliest convenience....
When I next visit N.Y. I'd like to see your "As You Like It."

1. Actress (1860–1916); in Daly's company for twenty years.
2. Actress (1821–1904); in Daly's company for thirty years. In later years she specialized in old-woman roles.

To Susan B. Anthony (HL)
Feb. 11. 1890.   The Shoreham [Hotel]. Washington, D.C.

Dear Miss Anthony;—
I heard that you had stated publicly that my paper was subsidized by liquor-dealers.[1] I did not believe the story and have taken the first opportunity I ever had to pay you respect by giving you the place of honor in my issue of Feb. 12th.[2] I did this half on your account, and half on account of the suffragists and pro-hibitionists who because I don't entirely agree with them, either slander me basely or let me severely alone. I can return good for evil and give anyone who is honest a fair hearing in my paper. I don't expect to get the least credit for a decent act. I merely want you personally to know my motive in having you called upon during my absences.

In "Washington Whispers" you will also find a reference to yourself written by... [page missing]

1. As women were not permitted to join the Sons of Temperance, Anthony organized the first women's temperance association, the Daughters of Temperance. The elite of the women's rights movement soon espoused her cause. Elizabeth Cady Stanton went so far as to urge women to refuse all conjugal rights to husbands who did not practice temperance.

2. Anthony's article on how she became a suffragist appeared in *KF's Washington* (12 Feb. 1890). Two KF interviews of Anthony appeared in the same paper (28 Feb. 1894 and 9 Mar. 1895).

To Mary Mapes Dodge (PUL-W)
Feb. 13. 1890.   The Shoreham [Hotel]. Washington, D.C.

Dear Dodgie;—
Check received.[1] It ought to be framed as the greatest evidence of faith in one editor by another. I take it in that spirit and thank you.

You said the other day that you found in "K.F.'s W" what was not in other papers; hence its interest. Are you willing to put something of this sort in a note that I can publish with others? It will do us good.

Do you know anyone who will get us subscriptions on enclosed terms? Women who go among well-to-do men and women are best.

I'm out gunning for Yosemite and am making converts.[2] Tell Mr. [Robert Underwood] Johnson.[3]

1. For a subscription to *KF's Washington*.
2. To make Yosemite a national park.
3. Associated with Gilder in the editorship of *Century Magazine*, Johnson (1853-1937) was also concerned with the preservation of Yosemite and published John Muir's articles on the subject, which culminated in the passage of the Yosemite National Park Bill by Congress.

To Laurence Hutton (PUL-H)
March 19. 1890.   The Shoreham [Hotel]. Washington, D.C.

Dear L.H.;—
I send you extra copies of this week's issue [of *KF's Washington*] to give where they'll have effect. I think this "Purity" business is disgraceful and should be put down so far as *calling* one's self "pure" is concerned.[1]

Send one to Lamb's Club please.²

Mr. [Albert M.] Palmer instructed me to send our paper to Players Club and to send bill to him. We send the paper of course but have not sent bill, as I think the Club ought to pay it as the paper has Mr. Booth's sanction and endorsement. What do you think?

Why don't you send us another *Grumble?* ...

1. In *KF's Washington* of 19 March, KF attacked the newly formed "Society of Young Girls of Pure Character on the Stage," principally because its members had committed "the unpardonable offence against decency and taste of labelling themselves 'Pure,'" thereby implying "that actresses outside of this immaculate sisterhood are *im*pure."

2. New York theatrical organization.

To Phoebe Apperson Hearst (UCB-P)

Phoebe Hearst (1842–1919) was the wife of George Hearst (1820–91), mine owner and U.S. senator. In 1887 her only son William Randolph Hearst (1863–1951) assumed charge of his father's *San Francisco Examiner*, the beginning of his communications empire.

April 4. 1890.   Victoria Hotel. New York

Dear Mrs. Hearst;—

J. R. Osgood, formerly the Boston publisher—now representing Harper in London—is here for a short time and has asked me to use my influence to get Congress to buy the only 3/4 portrait of Longfellow in existence and the only one well painted. It is by [George Peter] Healy[1] at his best and is endorsed by Lowell, Holmes, Aldrich, Howells &c in autograph letters. It occurs to me that your gallery is the place for such a painting—that is, in your place I'd want it, and so I drop you a line to ask whether you care to entertain the idea. I won't say a word elsewhere if you do.

Kindly reply here where I remain another week. So glad you are a patron of the [New York] Conservatory of Music.

Will the Examiner copy the enclosed, do you think? The only way to keep people awake is to beat the drum.

The portrait is worth $2000 at most. I know it well and it is very interesting—the only work of Healy I ever liked. Mr. Osgood has no place now to keep it.

1. American portraitist (1813–94). The portrait now hangs in the Museum of Fine Arts, Boston.

To Laurence Hutton (PUL-H)
May 11. 1890.   Victoria Hotel. New York

Dear L.H.;—
I should like to see Booth's portrait by [John Singer] Sargent. Is it possible?

To Samuel Langhorne Clemens (UCB-M)
May 13. 1890.   Victoria Hotel. New York

Dear Mr. Clemens;—
Will you read enclosed[1] and send me a word of denunciation for a column of authors that is to be in my next number? If you send, please let it be immediately.

You understand my reference to humor is not *against* humor. People buy it and you are the exception to rule.[2]

1. "A Nation of Pirates" (from *KF's Washington*, 14 May 1890), decrying the fact that Congress had failed to pass the International Copyright Bill.

2. In the article KF enclosed, she had written: "Men of letters . . . are poorly paid compared to their peers in painting, sculpture, law, medicine or trade. . . . Mark Twain is a humorist, and humor sells in literature as burlesque sells on the stage." Twain, apparently, did not oblige KF with the desired denunciation, as his name does not appear in the index to the 1890 volume of *KF's Washington*. Also, the Mark Twain Project at the University of California, Berkeley, does not have such a letter.

To Mrs. Cox (MHS-LFM)
Unidentified.
May 29 [1890?]   112 Fifth Avenue [New York]

Dear Mrs. Cox;—
The enclosed explains itself. We now have 600 subscribers [to *KF's Washington*] who have taken from one to twenty shares each.[1] Gen. Sherman and Gen. Schenck were our first Washington subscribers.

1. According to a circular signed by KF, her weekly, selling for ten cents a copy or four dollars for a year's subscription, aimed for a circulation of ten thousand. When the paper's circulation increased to forty thousand, KF halved the price per copy and subscription, a reduction more than recompensed by her numerous advertisers.

To Laurence Hutton (PUL-H)
Sept. 25. 1890.   Victoria Hotel. New York

Dear L.H.;—

It's a bit dangerous for me to give the reason why Dickens destroyed his correspondence,[1] as my memory is treacherous, but I think it was to prevent the Froude-Carlyle business.[2] Self-preservation or at least the preservation of his friends, who did not reciprocate apparently, as Dickens's [extant] letters are many.

Tell those artists that if they don't send me their ideas about [designs for] coins *at once,* they are "pathetical break-promisers" & deserve anathema.[3]

The latest in art from the seat of war is that Congress will reduce the tariff on [imported] art to 15 per cent—one half [the former tariff]. Perhaps half a loaf is better than no bread, but I'm disgusted.

I've seen [Augustus] St. Gaudens[4] today & got those "points" about Grant swindle.[5]

Having tested my idea of a national weekly for nine months and made a place for the bantling in that time, I'm about to form the [Washington Publishing] company which so far has only existed in name. It will be limited liability, with stock fully paid up—$100 a share. Capital $50,000, $24,000 of which stock will be for sale, i.e. 240 shares. Do you know of any persons likely to invest in such an idea? I'm always fighting for the stage & ought to be backed by rich actors but, so far, they have not materialized even as subscribers. Do you think Edwin Booth would take to such an organization? Of course I'd like to have the stock taken by a few persons, but I'll sell shares singly as well as in blocks if desired. If you have any suggestions to make, let me have them. I own a controlling interest in [the] paper.

Tell Mr. Harry Harper his firm have *not* advertised Mrs. [Elizabeth] Custer's book[6] in *K.F.'s W.* as he promised....

---

1. Dickens reported to Macready in 1865: "Daily seeing improper uses made of confidential letters in the addressing of them to a public audience that have no business with them, I made a great bonfire . . . and burnt every letter I possessed. And now, I always destroy every letter I receive not on absolute business" (*The Letters of Charles Dickens*, ed. Walter Dexter [London: Nonesuch Press, 1938], 2:20).

2. After Carlyle's death in 1881, James Anthony Froude (1818–94), Carlyle's literary executor, published a four-volume biography of his friend. It raised a storm of controversy, for unlike typical Victorian biography, it exposed Carlyle's weaknesses.

3. KF wanted U.S., not foreign, artists to design coins for the U.S. Mint.

4. Distinguished U.S. sculptor (1848–1907).

5. Concerning the yearslong squabble between the Grant family and the Sherman Monument Committee of New York, which planned to place the Saint-Gaudens statue of General Sherman, when

completed, in front of Grant's Tomb, a placement that the Grant family would not permit. The statue is now at the entrance to Central Park at Fifth Avenue and Central Park South.

6. *Following the Guidon* (1890). Mrs. Custer (1842–1933), the wife of Gen. George Armstong Custer (1839–76), had written two other books to preserve her husband's memory: *Boots and Saddles* (1885) and *Tenting on the Plains* (1887).

To Robert Underwood Johnson (BPL)
Dec. 16. 1890.   The Shoreham [Hotel]. Washington, D.C.

Dear Mr. Johnson;—

Enclosed is this week's dose of Copyright—"Dec. 17."[1]

As you want to impress [the copyright question on] Senators, why don't you order 100 copies of *K.F.'s W.* for May 21st marked & sent to every man in the Senate? What [Oliver Wendell] Holmes and Lowell[2] and all of you say in conclave should have weight—and the expense won't be more than $10 or $12.

This is my reply to your circular, as I have no senators to order about. This district [of Columbia] is well governed without them.

1. The "dose" was a clipping from the postdated *KF's Washington*. Like Johnson, KF campaigned for international copyright.

2. KF had published Holmes's and Lowell's letters on the copyright question in the 21 May issue. BPL has three of Holmes's letters to KF.

To Phoebe Apperson Hearst (UCB-P)
Dec. 24. 1890.   The Shoreham [Hotel]. Washington, D.C.

Dear Mrs. Hearst;—

I've just returned to town and called yesterday to inquire about [your husband] the Senator, who is reported ill, and to invite you to see that interesting portrait of Longfellow which is now in my possession. Do you care to know how the poet looked at his best? I've made no effort to sell the portrait since I wrote to you last Spring.

Are you interested in the Garrett Johns Hopkins idea?[1] I've heard it was under your charge here. If so, I'll help. I'm to see Miss Garrett in Baltimore at the earliest opportunity. . . .

1. From 1889 to 1893, Mary Elizabeth Garrett (1854–1915), philanthropist, was the principal donor

and fund-raiser in the founding of the Johns Hopkins Medical School, opened on her condition that women be admitted on the same terms as men.

To Lilian Whiting (LW)
[1891?] [The Shoreham Hotel, Washington, D.C.]

The difference between a life in a book and a newspaper sketch is very great. When I die—if between now and then I do anything worthy of record—my life [story] can be taken. While alive, I contend that lives in books are absurd.[1]

1. Refers to the request from Frances E. Willard and Mary A. Livermore to include KF in their *A Woman of the Century: Fourteen Hundred-Seventy Biographical Sketches Accompanied by Portraits of Leading American Women in All Walks of Life* (1893). KF's sketch and picture were included.

To Edmund Clarence Stedman (CU)
May 18. 1891. *Kate Field's Washington*
59 Corcoran Building. Washington, D.C.

Dear friend;—
Won't you write me a short note of approval about this [Art] Congress for print?[1] It will help.
Thank you for saying a good word [about *KF's Washington*] to Century Club. I ordered the paper sent on E[astman]. Johnson's[2] word.

1. KF was soliciting letters from artists, editors, literary figures, and government leaders to aid in the formation of a so-called Art Congress. One function of the Art Congress was to sponsor a national loan exhibition of paintings by American artists; another was to convince Congress to eliminate the tariff on imported art.
2. American genre painter (1824-1906).

To Edmund Clarence Stedman (CU)
June 20. 1891. The Shoreham [Hotel]. Washington, D.C.

Dear Poet;—
You turn such charming sentences I can't help quoting you again next week. Thanks for your generous subscription [to the Art Fund].[1] No money will be

needed for months. I've really raised one fifth of the sum I've asked for, $5000, but I dare say $10,000 will be needed to send the pictures to & fro and insure them. The National Museum [of the Smithsonian Institution] will permit no charge, so all expenses must be borne by voluntary contributions or *bullied* contributions, which is really what they generally mean, saving with two generous souls like yourselves.

I'll write to Miss [Emily] Howland.[2] Glad of the suggestion. . . .

   1. KF was encouraging donations to fund the so-called National Loan Exhibit, an event that would feature the hundred best works of American art at the Smithsonian for ten days. Through her paper, she raised one thousand dollars in one week.

   2. Philanthropist (1827–1929). In 1890 she became a director of the First National Bank of Aurora, New York, one of the first women to fill such a position in the United States.

To George Washington Cable (TU)
July 7. 1891.   Kate Field's Washington
                                            59 Corcoran Building. Washington, D.C.

Dear Mr. Cable;—

I don't believe you've ever seen my national review—"No gentleman's library is complete without it"—so I've ordered several numbers sent to you that you may read the story of the Art Congress, in which I should like to interest you.

If, after reading, you approve, will you send me a few lines for publication to help on the work? The cause is good.

To Thomas Gregg (MHS-T)
Aug. 1. 1891.   Kate Field's Washington
                                            59 Corcoran Building. Washington, D.C.

Dear Mr. Gregg;—

Don't take so gloomy a view of yourself. *All* our lives are failures. I'm sure mine is but I do the best I can.

I have simply had no time to read your book [*The Prophet of Palmyra*] and nobody else [on my staff] knows anything about Mormonism. As soon as I am able I shall review it, but believe me that *nobody* buys books on a subject so interesting to you and me. That's the reason I lectured. Not one publisher would take my ms.[1] And it turned out [for the] best.

1889-1894

I'm sorry but as [Robert] Browning never made money out of his poems until near his death, what can the rest of us expect?

Never mind my anti-prohibition [stand]. Let us agree to disagree.

I send you my paper with pleasure....

1. The only KF manuscripts on Mormonism published were a series of letters in the *Boston Herald* (1883-84); "Utah Politics and Morals," *New York Tribune*, 7 Sept. 1884; "Kate and the Mormons: Miss Field's Arraignment of the Apostolic Women of Utah," *Chicago Tribune*, 6 June 1886; and "Mormon Blood Atonement," *North American Review*, Sept. 1886.

To Charles Lawrence Hutchinson (NL)

Hutchinson (1854-1924) was president of the Chicago Art Institute and the Chicago Corn Exchange Bank.

Dec. 8. 1891.   Chicago

Dear Mr. Hutchinson;—

Here is the letter of introduction. I accidentally met Mr. Marshall Field[1] today who gave me $100 for the [Art] Fund.

I hope there will be no doubt of your presence tomorrow. Mrs. Potter Palmer[2] says whatever you endorse goes & she will probably do whatever you suggest. My talk will be short & if you will speak after or before me—better after— the [Art Fund] cause will be greatly advanced.

1. Department store magnate (1834-1906).
2. Bertha Honoré Palmer (1849-1918), social leader of Chicago whose husband (1826-92) was a real estate mogul and owner of the world-famous Palmer House.

To Phoebe Apperson Hearst (UCB-P)

Feb. 9. 1892.   *Kate Field's Washington*
                                                                              59 Corcoran Building. Washington, D.C.

Dear Mrs. Hearst;—

I've got back [from Chicago] all in one piece and am now wrestling with the Art Congress. You'll be glad to learn that [Albert] Bierstadt[1] will be an active worker here and that [Daniel] Huntington,[2] [John] La Farge,[3] Eastman Johnson, Millet, [William Merritt] Chase[4] promise to come to Washington. We have fixed the time for the middle of May when you'll be in town.

If you now feel like sending your subscription[5] I'll be glad, as I want to know what we have to depend upon.

Can't you inspire an art meeting in San Francisco? What pictures do you want exhibited?

1. Bierstadt (1830-1902) was an American painter of Western scenery.
2. Huntington (1816-1906) was an American painter and vice president of the Metropolitan Museum of Art.
3. American muralist and designer of stained glass (1835-1910).
4. American painter (1849-1916).
5. Mrs. Hearst sent KF five hundred dollars for the Art Fund.

To [?] (UV-F)
April 16. 1892.   The Shoreham [Hotel]. Washington, D.C.

Dear Sir;—

Will you kindly inform me whether Senator [John Percival] Jones's[1] two paintings by Bierstadt are still hanging in your gallery, and if so, will you permit me to see them? Mr. Bierstadt [on our committee] would like to have the smaller exhibited at the coming National Loan Exhibit [of Art].

I enclose a circular of a new art organization[2] which we'll be happy to interest you in if you believe in *free* [untaxed imported] *art.*

1. Elected from Nevada in 1873, Jones (1829-1912) served in the U.S. Senate for thirty years.
2. The National Art Association of which KF was secretary.

To an Unidentified Artist (MHS-LFM)
May 2. 1892.   Victoria Hotel. New York

Dear Sir;—

Please read inclosed and state whether you care to join our [National Art] Association, whether you can be present at the convention and whether you can send a medium sized picture to the exhibit. I called at your studio today and obtained your present address. I greatly regret not seeing you, for letters poorly tell a story in which I am deeply interested.

The pictures will be collected by J. H. Mills, 147 E. 23d St., on Thursday & Friday of this week. They are packed unboxed in one car and will be returned the end of the month, being insured by Ass'n. Kindly telegraph me to above address up to Wednesday night. I leave here Thursday a.m. when my address will be The Shoreham [Hotel], Washington, D.C.

If you have a picture ready here in town it will be well to notify Mills at the same time you do me & thus save time.

Hoping you can come to Washington, bringing your wife if you are married.

To Phoebe Apperson Hearst (UCB-P)
July 12. 1893.   Lexington Hotel. Chicago

Dear Mrs. Hearst;—

My silence has not been due to forgetfulness. I wanted to write immediately after receiving your telegram to tell you how sorry I felt for you, as the news meant additional care and disappointment to you.[1] I knew too what pain it gave you to send the telegram and I've been waiting for the clouds to lift as you have trouble enough of your own and need cheering. The clouds however still hang over me and I can wait no longer or you'll think me unfeeling and ungrateful. I am neither.

The financial condition must give you great anxiety and where and when relief will come, who can say? I fervently hope the best fortune may come to you soon.

For myself, I feel like a hunted animal driven into a corner. After you left, The [Chicago] Herald broke the contract with me which was for six months, giving the plea of poverty. My engagement with the Herald made me so conspicuous that of course no other Chicago paper could be approached. The [Chicago] Tribune would have made a better contract in the beginning, but, being jealous, sulked at having a second choice. So I've lost that income and am hanging on by the eyelids. How long I can endure the strain I don't know. I work constantly and keep up my nerve, but I see no light. This is the reason of my silence. I would not tell you this did I not think I ought to be truthful.

Would it be possible for the subscription agent of [your son's San Francisco] Examiner to get subscribers for [KF's] *Washington* on commission? Is it worth considering?

The Fair[2] is greater than ever but the management makes one ill and disgusted. I could tell you *such* stories!

Dear Mrs. Hearst, may all your kind deeds come home to roost and fill your life with good cheer. . . .

---

1. Mrs. Hearst's husband had died two years earlier; now she was fearful of the effect of the current financial panic—overall, the worst of the century—on her investments.

2. The World's Columbian Exposition, held in Jackson Park from May to November 1893 to com-

memorate the quadricentennial of Columbus's coming to America. KF was there the entire time as a reporter for *KF's Washington*. When the fair ended, KF tried to save the buildings from destruction. Her only success was in saving John Brown's "fort," the armory engine house. "It is the single most important historic structure in our park," writes Francis Schultz-DePalo, the curator of Harpers Ferry National Historical Park. Mary Johnson, the museum director of the park, used to show an enlarged photograph of KF to visitors, saying, "This is Miss Kate Field—she is the lady who saved this fort from being destroyed" (*St. Louis American*, 22 Sept. 1964).

To an Unidentified Editor (MNP)
July 21. 1893.   Lexington Hotel. Chicago

Dear Sir;—
 As my price is generally $50.00 an article for 1500 words or less, you can understand that your offer is not tempting. It may be I shall have some message for women which needs circulation. In that event money is a secondary consideration. Allow me to ask whether you make no exception to a cent a word? Are names of no value?
 You did not inclose the sample of matter desired.

To Phoebe Apperson Hearst (UCB-P)
Aug. 27. 1893.   Lexington Hotel. Chicago

Dear Mrs. Hearst;—
 ... I have been quite ill but am much better and work constantly over the news of the day and sketches of the Fair, thus addressing several millions of readers in syndicate matter, helping others I'm told, though not of much use to myself. I send you two articles. Of course you see K.F.'s W[ashington]. Hoke Smith's[1] representative told me I had inspired him to inspire the Georgians to come to Chicago. It was a comfort to feel the arrow had not been shot in vain.

 1. Smith (1855–1931), a former Georgian lawyer, was at the time Secretary of the Interior.

To Andrew Varick Stout Anthony (HC)
Nov. 4. 1893.   Lexington Hotel. Chicago

Dear Mr. Anthony;—
 I am still here, trying to make some people here appreciate the work I have

done for the Fair this Summer. I know just how anxious you are because I have been on that same gridiron for months. People don't pay their debts and the result is disastrous. How long it may last,[1] and whether it lasts longer than I do, remains to be seen.

I can't help you one bit and it hurts me to admit it. Chicago papers are cutting down expenses and other papers are doing the same. The situation is deplorable and it takes all my courage to face it. God help us all is the prayer of Your sincere friend, Kate Field

For such work as suits our paper we pay $5.00 a column. If you are willing to try, I shall ask my editor [Caroline Gray Lingle] what she thinks about paragraphs on art & club life. Suppose you write K.F.'s W. what you can do in that line.

1. The Panic of 1893 lasted four years.

To Phoebe Apperson Hearst (UCB-P)
April 8. [1894]   The Shoreham [Hotel, Washington, D.C.]

Dear Mrs. Hearst;—

... I go to Chicago on Saturday to lecture before the Press Club on *America for Americans*. There may be a demonstration[1] as I shall appear in Central Music Hall and appeal to the people.

1. Given the title of her lecture, KF was said to be in league with the American Protective Association, an anti-foreigner, anti-Catholic organization created in 1887 that claimed a million militant members. In Chicago, whose one million immigrants outnumbered its two hundred thousand native-born, she could well have expected a demonstration. For more about the lecture, see *To an Unidentified Lyceum Agent*, 16 Oct. 1894, n. 1.

To Laurence Hutton (PUL-H)
May 8. [1894]   Victoria Hotel. New York

Dear L.H.;—

I understood you to say that we could have your article[1] gratis and so informed my editor. She incloses your letter and asks me to explain. Am I dreaming? Had I not thought it was gratis, it would not have been accepted, *not* because it doesn't deserve to be paid for, but because I am forced to rigid economy in these hard times in order to live at all.

I shall pay that money, whatever it be, out of my own pocket and thus keep my word with the paper. I have sent *K.F.'s W.* to you as a gift with pleasure for four years and more. Is it worth paying for hereafter? I'm going to cut down the free list and be a dragon. . . .

    1. Hutton's satire alleging that Bacon and Shakespeare were the sons of Queen Elizabeth; it had been rejected by other journals.

To Laurence Hutton (PUL-H)
May 9. [1894]   Victoria Hotel. New York

Dear L.H.;—

Here you are. I am thankful I am not insane, for my staff are beginning to doubt my word from just such things as this. Yours was the last straw and the worm turned. It is really a relief to me to have you substantiate my own statement [that you had submitted your article gratis].[1] It is now all right and as Douglas Jerrold once exclaimed, "Thank God, I am not mad."[2]. . .

    1. See *To Laurence Hutton*, 8 May [1894].
    2. When Jerrold (1803–57) was recovering from a severe illness, his family gave him his first piece of convalescent reading: Browning's *Sordello*. Unable to make any sense of the poem, Jerrold became more and more convinced that his family had kept the hideous truth from him—that his illness had made him insane. "My God!" he cried out, "I'm an idiot. My health is restored but my mind's gone. I can't understand two consecutive lines of an English poem!" Stricken, he handed the book back to his family. But when he saw how each of them showed complete bewilderment as they read, he exclaimed, "Thank God, I am not mad" (Donald S. Thomas, *Robert Browning: A Life Within Life* [London: Weidenfeld & Nicolson, 1982], 82).

To an Unidentified Lyceum Agent (NYH)
Oct. 16. 1894.   The Virginia. Hot Springs Bath Co. Virginia

Dear Sir;—

You understand that $100 represents my lowest fee for lectures and does *not* refer to my musical monologues.

You can have Dec. 3d for Ironton [Ohio]. I must be in Cairo (Ill.) for Dec. 10th and if you can arrange lectures on the route please let me know *at once*, addressing me as above. If you don't want Ironton, let me be notified in order to make other plans.

I'd like to give my America for Americans[1] in Cincinnati. It suits loyal Germans perfectly well. No A.P.A.[2] about it.

> **REPUBLIQUE FRANÇAISE.**
> Ministère De L'Instruction Publique Et Des Beaux-Arts.
>
> Le Ministre de l'Instruction publique et des Beaux-Arts,
> Vu l'article 32 du décret organique du 17 mars 1808;
> Vu les ordonnances royales des 14 Novembre 1844, 9 Septembre 1845 et 1 er Novembre 1846;
> Vu les décrets des 9 Décembre 1850, 7 Avril et 27 Décembre 1866, et 24 Décembre 1885,
> Arrête:
> Miss Kate Field, Conférencière à Washington est nommé Officier de l'Instruction publique.
>
> (SEAL) Pour Ampliation: Le Chef du Cabinet, Mehumel.
>
> Fait à Paris, le 21 Septembre 1893.
> Le Ministre de l'Instruction publique et des Beaux-Arts,
> Signé: Léon Bourgeois.

Brevet presented to Kate Field to certify that the French Republic had awarded her the *Palmes académique*, the highest distinction the French could bestow on an individual for service to literature and art.

1. The lecture opposed what KF called the "criminal looseness of naturalization laws passed by thoughtless State legislatures." In sixteen states, she charged, foreigners were allowed to vote or were naturalized to vote just before an election. She also said, "No alien living five years in this country without using soap and learning our language deserves citizenship" (*KF's Washington*, 25 Apr. 1894).

2. American Protective Association.

To John Augustin Daly (FL)
Oct. 26. [1894]   The Shoreham [Hotel, Washington, D.C.]

Dear Mr. Daly;—
  ... Will you tell me the story of your imported employe? I am wild against that Contract Labor Law[1] and take every opportunity to criticize it.

1. The law, passed in 1885, prohibited the immigration of laborers under contract to work for the cost of their passage, except for skilled, professional, and domestic workers.

To Jules Patenotre (LW)
Nov. 17. 1894.   Washington [D.C.]

To His Excellency the Ambassador of France.
Sir;—
  The honor conferred upon me as editor of a national review by the govern-

ment of France through you, who so ably represent the great republic of Europe, is the more delightful for being unexpected. I will not affect modesty, preferring to emulate the example of that eminent diplomatist and lawyer, the Hon. Edward J. Phelps,[1] who, after listening to his own praises at a banquet in New York, replied that he "had quite made up his mind it was far pleasanter to *receive* plaudits than to have the merit to deserve them." Accept my heart's assurance that I am profoundly grateful to your Government for decorating me with the palms of the Academy,[2] the possession of which will be a constant inspiration.

> "Perhaps the longing to be so
> Helps make the soul immortal,"

sings Lowell [in "Longing"]. Perhaps the longing to deserve this great recognition will help make me worthy of it.

That the union between your country and mine may be as close as that which unites you, dear sir, to one of America's fairest daughters,[3] is the fond prayer of, / Yours truly and gratefully, / Kate Field

1. Phelps (1822–1900) was former U.S. minister to Great Britain.

2. In recognition of her service in eliminating the U.S. tariff on imported art and artifacts. This was the highest distinction the French Republic could bestow on an individual for service to literature and art. Earlier, KF had refused the honor because her work had been only partly accomplished; for the tariff, though reduced, was not eliminated until 1894.

3. Patenotre was married to an American.

To Lydia Avery Coonley (UV-C)
  Coonley (1845–1924) was a poet and leader in the social and cultural life of Chicago.
Dec. 12. 1894.   Victoria Hotel. Chicago

Dear Mrs. Coonley;—

I returned today and found your invitation. How I wish I could [accept], but I lecture every night this week and am a slave. On Saturday night Galesburg [Illinois]. Then (D.V.) I'm to take a train & get here on Sunday afternoon to remain until the early morning when I go to Madison [Wisconsin] and then to Iowa, returning here Dec. 23d en route to Washington.

I should much like to give a course of lectures in Chicago as I did in Washington last Spring, but I don't know the modus operandi here, so I shall make no effort unless engaged as I was tonight by a club.

To Mr. Stilson Hutchins (HC)
  Hutchins (1838–1912), a businessman, founded the *Washington Post* in 1877, which he sold in 1889. A millionaire, he summered on Governor's Island, New Hampshire (an island he owned), and wintered in Washington, D.C.
Dec. 23. 1894.   Victoria Hotel. Chicago

Dear Mr. Hutchins;—
  I have just received your letter of the 17th, which is not what I expected, assuming I had any reason to expect anything. My talks with Mr. [William Eaton] Chandler[1] led me to think that the one and only thing I wished, the sale of some stock [in *KF's Washington*], could be accomplished.
  As this does not enter into your proposition,[2] I can not consider it.
  I shall be happy to see you in Washington, however, regardless of business.

  1. Chandler (1835–1917) was a U.S. senator from New Hampshire.
  2. Presumably Hutchins wanted to buy KF's weekly outright.

Part Ten: 1895–1896

En Route to San Francisco
and Hawaii
Final Days

To Charles Warren Stoddard (CWS)
Stoddard (1843–1909), a California poet, became famous for his travel books on the South Sea Islands, which inspired Robert Louis Stevenson to write on the same subject. Stoddard first met KF in Washington in the early 1890s when their mutual friend, the artist Frank D. Millet, brought him to KF's apartment in the Shoreham Hotel.
Feb. 14. 1895. [The Shoreham Hotel, Washington, D.C.]

Dear Valentine;—

Your papers[1] are delightful and are worth $250. That's what I wish I could send you. I feel very proud to publish so charming a glimpse of a great man. You are entitled to all the papers you want at any time and orders are so given at the office. The Stevenson articles are most valuable and I only wish I could make it worth your while to be a constant contributor.

I live in hope.

I've heard so much praise of your articles on Robert Louis Stevenson it makes me ache to have money enough to ask you to become a regular contributor. O! why have I been cheated out of my fortune?[2]

Discipline can go too far.

---

1. Refers to Stoddard's three articles on his friend Robert Louis Stevenson, published in *KF's Washington* (26 Jan., 2 Feb., and 9 Feb. 1895).

2. See *To Charles Warren Stoddard*, 21 June 1895, n. 1.

To Laurence and Eleanor Hutton (PUL-H)
May 29. 1895.   The Shoreham [Hotel]. Washington, D.C.

Dear friends;—

It was a case of self-preservation.[1] The paper has been a great success and can be more so in better times and with better business management.

How long shall you be in N.Y.? I expect to be there next month en route to Hawaii. I have joined the staff of the Chicago *Times-Herald* and may go round the world before I stop.

---

1. The termination of *KF's Washington* after more than five years of uninterrupted publication.

To Charles Warren Stoddard (BU)
June 21. 1895.   *Kate Field's Washington*
                                          59 Corcoran Building, Washington, D.C.

Dear Poet;—

I have mislaid your letter sent to me when I was in Newport contesting a Will.[1] Jury disagreed of course because my claim was righteous. My cousin [George Riddle] refuses to join me in a second trial and I am forced thereby to let crime triumph. Such is life.

Whatever you asked for is yours. I now send by express 20 copies each of the three [Robert Louis] Stevenson articles[2] [from *KF's Washington*]. If you want more, say so at once as I am packing up to go to Chicago & thence to Hawaii. Won't you come & see me before I leave? If not at the Shoreham [Hotel] I'll be at this office. If you'll dine with me on Sunday without ceremony at 7 p.m. so much the better.

Can you give me letters or suggestions for Hawaii?

---

1. KF and her cousin George Riddle had contested the will of their aunt, Cordelia Sanford (whose husband had died in 1883), though they were among her twenty-four beneficiaries. They attempted to "prove that undue influence was brought to bear by the person in whose favor the will was made [presumed to be Alla Newton, Mrs. Sanford's friend, though Riddle was the chief beneficiary]. It is not a contest for money, the whole sum [bequeathed to Alla Newton] being not over $30,000, but it is a fight for an idea, a principle" (interview with KF in *New York Tribune*, 29 Apr. 1895).

2. Written by Stoddard.

To Lilian Whiting (LW)
[Summer 1895]   [Chicago]

Did I ever tell you that I only missed having an original poem from Lowell to recite on the occasion of the Stratford-on-Avon festival for the benefit of the theatre when I recited one written by Dr. Marston? I had written to Mr. Lowell, begging he would do the Shakespeare Memorial Association this great favor, and I enclose you his reply.[1]

    1. Lowell, then Ambassador to Spain, replied that he could not satisfy KF's request for an original poem; instead, he asked for a copy of her *Ten Days in Spain*.

To Charles Warren Stoddard (CWS)
Oct. 28. 1895.   [Knutsford Hotel] Salt Lake City, Utah

Dear Savage:[1]

I never dreamed of your helping the John Brown fort. Don't you suppose I know how many uses you have for your hard-earned salary? All I meant was, could you suggest anything? I have raised almost all the money, and the fort is now going up at Harper's Ferry.[2] I wish that you could take a Sunday off and go up there and see what is being done and tell me what you think of the situation.

If you can, if you will call at the B[altimore]. and O[hio]. ticket office and ask for the gen'l pass'gr ag't, who is very nice and very good-looking, and show him this letter and tell him who you are, I am sure he will give you a pass both ways. If you have not visited Harper's Ferry, you ought, for it is one of the loveliest spots in the United States.

Owing to the report of cholera I have been detained in Salt Lake City, and I look upon it as fate, for the most crucial period of history in this territory has arrived. I am doing what I can to prevent statehood, but I shall not succeed, for both parties are playing into the hands of the Mormons and will vote for it on the 5th of November.

Immediately after the election I go to San Francisco, where I shall stop a few days at the Occidental [Hotel] and there go on to Honolulu [for my health].[3] Mr. [Lorrin Andrews] Thurston[4] has invited me to visit him, but I think that I ought not to commit myself to either party[5] in the beginning. Will the Honolulu Hotel be good quarters, and have they means there of keeping away mosquitoes? I absolutely dread those beasts. . . .

    1. "Savage" alludes to Stoddard's living among the natives of the South Sea Islands.
    2. See *To Phoebe Apperson Hearst*, 12 July 1893, n. 2.

3. To defray expenses, KF planned to write travel letters for the *Chicago Times-Herald*.

4. The *Honolulu Commercial Advertiser*'s editor and principal owner (1858–1931); a leader of the 1893 revolution that overthrew Queen Liliuokalani.

5. The parties differed on whether Hawaii should or should not be annexed by the United States.

To Lilian Whiting (LW)
[Oct. 1895] [Knutsford Hotel, Salt Lake City, Utah]

I did not expect to see my press letters quoted in Utah, for the reason that I was not partisan. Fancy my amazement at seeing both sides making "elegant extracts." They take what agrees with their complexion and leave out the rest; and the "[Salt Lake City] Herald" had the gall to reproach the "[Salt Lake City] Tribune" for ignoring what wouldn't be to its advantage to print. Thereupon the "Tribune" makes a bluff by declaring that when Miss Field writes about the glories of Salt Lake, it is its business to assist Zion by copying the same, but it does not propose to resurrect graveyard reminiscences. This is a specimen of the way the press goes on in Utah; both sides think one thing and write another. The atmosphere reeks with insincerity. There is more lying to the square foot in Utah than any place on the habitable globe, I verily believe. That the Republican party and the Mormon Church should now be embracing each other is a spectacle for gods and men.[1] The rupture begun by the Democratic re-convention cannot be snuffed out if there be one particle of manhood in young Utah. It gives me great hope, and it would not surprise me, if I live five years and come back to Utah, to be received with open arms by the very people who now think me their worst foe. Those people are Mormon Democrats. Was there ever anything stranger than this evolution?

1. Echo of 1 Cor. 4:9: "We are made a spectacle unto the world, and to angels, and to men."

To Cornelia B. Field (DU)
Nov. 2. 1895. Knutsford Hotel. Salt Lake City. Utah

Dear Aunt Cornelia;—

The reason why the paper stopped was because my health broke down and I am now en route to Hawaii, where I expect to be absent for several months. . . . It was a great blow to me to be obliged to relinquish the Washington, but it was "Hobson's choice."[1] My physician told me I must either give it up for the present or give up my life; and of the two evils I chose the lesser. I hope that my expedition Westward will give me the recreation and change I so greatly need. During

1895-1896

my absence I shall correspond for the Chicago Times-Herald, so if you want to know where I am and what I am doing, I refer you to that very well-edited paper.

I do hope that you are all well and that the world is treating you kindly. It seems to give us all pretty hard rubs, but I suppose that is what we are here for.

1. Thomas Hobson (1544–1631), an English liveryman, gave his customers only one choice: to take the nearest horse.

To Lilian Whiting (LW)
[Nov. 1895] [San Francisco]

I arrived here last night.... The journey from Salt Lake City is thirty-six hours, and I spent the time in bed [in the Pullman car]....

The Press Club gives me a reception to-morrow afternoon, and I shall be dining out a bit....

I have engaged passage on the "Mariposa" that sails on November 14 for Australia and stops at Honolulu. I've a room on deck that the Captain takes me to look at to-morrow, and I shall get as much comfort as I can out of what I detest,—a sea voyage. Six days, however, do not last forever.

To Lilian Whiting (LW)
[Nov. 1895] [San Francisco]

... It was perfectly natural that my dear mother should have dreaded to leave me alone, but she understands it all now and knows that I am far better alone than I should be with ———[1] Marriage is not a panacea—very good when right—terrible when wrong—I have escaped several probabilities of misery and am to be congratulated.

1. Name excised by Whiting (LW, 533), but very likely that of Albert Baldwin.

To Lilian Whiting (LW)
[Dec. 1895] [Honolulu]

Life here is one long summer day with mosquitoes thrown in. I don't think women's clubs are worse than mosquitoes, as you believe, because you *can* ignore clubs and mosquitoes *won't* let you alone night or day. However, there's a deal to interest here as long as the political situation remains doubtful. . . .

The climate in the island of Hawaii is said to be more bracing, and I may remain there a month, writing meanwhile and reading. After those come the islands of Maui and Kauai. Then I must look into the conditions of Japanese, Chinese, [and] Portuguese, all of whom swarm here and are crowding out natives and whites. It's a very serious problem, this Asiatic invasion, and bodes no good to the United States.

To Lilian Whiting (LW)
Dec. 25. 1895   Honolulu.

Accidentally a ship goes to the coast today and I send you a little Xmas greeting. I dine with President and Mrs. Dole,[1] so you see I am not forlorn. People are very hospitable here and the way my time is taken up is awful for work. I have gained in flesh and am told I look much better than on arrival. It does not look now as if I'll return in February as I expected. . . .

I've just returned from a visit to the lepers.[2] Very pathetic and very interesting. . . .

I think I'm in favor of annexation [by the United States], but shall not make up my mind in a hurry. . . .

I've written a dozen letters for publication, but only one of them has national importance,—an interview with President Dole.[3] It is the first time he has allowed himself to speak [to the press]. . . .

  1. Sanford Ballard Dole (1844–1926), first president of the Republic of Hawaii, married Anna Prentice Cate (1842–1918), a Maine woman, in 1873.

  2. The Molokai leper colony, located on Kalaupapa Peninsula, was established in 1860 and, separated from the rest of the island by a mountain wall, is reached only by negotiating a two-thousand-foot pass.

  3. The *Honolulu Commercial Advertiser* (9 Jan. 1886) reported that KF's "interview with President Dole has done more to set this Government before the American people in its true light than anything that has thus far been written" (LW, 544).

To Lilian Whiting (LW)
[Dec. 1895]   [Honolulu]

. . . The U.S.S. "Bennington" is here, and at the concert two nights ago, when I sang for the benefit of the lepers, the officers loaded me down with flowers. It was a great success, my Spanish song just suiting the audience, who applauded wildly and encored me to the echo. We made several hundred dollars, to be expended in Christmas gifts to the lepers who are segregated on the island of Molokai fifty miles away.

No mail to the U.S. for twenty days. It is awful. If Congress does not give these islands a cable, the people will eat each other up for lack of other excitement. If you can stir any papers up on this matter, please do. A cable is now being proposed and is before Congress. Were you here, you would write poems about the sea and sky and mountains, all of which are my daily food. As I'm here for politics, I'm obliged to study the history and the people before paying my compliments to Nature. Really, I wish I had nothing to do but loaf and invite my soul.[1] It is all this climate is good for. Yet, my dear, I can't escape a "woman's edition" of a newspaper even here. I've just sent a contribution to one gotten up for the benefit of the kindergartens. Yes, they've all the religions and all the crazes and all the fads out here in the middle of the Pacific.

1. Echo of Whitman's "Song of Myself," line 4: "I loafe and invite my soul."

To Lilian Whiting (LW)
[1896]   [Honolulu]

That's a strange experience of yours concerning ———,[1] but it does not seem to me at all unlikely. Of course, materialists would laugh the idea to scorn, but I'm not one of that sort, thank God. I believe in a spiritual existence, and it's most natural to suppose that a spirit will at first hardly realize the change and will linger about old haunts. I've long since put you down as very mediumistic. You are extremely susceptible to atmospheres.[2]

1. Name excised by Whiting (LW, 535).
2. In *After Her Death: The Story of a Summer* (1897), Whiting reported communicating with KF, who had died the previous year.

To Lilian Whiting (LW)
[March 18, 1896]   [Honolulu]

I have now been around this island [Oahu] riding and driving, and enjoyed the experience immensely. On the 24th I sail for Hawaii (another island), where I may remain a month, going around it and visiting the volcano.... Any one who thinks these islands can be seen quickly and intelligently reckons without a host of problems.... The islands are eight in number, and I must visit at least three more, Hawaii being the largest and the home of the great volcano. I hope the goddess Pele[1] will perform for my benefit. If she doesn't, the great sensation of the islands will be lost....

Of one thing you may be assured,—the [Liliuokalani] monarchy can never be restored.

   1. Goddess of the volcano.

To Lilian Whiting (LW)
[March 28, 1896] [Hilo, Hawaii]

I'm at last on the road to the volcano, but as the distance by road is 30 miles, and as the journey must be made in the saddle and will take several days, you can imagine I'm as far from it as Omaha is from N.Y. I reached Hilo after the worst sea voyage I ever took . . . but now I'm in this strange land among natives. I'm very glad I came.

To the President of the Kodak Club (U V-F)
April 20. 1896. Hilo. Hawaii

Dear Sir;—

Thank you very much for making me a member of your Kodak Club. As I am now wrestling with "No. 2. Bullet,"[1] I fully appreciate the compliment.

After I have gone round the island of Hawaii,[2] I hope to "do" Kauai. How long will it take? Have you any town large enough to command a lecture audience?

   1. Name of a camera introduced by Kodak in 1895 with cartridge-type film that could be loaded in broad daylight.
   2. KF contracted pneumonia while traveling on horseback around the island of Hawaii. Taken by steamer to Honolulu for medical attention, she fell into a coma and died there on 19 May 1896.

APPENDIXES

INDEX

Appendix A

Calendar of Additional Kate Field Letters

Date	Recipient	Location
1856		
June 19	Noah Miller Ludlow	MHS-LFM
Sept. 9	Solomon Franklin Smith	MHS-S
1860		
June 6	Cordelia Riddle Sanford	LW
Summer	Cordelia Riddle Sanford	LW
Summer	Cordelia Riddle Sanford	LW
Summer	Cordelia Riddle Sanford	LW
Summer	Cordelia Riddle Sanford	LW
Summer	Cordelia Riddle Sanford	LW
1861		
Mar. 31	Cordelia Riddle Sanford	LW
June 21	Cordelia Riddle Sanford	LW
[?]	Cordelia Riddle Sanford	LW
1865		
Dec. 4	John Weiss	UV-F
Dec. 19	Henry Theodore Tuckerman	UV-F
1866		
Jan. 18	Mrs. James Lorimer Graham	BPL
Jan. 26	James Lorimer Graham	BPL
Mar. 9	James Lorimer Graham	BPL
Apr. 2	Noah Miller Ludlow	MHS-LFM
1867		
Mar. 21	Cornelia Ludlow Field	MHS-LFM

	June 28	Noah Miller Ludlow	MHS-LFM
	[?]	Cornelia Ludlow Field	MHS-LFM
1868			
	June 12	Noah Miller Ludlow	MHS-LFM
	June 24	Noah Miller Ludlow	MHS-LFM
1869			
	Feb. 18	Harry A. McGlenen	HC
	Apr. 14	Mary Elizabeth Sargent	BU
	Apr. 28	Mary Louise Booth	MNP
	June 8	Whitelaw Reid	MU
	June 29	Whitelaw Reid	MU
	June 30	Whitelaw Reid	MU
	July 4	Mary Aurelia Anthony	HC
	Aug. 10	Whitelaw Reid	MU
	Aug. 17	Whitelaw Reid	MU
	Aug. 31	Whitelaw Reid	MU
	Oct. 30	Unknown	MHS-T
	Nov. 20	Whitelaw Reid	MU
	Dec. 18	Whitelaw Reid	MU
	Dec. 26	Ira F. Hart	UV-F
1870			
	Jan. 16	Whitelaw Reid	MU
	Mar. 25	Whitelaw Reid	MU
	Mar. 28	Whitelaw Reid	MU
	May 14	Whitelaw Reid	MU
	May 28	Whitelaw Reid	MU
	June 3	Charles Mumford	WV
	July 1	Whitelaw Reid	MU
	Aug. 10	Whitelaw Reid	MU
	Aug. 20	Whitelaw Reid	MU
	Aug. 26	Whitelaw Reid	MU
	Sept. 22	Whitelaw Reid	MU
	Sept. 29	Whitelaw Reid	MU
	Oct. 7	Whitelaw Reid	MU
	Oct. 12	Whitelaw Reid	MU
	Oct. 17	William Claflin	RBH
	Oct. 18	Whitelaw Reid	MU
	Nov. 29	Whitelaw Reid	MU
	Dec. 26	Whitelaw Reid	MU

Calendar of Additional Letters 239

1871

Jan. 8	Whitelaw Reid	MU
Jan. 21	Whitelaw Reid	MU
Jan. 22	Whitelaw Reid	MU
Feb. 5	Whitelaw Reid	MU
Feb. 16	Whitelaw Reid	MU
Feb. 24	Mary Aurelia Anthony	HC
Mar. 12	John Augustin Daly	FL
Mar. 20	Whitelaw Reid	MU
Mar. 30	Mary Claflin	RBH
Apr. 5	Whitelaw Reid	MU
Apr. 16	Whitelaw Reid	MU
Apr. 23	Whitelaw Reid	MU
May 12	Whitelaw Reid	MU
June 4	James Lorimer Graham	BPL
July 2	Whitelaw Reid	MU
Sept. 1	Mary Mapes Dodge	PUL-W
Nov. 8	Whitelaw Reid	MU
Nov. 24	Whitelaw Reid	MU
Dec. 5	Whitelaw Reid	MU

1872

Jan. 3	Whitelaw Reid	MU
Feb. 7	Whitelaw Reid	MU
[Spring]	Milton H. Sanford	LW
[June]	Cordelia Riddle Sanford	LW
Sept. 1	Whitelaw Reid	MU
Oct. 10	Whitelaw Reid	MU
Oct. 23	Whitelaw Reid	MU
Oct. 24	Mary Aurelia Anthony	HC
Oct. 29	Whitelaw Reid	MU
Nov. 10	Whitelaw Reid	MU
Nov. 13	William Warland Clapp	HC
Nov. 15	Whitelaw Reid	MU
Nov. 20	Whitelaw Reid	MU
Nov. 24	Whitelaw Reid	MU
Nov. 25	Whitelaw Reid	MU
Dec. 6	Whitelaw Reid	MU
Dec. 10	Whitelaw Reid	MU
Dec. 18	Whitelaw Reid	MU
Dec. 21	Whitelaw Reid	MU
[?]	Whitelaw Reid	MU

[?]	Cordelia Riddle Sanford	LW

1873
Mar. 16	John Augustin Daly	FL
Apr. 7	William Winter	FL
Apr. 30	James Fairbanks Colby	BU

1874
Jan. 14	William Winter	FL
May 26	John Augustin Daly	FL
June 1	William H. Huntington	BU
July 4	Edmund Clarence Stedman	NYH
Aug. 1	Mary Aurelia Anthony	HC
[Nov.]	Edmund Clarence Stedman	CU
Nov. 23	Edmund Clarence Stedman	CU
Dec. 8	Edmund Clarence Stedman	CU

1875
Apr. 3	Edmund Clarence Stedman	CU
May 19	Unknown	BC
June 15	John Bigelow	UC
June 25	John Bigelow	UC
July 28	James Lorimer Graham	BPL
Oct. 5	Edmund Clarence Stedman	CU
[?]	Edmund Clarence Stedman	CU

1876
Feb. 1	Laura Woodworth Stedman	CU
Feb. 9	Edmund Clarence Stedman	CU
May 19	Edmund Clarence Stedman	CU
June 17	Edmund Clarence Stedman	CU
June 23	Edmund Clarence Stedman	CU
July 25	John Augustin Daly	FL
Aug. 3	Edmund Clarence Stedman	CU
Aug. 9	Murat Halstead	WV
Aug. 9	Laurence Hutton	PUL-H
[Aug.]	Thomas B. Connery	CU
Aug. 20	Edmund Clarence Stedman	BU
Aug. 22	Laurence Hutton	PUL-H
Aug. 25	Mary Aurelia Anthony	HC
Aug. 27	Edmund Clarence Stedman	CU
Sept. 4	Edmund Clarence Stedman	CU
Sept. 11	Edmund Clarence Stedman	CU

Calendar of Additional Letters

Sept. 18	Edmund Clarence Stedman	CU
Oct. 11	Edmund Clarence Stedman	CU
Nov. 20	Edmund Clarence Stedman	CU

1877

Jan. 14	Edmund Clarence Stedman	CU
Jan. 18	Edmund Clarence Stedman	CU
Feb. 6	Edmund Clarence Stedman	CU
Mar. 14	William Moy Thomas	UR
Mar. 15	John Sleeper Clarke	UV-F
Mar. 31	Frederick Stedman	CU
Apr. 9	William Moy Thomas	UR
May 28	William Winter	FL
July 4	William Winter	IU
July 11	William Winter	FL
July 11	Edmund Clarence Stedman	CU

1878

June 7	Edmund Clarence Stedman	CU
June 21	Edward Pigott	FL
June 27	Edmund Clarence Stedman	CU
July 21	Laurence Hutton	PUL-H
Sept. 1	Laurence Hutton	PUL-H
Sept. 14	John Augustin Daly	FL

1879

Jan. 18	John Augustin Daly	FL
[Apr.]	Cordelia Riddle Sanford	LW
May 20	Edmund Clarence Stedman	CU
June 17	Edmund Clarence Stedman	CU
June 24	Edmund Clarence Stedman	CU
[Oct.]	Edmund Clarence Stedman	CU
Dec. 30	William Winter	FL

1880

Feb. 16	Edmund Clarence Stedman	CU
Mar. 3	Mrs. [?] Wilson	HC
Mar. 18	William Warland Clapp	HC
May 27	John Augustin Daly	FL
July 15	Frederick Stedman	CU
July 23	Laurence Hutton	PUL-H
Aug. 2	Eliza Ann Hutton	PUL-H
Dec. 26	William Winter	FL

1881

Apr. 13	Laurence Hutton	PUL-H
May 20	Laurence Hutton	PUL-H
May 28	Murat Halstead	CHS
June 1	Mary Louise Booth	BPL
June 3	Laurence Hutton	PUL-H
Aug. 11	Laurence Hutton	PUL-H
Aug. 17	Edmund Clarence Stedman	CU
Dec. 15	Edmund Clarence Stedman	CU

1882

Jan. 23	J. O. Woods	PUL-P
Apr. 5	Edmund Clarence Stedman	CU
Apr. 27	Laurence Hutton	PUL-H
Apr. 29	Mrs. [?] Locke	MNP
May 27	Jeanette Gilder	UV-F
June 15	Frederick Stedman	CU
[July]	Lilian Whiting	LW
July 21	Laurence Hutton	PUL-H
Oct. 15	Curtis Guild	MH
Oct. 17	Curtis Guild	MHS-LFM
[?]	Edmund Clarence Stedman	CU

1883

Jan. 12	Frederick Stedman	CU
May 22	Unknown	MHS-T
Aug. 17	Edmund Clarence Stedman	CU
Dec. 21	Laurence Hutton	PUL-H
[?]	Laurence Hutton	PUL-H

1884

Jan. 26	Laurence Hutton	PUL-H
Feb. 1	Laurence Hutton	PUL-H
Sept. 11	Edmund Clarence Stedman	CU
Nov. 14	Sallie Joy White	RC
Nov. 20	Charles F. Dunbar	BPL
Dec. 18	Mrs. [?] Kimball	WV

1885

Jan. 5	Edmund Clarence and Laura Stedman	PUL-D
Mar. 3	Spencer Fullerton Baird	HL
Apr. 8	Laurence Hutton	PUL-H
Apr. 12	Eleanor Mitchell Hutton	PUL-H

Calendar of Additional Letters

Sept. 25	Laurence Hutton	PUL-H
Oct. 23	James Parton	HC
Nov. 11	Laurence Hutton	PUL-H
Nov. 13	Mary Mapes Dodge	PUL-W
Dec. 11	John Augustin Daly	FL
Dec. 30	James G. Woodward	UV-F

1886

Mar. 14	Laura Woodworth Stedman	CU
Mar. 21	Laura Woodworth Stedman	CU
[June]	Lilian Whiting	LW
Dec. 18	Laurence Hutton	CU
[?]	Lilian Whiting	LW

1887

Feb. 2	Laurence Hutton	PUL-H
June 29	Eugene Woldemar Hilgard	UCB-H
July 29	Lilian Whiting	LW
Oct. 19	Lilian Whiting	LW
[?]	Lilian Whiting	LW
[?]	Lilian Whiting	LW
[?]	Lilian Whiting	LW
[?]	Lilian Whiting	LW
[?]	Lilian Whiting	LW
[?]	Lilian Whiting	LW
[?]	Lilian Whiting	LW

1888

Jan. 3	Robert Whitney Waterman	UCB-W
Jan. 4	Laurence Hutton	PUL-H
[Jan.]	Lilian Whiting	LW
[Jan.]	Lilian Whiting	LW
Jan. 11	Laurence Hutton	PUL-H
Jan. 16	Laurence Hutton	PUL-H
Jan. 19	Laurence Hutton	PUL-H
Jan. 28	Laurence Hutton	PUL-H
[Feb.]	Lilian Whiting	LW
Feb. 13	Sarah B. Cooper	MHS-LFM
Feb. 25	Laurence Hutton	PUL-H
Mar. 1	Lilian Whiting	LW
Mar. 2	Laurence Hutton	PUL-H
Mar. 20	[?] Clemens	IU
Apr. 9	Melville E. Stone	NL

Apr. 16	Laurence Hutton	PUL-H
May 5	Laurence Hutton	PUL-H
[June]	Lilian Whiting	LW
Dec. 17	Edmund Clarence Stedman	CU
Dec. 19	Edmund Clarence Stedman	CU
Dec. 28	Edmund Clarence Stedman	CU

1889

Jan. 8	Edward Henry Clement	MHS-LFM
Mar. 29	B. W. Austin	HC
May 1	Charles Wells Moulton	B&E
[June]	Lilian Whiting	LW
July 30	Louis Ferdinand Gottschalk	MHS-T

1890

Feb. 9	Charlotte Botta	WV
Feb. 20	Laura Woodworth Stedman	CU
[Mar.]	Edmund Clarence Stedman	CU
Apr. 16	Henry Stoddart	HC
May 29	Andrew Varick Stout Anthony	BC
June 9	Robert Underwood Johnson	BPL
Dec. 8	Robert Underwood Johnson	BPL
Dec. 19	Edna Dean Proctor	NH
Dec. 29	Edmund Clarence Stedman	CU

1891

Mar. 26	John Augustin Daly	FL
Mar. 27	Charles Stebbins Fairchild	UV-F
Apr. 30	Hugh McCulloch	IU
May 10	Hugh McCulloch	IU
June 9	Charles Warren Stoddard	CWS
June 15	Edmund Clarence Stedman	CU
Aug. 3	Susan Maria McCulloch	IU
Aug. 21	Laura Woodworth Stedman	CU
Dec. 20	Melville E. Stone	NL
Dec. 28	Charles Warren Stoddard	CWS
Dec. 30	Charles Warren Stoddard	CWS
[?]	Lilian Whiting	LW

1892

Feb. 23	Phoebe Apperson Hearst	UCB-P
Feb. 25	Unknown	NYH

Calendar of Additional Letters

	Apr. 14	Melville E. Stone	NL
	Apr. 16	Lilian Whiting	LW

1893
	[Spring]	Lilian Whiting	LW
	May 14	Andrew Varick Stout Anthony	HC
	Oct. 1	Lilian Whiting	LW
	Nov. 28	Lydia Avery Coonley	UV-C
	Dec. 2	Lydia Avery Coonley	UV-C

1894
	July 4	Laurence Hutton	PUL-H
	Oct. 27	John Augustin Daly	FL
	Nov. 13	Unknown	UV-F

1895
	May 15	Susan Maria McCulloch	IU
	May 19	Lilian Whiting	LW
	Summer	Lilian Whiting	LW
	Summer	Lilian Whiting	LW
	Summer	Lilian Whiting	LW
	Summer	Lilian Whiting	LW
	June	Charles Warren Stoddard	CWS
	July 14	Unknown	LW

1896
	[?]	Lilian Whiting	LW

Letters Undatable by Year
	Apr. 12	Mary Louise Booth	BC
	Apr. 20	Edmund Clarence Stedman	CU
	1890–95	Charles Warren Stoddard	CWS

Appendix B
Selected Works of Kate Field

This listing does not include Kate Field's magazine and newspaper articles, conservatively estimated to be no less than three thousand. Articles that are mentioned in her letters are listed in the index.

BIOGRAPHIES

Adelaide Ristori: A Biography. New York: J. A. Gray & Green, 1867.
Charles Albert Fechter. American Actor Series. Boston: J. R. Osgood, 1882.

TRAVEL BOOKS

Hap-Hazard. Boston: J. R. Osgood, 1873.
Ten Days in Spain. Boston: J. R. Osgood, 1875.

MISCELLANEOUS BOOKS

Pen Photographs of Charles Dickens' Readings: Taken from Life. Boston: Loring, 1868. A 38-page pamphlet.
Planchette's Diary. New York: J. S. Redfield, 1868.
Pen Photographs of Charles Dickens's Readings: Taken from Life. Boston: Loring, 1868. A 58-page hardback edition.
Pen Photographs of Charles Dickens's Readings: Taken from Life. Boston: J. R. Osgood; London: Trübner & Co., 1871. A 152-page hardback edition with illustrations.
The History of Bell's Telephone. London: Bradbury, Agnew, 1878.
The Drama of Glass. Toledo, Ohio: Libby Glass Co., [1894].

PUBLISHED PLAYS

Mad on Purpose: A Comedy in Four Acts Translated from the Italian of Baron Cosenza. New York: J. A. Gray & Greene, 1868.
Extremes Meet: A Comedietta. London: S. French, 1877.
Plato & Cupid: A Christmas Comedietta. Kate Field's Washington 1 (1 Jan. 1890).
Caught Napping: A Comedietta Adapted from the French. Kate Field's Washington 1 (29 Jan. 1890).
The Shadows of Christmas Eve. Kate Field's Washington 2 (24 Dec. 1890).

Dead to the World: A Drama, in a Prologue and Five Acts, Adapted from the French. Kate Field's Washington 4 (30 Sept. 1891).

UNPUBLISHED PLAYS

(Preserved in the Kate Field Collection at the Boston Public Library.)

The Blind Side: A Comedietta Adapted from the French.
The Cost of Five Gowns.
Gabrielle, or a Night's Hazard: A Revision of Joseph M. Field's Adaptation from the French.
Olympe.
The Opera Box: A Comedy in One Act Adapted from the French.
Oshkosh in London.
The Wrong Flat.
Three additional plays, untitled.

UNLOCATED PLAYS

Eyes and Ears in London.
Eyes Right.
Folie Musicale.
Two Fighting Cousins.

SHORT STORIES

"Love and War: A Story of 1865." *The Public Spirit: A Magazine of Choice Original Literature* 2 (Jan. 1868): 312–21. Reprinted in the *Springfield Republican*, 13 Jan. 1868.
"Our Summer's Outing." *Harper's New Monthly Magazine* 75 (Oct. 1887): 651–66.

CHAPTERS IN BOOKS

"Charles Fechter." In *Actors and Actresses of Great Britain and the United States*, 5 vols., edited by Brander Matthews and Laurence Hutton, 4:207–28. New York: Cassell & Co., 1886.
"North of the Golden Gate." In *Picturesque California and the Region West of the Rocky Mountains*, 2 vols., edited by John Muir, 1:219–32. San Francisco and New York: J. Dewing Co., 1888.

Index

KF   Kate Field
KFW   *Kate Field's Washington*
LDA   Ladies' Co-operative Dress Association
SMT   Shakespeare Memorial Theatre

Albert, Prince Consort, 124
Aldrich, Thomas Bailey, 69, 211; letter to, 181
American Publishing Co., letter to, 186
Anthony, Andrew Varick Stout, 83, 104n, 221; letter to, 220
Anthony, Mary Aurelia (Mrs. Andrew Varick Stout), letters to, 42, 44, 54, 68, 71, 83, 92, 104, 149, 155
Anthony, Susan B.: as lecturer, xxii; KF endorses, xxiv; and *The Revolution*, 51n, 84n; on Temperance, 210n; mentioned, 45, 46n; letter to, 209
Argyll, John Campbell, 9th Duke of: marries Queen Victoria's daughter, 82n; publishes book, 115; mentioned, 84, 122, 126
Arnold, Matthew: lectures in U.S., 175; mentioned, 39n
Art Congress, KF promotes, 215, 216, 217

Bailey, Isaac H.: and John Brown's farm, 50n; mentioned, 66, 79, 88, 91n
Baldwin, Albert: KF's love affair with, 24, 35–37, 90, 126, 131n, 231; letter to, 35
Ballou, Maturin Murray, letter to, 207
Bancroft, George: KF on, 102; mentioned, 11n
Barrett, Lawrence, 147, 161
Beecher, Rev. Henry Ward: and KF, 41, 42; on lecture circuit, 72n; reputed seducer, 91, 92n; mentioned, 31, 40, 54, 196
Bell, Alexander Graham, KF promotes telephone of, xxi, 138, 139n
Benedict, Sir Julius, and SMT, 151
Bennett, James Gordon, Jr.: and Ida Lewis, 47n;

employs KF, 61–62, 74, 75, 103, 104, 120, 123–24, 128, 136, 138; finances Stanley, 124n; moves to Paris, 128, 129n, 135, 136n, 207
Bernhardt, Sarah, KF on, 169–70
Bigelow, John: invests in LDA, xxi; on KF, 137n; KF invites to lecture, 188; letters to, 137, 188
Blagden, Isa: and KF, xix, 15, 18; at Barrett Browning's deathbed, 26, 27; and funeral, 28; and Robert Browning's grief, 29–30; mentioned, 20
Blanc, Louis, KF interviews, 137
Booth, Edwin: promotes SMT, 143; Sargent paints, 212; mentioned, xxx, 22, 147, 206, 211, 213
Booth, John Wilkes, 22n
Booth, Junius Brutus, KF's mother acts with, xvii, 80
Booth, Mary Louise, letter to, 38
Botta, Anne Charlotte Lynch: and KF, 39, 43, 44; mentioned, 81, 102
Bowles, Samuel: on KF's acting, xxvi; publishes KF, 53, 54n; mentioned, 100, 125
Boyd, Andrew Kennedy, maligns KF, 126, 127
Briggs, Charles Frederick, criticizes KF, 47–48
Brooke, Rev. Stopford, on KF, 147
Bross, Jessie: and SMT, 142; mentioned, 94; letter to, 142
Brown, John: KF on grave and farm of, 49, 50, 53, 64, 86; KF saves "fort," 220n, 229
Brown, John, Jr., letter to, 64
Brown, Mary Ann Day (Mrs. John), sells farm, 64
Browning, Elizabeth Barrett: and KF, xix, 13, 15, 16, 20; on Landor, 26; KF on death and funeral of, 26–28; mentioned, xxii, 58, 84n, 180
Browning, Robert: and KF, xix, 13, 15, 16, 18, 20, 23, 29, 96; manages Landor's finances, 24n; and wife's death, 26–27, 28, 29; on Joaquin Miller, 91; mentioned, 30, 217, 222n
Browning, Robert Wiedemann Barrett: and mother's death, 27, 28; mentioned, 20, 21n, 30
Bryant, William Cullen, xxii, 11n, 39
Buel, Clarence Clough, letter to, 170

249

Bull, Ole Bornemann, 4, 5n
Bullard, Laura Curtis: and KF, 83, 84n, 85, 88, 89, 91, 105; mentioned, 102, 134

Cable, George Washington, 170; letter to, 216
Cesnola, Luigi Palma di: KF on collection of, 127, 128; competes with Schliemann, 129n
Church of Jesus Christ of Latter-Day Saints. *See* Mormonism
Claflin, Agnes, letter to, 34
Claflin, Mary Davenport (Mrs. William), letter to, 33
Claflin, Gov. William: KF on, 33; attends KF's lecture, 40; KF on John Brown's farm, 50; letter to, 50
Clapp, William Warland, letters to, 19, 160–61, 163, 164, 202, 207
Clemens, Olivia Langdon (Mrs. Samuel): KF on, 69; joins KF's LDA, 160, 166; letters to, 160, 166
Clemens, Samuel Langhorne: on Dickens, xxiii; and *Colonel Sellers*, 26; KF meets, 69; on KF, 71n; lectures for Redpath, 72n; KF offers ms., 190; KF solicits article from, 212; mentioned, xx, 186n; letters to, 190–91, 212
Cleveland, Pres. Grover: KF sends "Mormon scraps" to, 190; letter to, 189
Cobbe, Frances Power: describes KF, xix; and KF, 18, 85; mentioned, 20
Collins, Wilkie: and KF, 74, 75, 76, 160n, 165; mentioned, 169, 170
Collyer, Rev. Robert, promotes SMT, 142–43, 144
Columbian Exposition, and KF, 219, 220, 221
Conway, Moncure Daniel: KF on, 120; congratulates KF, 122; mentioned, 158
Coonley, Lydia Avery, letter to, 224
Coues, Elliott, letter to, 202
Couzins, Phoebe: Sorosister, 45; Reid on, 56
Cox, Mrs., letter to, 212
Croly, David Goodman: publishes KF, 126; mentioned, 125, 140
Cushman, Charlotte: KF meets in Rome, 13; acts with KF's mother, 80; mentioned, xxx, 9, 14, 18, 22, 79

Daly, John Augustin, letters to, 189, 208, 223
Dickens, Charles: on Prohibition, xxiv–xxv; KF discusses, 19; flirtatious exchange with KF, 34n, 35; farewell dinner to, 39n; in ill health, 45, 46n; on death of, 57; KF and *No Thoroughfare*, 74, 75, 76; Gail Hamilton on, 92n; KF dedicates *Fechter* to, 167n; destroys letters, 213; mentioned, 2, 20, 34, 63n, 67, 68n, 71, 74, 139n, 159; letters to, 34n, 35. *See also* KF, works mentioned, books, *Pen Photographs of Charles Dickens's Readings*
Dickinson, Anna: as lecturer, xxii; on Jeanne d'Arc, 66n; mentioned, 62, 63n, 140n
Dilke, Sir Charles: and KF, 85, 96–97, 98, 109; in U.S., 117; on Stanley, 124n; mentioned, 82
Dodge, Mary Mapes: on *KFW*, 210; mentioned, 81, 82n; letters to, 114, 210
Dole, Sanford Ballard, KF interviews, 232
Douglass, Frederick, nominated for vice presidency, 94n

Eliot, George (Mary Ann Evans, Mrs. Lewes): KF on, xix; KF meets, 19; KF on *Mill on the Floss*, 21; corresponds with KF, 93; KF visits, 96; mentioned, 100. *See also* Lewes, George Henry
Emerson, Ralph Waldo: KF on, 37–38; mentioned, 39n
Erichsen, Hugh, letter to, 180
Every Saturday, 86, 104n

Faithfull, Emily: and KF, 101–2, 140; letter to, 140
Fechter, Charles Albert: and CD, 57, 74; manages *Globe*, 58; and KF, 61, 63, 159, 165; acts in Chicago, 72, 73, 74n; acts with Rachel, 161n. *See also* KF, works mentioned, books, *Charles Albert Fechter*
Field, Cornelia B. (Mrs. Matthew), letter to, 230
Field, Eliza Riddle (KF's mother): actress, xvii, 2, 79–80; in Florence, 17, 18; and Brownings, 20, 29; illness of, 43, 44, 45, 75; death and burial of, 77, 83, 84n; letters to, 2–3, 4, 6–8, 10, 12–16
Field, Eugene, and KF, 173
Field, Joseph Matthew (KF's father): careers, xviii, 1, 5–6, 10, 11n, 80; and Dickens, xx; illness and death of, 8, 9n, 88; reputation of, 71, 72n, 79; and Forrest, 136; letters to, 1, 9
Field, Joseph Matthew, Jr. (KF's brother), 4
Field, Kate (Mary Katherine Keemle)
 background: birth, parentage, death, xvii–xviii, xxx, 234n; biographical sketch, xvii–xxx
 careers
  actress: career reviewed, xxv–xxvii; debuts in *Masks and Faces*, 110, 112n; and reactions to debut, 112, 114, 115; debuts on English stage, 116, 117, 121–23

author, career reviewed, xxi–xxii. *See also under* works mentioned; appendix B
journalist, career reviewed, xix–xxi, xxviii–xxix. *See also under* works mentioned
lecturer, career reviewed, xxii–xxv. *See also under* works mentioned
playwright. *See under* works mentioned; appendix B
See also Kate Field's Washington; Ladies' Co-operative Dress Association
works mentioned
  books: *Adelaide Ristori*, xxi–xii; *Charles Albert Fechter*, xxii, 57n, 159, 160n, 161, 165, 166, 167, 170; *Drama of Glass*, xxii; *Hap-Hazard*, xxi, 56n; *History of Bell's Telephone*, xxi, 140, 141n, 144; *Pen Photographs of Charles Dickens's Readings*, 20, 33, 35, 85, 86n, 95, 97, 119; *Planchette's Diary*, xxii, 38, 39n; *Ten Days in Spain*, xxi, 197, 229n
  lectures: "Alaska," 196, 197, 199; "America for Americans," 221, 222; "Among the Adirondacks," 49n, 51n, 52, 53, 138; "Charles Dickens," 57, 58, 61n, 62, 63, 64, 66, 68, 71n, 72n, 85, 88, 138, 139, 175n; "The Intemperance of Prohibition," 198; "Mormonism," 178, 179, 181, 182, 183, 184, 186, 187–88, 189, 191; "Woman in the Lyceum," xxiii, 39, 40, 41, 42, 44, 48, 129
  magazine articles and reviews: "Anthony Trollope on North America," 31; "Archibald Forbes," 153n; "Arthur Sullivan," 152n; "Charles Albert Fechter," 58n; "Elizabeth Barrett Browning," 30, 31; "English Authors in Florence," 19n; "Fechter as Hamlet," 58n, 61, 75, 136; "The Great Public Reception [for Stanley] by the Geographical Society," 140–41; "Henry Schliemann," 134; "In and Out of the Woods," 51n; "Intercepted Letters," 132, 133n, 138, 153; "Last Days of Walter Savage Landor," 26n; "Letter from Kate Field [on Knowles's lecture on *Macbeth*]," 123n; "A Morning with Sir Julius Benedict," 125n; "Mrs. Browning's Essays on the Poets," 33; "Our Ignorance of Alaska," 195, 198n; "Reply to Andrew Kennedy Boyd," 126n, 127; "Review of George Wilkes's *Shakespeare from an American Point of View*," 130n; "Review of Stedman's *Victorian Poets*," 138; "W. S. Gilbert," 129n, 131, 132, 152n
  newspaper articles: "Americans Abroad," 56n; "Hawaii," xxix, 231, 232; "Henry Schliemann," 133n; "Interview of Boucicault," 123; "Interview of Sanford B. Dole," 232; "Interview of Stanley," 102n; "Kate and the Mormons," 217n; "Leaves from a Lecturer's Notebook," 56n, 73; "Letter on Cesnola Collection," 128; "Recollections [of George Eliot]," xix; "Review of *No Thoroughfare*," 74, 75, 76; "The Telephone," 139n; "The Turf," 104n; "Utah Politics and Morals," 181n, 217n; "Woman in the Lyceum," 57. *See also Kate Field's Washington*
  plays: *Dead to the World*, 133n, 134, 139, 140; *Extremes Meet*, 130, 131–32, 133, 135, 136, 138, 140, 176; *Eyes and Ears in London*, xxvi, xxvii, 153, 154, 155, 158, 173, 175n, 181; *Eyes Right*, 145, 146, 148n; *Folie Musical*, 118; *Gabrielle*, xxvi, 133; *The Opera Box*, xxvi; *Two Fighting Cousins*, 136
  poem, "Forty to Twenty," 128n, 131, 132
Field, Matthew C. (KF's uncle): journalist, xviii, 12n; death of, 88; mentioned, 34n
Field, Nathan (KF's ancestor), 141n
Fields, Annie Adams (Mrs. James T.): and KF, 17, 38; and Dickens, 34n; on Emerson, 38; and Temperance, 110; letter to, 110
Fields, James T.: and Thackeray, 7; meets KF, 17; attends KF's lectures, 40, 44, 61n, 62, 63; and Dickens, 45, 46n; mentioned, xxx, 145n
Flower, Charles Edward: founder of SMT, xxvii, xxviii, 141, 143, 145; letters to, 141, 144. *See also* Shakespeare Memorial Theatre
Forbes, Archibald, KF writes on, 153
Forrest, Edwin: acts with KF's mother, xvii; KF on, 136
Forster, John: and Landor, 24n, 25, 26n; and KF's *Pen Photographs*, 95
Frothingham, Rev. Octavius Brooks, 81, 129
Furness, Horace Howard, quotes KF on Fechter, 136
Furnivall, Frederick James, and SMT, 147

Garcia, Manuel: singing master, 14, 76; and KF, 82, 83, 93, 96; Pauline Viardot's brother, 93, 94n
Garrison, William Lloyd, on KF, xxiii

Gilbert, William Schwenck: KF writes on, 128, 129n, 151, 152, 154; mentioned, xx
Gilder, Jeannette: on KF's *Pen Photographs*, xx; writes obituary of KF, 118n; mentioned, 159
Graham, John (KF's cousin), 4
Greeley, Horace: KF freelances for, xx, 43, 74; and spiritualism, xxii, 11n; attends KF's lecture, 44; on lecture circuit, 62, 72n; on women lecturers, 90; on free love, 90, 92n; presidential candidate, 101n; death of, 105; fund for statue of, 106; mentioned, 53, 66, 102
Gregg, Thomas, letters to, 177–80, 188, 192, 216
Grisanowski, Dr. E. G. F.: Barrett Browning's physician, 27, 28n; mentioned, 30
Grossmith, George, collaborates with KF, 153

Hamilton, Gail (Mary Abigail Dodge): on Dickens and Georgina Hogarth, 90, 92n; maligns women journalists, 91
Harrison, Russell Benjamin, letter to, 206
Harte, Bret: KF on, 72; receives lucrative offers, 72n, 73n; mentioned, 91, 94
Hawthorne, Nathaniel, KF meets, 13
Hay, John: KF quotes, 65; mentioned, 73, 99, 177; letter to, 157
Hayes, Lucy Ware Webb (Mrs. Rutherford B.), letter to, 157
Hearst, Phoebe Apperson, letters to, 211, 214, 217, 219–21
Hearst, William Randolph, 211
Hennessy, William John, and KF, 78, 81n, 83, 84, 122, 129, 134, 135, 137, 147, 149
Higginson, Mary Elizabeth Channing (Mrs. Thomas Wentworth), letter to, 40
Higginson, Thomas Wentworth: KF submits poems to, 37; mentioned, xix, xxx, 40; letters to, 37, 99–100
Hilgard, Eugene Woldemar, letter to, 197
Hillard, George Stillman, attends KF's lecture, 53, 61n
Hogarth, Georgina, Gail Hamilton on, 90, 92n
Holmes, John H., letter to, 176
Holmes, Oliver Wendell, xxx, 211, 214
Hood, Thomas: KF recites poems of, 54, 110n, 111; mentioned, 189
Hosmer, Harriet, and KF, 13, 18
Houghton, Richard Monckton Milnes, 1st Baron: Stedman escorts, 115, 119; KF on, 119; KF attends ball given by, 152
Houghton Mifflin Co., letter to, 197
Howe, Julia Ward: invests in LDA, xxi; lectures, 72n; KF invites to lunch, 99; mentioned, xix, 102
Howells, William Dean: Reid's friend, 45, 46n; mentioned, 69, 211
Hughes, Thomas, KF covers lecture of, 59, 60, 61n
Hugo, Victor, inscribes book to KF, 137
Hunt, Helen. *See* Jackson, Helen Hunt
Hutchins, Stilson, letter to, 225
Hutchinson, Charles Lawrence, letter to, 217
Hutton, Eleanor Varnum Mitchell (Mrs. Laurence), letters to, 193, 228
Hutton, Laurence: on KF, 66–67; edits KF's Fechter biography, 159n, 160n, 165, 166, 167, 170; and *Harper's Monthly*, 201n; contributes to *KFW*, 206, 207, 211, 221, 222n; opposes tariff on imported art, 208n; mentioned, 124; letters to, 66–67, 126–27, 131, 133–34, 139, 149–51, 154, 158–60, 163, 165–67, 169–70, 175, 182, 191, 195, 197–200, 206–7, 210, 212–13, 221–22, 228

"Intercepted Letters." *See under* KF, works mentioned, magazine articles and reviews
International copyright, KF promotes, 212, 214
Irving, Henry: and SMT, xxvii, 144, 145, 150; mentioned, 130, 146

Jackson, Helen Hunt: on Mormonism, 177n; KF on, 186–87; mentioned, xix
James, Henry, Sr.: on free love, 90, 92n; mentioned, xix
Johnson, Robert Underwood, letter to, 214

Kate Field's Washington, xxi, xxviii–xxix, 205–25, 230
Kean, Charles, KF's mother acts with, 80
Keemle, Charles, and KF's father, xviii
Kemble, Fanny: and KF's mother, 79; attends KF's lecture, 86n
Knowles, Sheridan, 79, 81n, 123n

Ladies' Co-operative Dress Association, 156, 157, 160, 161–62, 163, 164, 165n, 166, 170–71, 174
Lamon, Ward Hill: on Lincoln and Temperance, 203; letter to, 203
Landor, Walter Savage: and KF, xix, 15, 20–21, 23–24, 25–26; gives KF unique author's volumes, 24; KF's article on, 26n; and valuable album of art, 135n, 168n; mentioned, 28, 49
Lasell Female Seminary: KF attends, xviii–xix, 6–11; KF describes curriculum of, 10

Leonowens, Anna Harriette, 102
Lewes, George Henry, and KF, xix, 19. *See also* Eliot, George
Lewis, Ida, 47, 51
Lincoln, Abraham, and Temperance, 203
Lind, Jenny: model for KF, xix, 3; studies with Garcia, 14; mentioned, 4, 76n
Livermore, Mary Ashton Rice, 45, 215n
Livingstone, David, KF at ceremony for, 124
Logan, Olive: KF detests, 45, 70, 71n, 75n, 89; lectures for Redpath, 72n; and George Dolby, 94. *See also* Sikes, William Wirt
Longfellow, Henry Wadsworth: KF on *Hiawatha*, 6; attends KF lectures, 61n, 155; and Craigie House, 81n; invites KF to home, 156; portrait of, 211, 214; mentioned, xxx, 145n; letters to, 155-56,
Lotus Club, 102, 147, 154
Louisville Courier-Journal. *See* Watterson, Henry
Lowell, Augustus: rejects KF's offer to lecture at Lowell Institute, 186n; letters to, 184-85
Lowell, James Russell: and KF's *Ten Days in Spain*, xxi, 229n; KF meets, 38; KF on, 196; mentioned, xxx, 192, 211, 214, 224
Ludlow, Noah Miller, letters to, 11, 33, 48
Lytton, Edward Robert Bulwer-: and KF 15, 30; at Barrett Browning's funeral, 28

Mackay, John William, 135, 136n
Macready, William Charles, acts with KF's mother and father, xvii, 80
Marquis of Lorne. *See* Argyll, John Campbell, 9th Duke of
McClure, J. H., letter to, 145
McClure, Samuel Sidney, letter to, 198
McCulloch, Hugh, letter to, 183
McCulloch, Susan Maria (Mrs. Hugh), letter to, 184
McGlenen, Henry A., letter to, 41
McVicker, James H., and SMT, 143
Miller, Joaquin, KF on, 91, 94
Millet, Francis Davis: paints KF, 160; KF invites to meet Wilde, 164; introduces Stoddard to KF, 227; mentioned, 166
Monsieur Tonson, 62, 63n
Montez, Lola, performs at KF's father's theatre, 5
Mormonism: KF investigates, xxiv, 174; KF writes on, 175n, 186, 189, 192; mentioned, 176, 229, 230
Morton, Levi Parsons, 201, 206
Moulton, Louise Chandler: on KF's lecture, 63; dines with KF, 105; reviews Stedman's *Victorian Poets*, 138; mentioned, 62, 106, 124, 129
Muir, John: publishes KF, xxii, 199; and Yosemite, 210n
Mumford, Mr., letters to, 58, 63
Murdoch, James Edward: writes on KF's mother, father, and KF, 164n; mentioned, 34
Murray, William Henry Harrison, writes on Adirondacks, 49

Nasby, Petroleum (David Ross Locke), attends KF's lecture, 61n
National Loan Exhibit of Art, KF promotes, 216n, 217, 218-19
New Orleans Picayune. *See* Field, Joseph Matthew; Field, Matthew C.
New York Herald. *See* Bennett, James Gordon, Jr.
New York Tribune. *See* Greeley, Horace

Osgood, James R.: publisher, 43-44, 72; on KF's tribute to John Brown, 53; sells portrait of Longfellow, 211; mentioned, 45, 70, 94, 104, 110, 166

Palmer, Harry, promotes SMT, xxvii, 147
Parker, Theodore: and Cobbe, 20; buried in Florence, 28; mentioned, 20, 21n
Patenotre, Jules: and KF's *Palmes académique* award, 223, 224n; letter to, 223
Patience (Gilbert and Sullivan), Wilde acts in, 165n
Phillips, Wendell, KF on, 176
Pierce, Franklin, KF meets, 13, 14
Pierrepont, Edwards, and SMT, 147
Pigott, Edward, on KF and SMT, 148
Planchette, described, 39n
Poe, Edgar Allan: KF's father helps, xviii; mentioned, 39n
Pond, Major James Burton: buys Redpath Lecture Bureau, 72n; as KF's theatrical agent, 153, 154
Poore, Benjamin Perley, letter to, 191
Powers, Hiram, at Barrett Browning's funeral, 28
Prohibitionists, malign KF, and her reply to, xxv, 201, 209
Pulbrook, Anthony: mismanages LDA, xxi, 160, 171; KF sues, 161, 162n; maligns KF, 163

Rachel (Élisa Rachel Félix): KF on, 21; acts with Fechter, 160, 161n; mentioned, 8, 9n, 159
Raymond, John T., KF acts with, xxvi

Reade, Charles: KF acts in *Masks and Faces* by, xxv, xxvi, 112n, 114, 115; KF's relations with, 116–17; mentioned, 122

Redpath Lyceum Bureau: booking arrangements of, 72n; manages KF lectures, 189

Reid, Whitelaw: and *Tribune*, xx, 45, 107, 108n; KF meets, 43; attends KF's lecture, 44; Howell's friend, 45, 46n; on KF, 51n, 112, 114; letters to, 46–47, 49–53, 56–57, 59–66, 68, 73–77, 82, 84, 88, 94–101, 103–7

Riddle, Edward (KF's uncle), 24n, 38n

Riddle, George (KF's cousin): and SMT, 149; reads KF's play, 176; contests aunt's will, 228; mentioned, 24n, 145n

Riddle, Mary Lapsley (KF's grandmother): coaches Forrest, 136; mentioned, 12n

Ripley, George: *Tribune*'s literary critic, 43, 49; on KF's lecture, 44

Ristori, Adelaide: KF on, 21, 22, 150; KF visits, 149; mentioned, xx

Sanford, Cordelia Riddle (KF's aunt): estates of, 7n, 12, 57, 58; urges KF to study singing, 8; and death of sister, 79, 80; illness of, 83, 101, 102, 103, 152, 154, 155; KF contests will of, 228; mentioned, 10, 11, 45, 47, 53, 76n, 84, 88, 104; letters to, 1, 4, 5, 17–26, 28–30, 86–87, 150, 174

Sanford, Milton Holbrook (KF's uncle): financial relations with, xviii, 6n, 8, 95, 101; disinherits KF, xx, 25, 65; estates of, 7n, 12, 57, 58; and horse racing, 45n, 88, 93, 104; death of, 174; mentioned, 5, 10, 11, 33, 42, 45, 65, 75, 84, 89, 103, 152, 176; letters to, 95, 101, 108

Sarony, Napoleon, photographs KF and parents, 81, 82n, 86

Schliemann, Henry: and SMT, xxvii, 142; and Cesnola, 129n; KF interviews, 132–33; KF recommends for U.S. consul, 157–58; mentioned, xx, 127n, 134, 140

Sedley, Henry (KF's cousin), 79, 81

Sedley, Sarah Riddle (KF's aunt): actress, 11; mentioned, 12

Sedley, William Henry (KF's uncle), xix, 12n

Shakespeare, William (singing master): and SMT, 151n; trains KF's voice, 154

Shakespeare Memorial Theatre, KF promotes, xxvii–xxviii, 141, 142–48, 149, 150, 151, 229

Shepherd, Miss, letter to, 187

Sikes, William Wirt: maligns KF, 70, 71n, 89–90; Olive Logan's husband, 71n

Simpson, Palgrave, letter to, 130

Smalley, George Washington: *Tribune*'s London correspondent, 68; helps KF, 73, 75, 81, 82, 85, 88, 91n, 100, 117, 119, 138

Smith, W. H., stage name of William Henry Sedley, 12n

Smith's Seminary: KF attends, xviii; mentioned, 71

Sorosis Club: maligns KF, 39; KF helps found, 39n; KF detests, 45

Stanley, Henry Morton: and Livingstone, 124; mentioned, xx, 102, 140–41

Stanton, Elizabeth Cady: as lecturer, xxii; agitates for women's rights, 46n; and *Revolution*, 51n, 84n; on Temperance, 210n; mentioned, 45

Stebbens, Emma, 13, 18

Stedman, Edmund Clarence: defends KF's acting, 112, 114; escorts Lord Houghton, 115; and brokerage office, 120, 174n, 177; writes poem on KF, 126n; on Schliemann's discoveries, 128; refuses to meet Wilde, 164n; mentioned, 110, 117, 119, 141n; letters to, 110–12, 114, 115, 118, 120–21, 123, 125–28, 130, 132, 135, 137, 140, 151–54, 158, 161–62, 164, 169–71, 174, 177, 215. *See also* Stedman, Frederick

Stedman, Frederick (Edmund Clarence Stedman's son): peculations of, 174n; mentioned, 125, 128, 129

Stevenson, Robert Louis, Stoddard inspires, 227

St. Louis Reveille. *See* Field, Joseph Matthew; Field, Matthew C.

Stoddard, Charles Warren: on Robert Louis Stevenson, 227, 228; letters to, 227–29

Stoddart, Joseph Marshall, letter to, 164

Stone, Lucy, as lecturer, xxii

Story, William Wetmore: and Theodore Parker, 20, 21n; at Barrett Browning's funeral, 28

Stowe, Harriet Beecher: KF on *Uncle Tom's Cabin*, 5; KF meets, 17, 18n; on KF's lecture, 42; mentioned, xix, 19

Sullivan, Arthur: attends KF's *Extremes Meet*, 131; KF on, 152, 154; mentioned, 120, 151n, 153

Sumner, Charles, xxx, 33

Swedenborg, Emanuel, KF on, 11

Swinburne, Algernon Charles: and Lord Houghton, 119; KF on, 120–21

Tariff on imported art, xxviii, 208, 213, 215n, 218, 224n

Taylor, Bayard, on *Tribune* staff, 120

Taylor, Clementia (Mrs. Peter Alfred): and KF, 82, 83–84, 85; mentioned, 100
Taylor, Peter Alfred. *See* Taylor, Clementia
Terry, Ellen, and SMT, 145
Thackeray, William Makepeace: KF on, 6–7; mentioned, 31n
Ticknor, Benjamin, letter to, 167
Tilton, Theodore: writes memorial on Barrett Browning, 31–32; attends KF lecture, 41; on divorce and women's suffrage, 91, 92n; publishes sketch of Victoria Woodhull, 94; mentioned, 31, 32n; letters to, 31, 39
Times (London), KF publishes in, xxi, 138, 139n. *See also* Walter, John
Todd, Mabel Loomis: records KF's final hours, xxx; editor of Emily Dickinson, 37
Trollope, Anthony: KF meets, xix, 23; and SMT, xxviii; corresponds with KF, 23n; KF reviews *North America*, 31; invites KF to Christmas dinner, 127; KF sends "Woman in the Lyceum" to, 129; mentioned, 17n, 31n, 145n
Trollope, Beatrice, 23
Trollope, Frances: KF meets, xix; mentioned, 17n
Trollope, Thomas: and KF, xix, 16, 17n, 19, 23, 33, 86n, 87; at Barrett Browning's funeral, 28; mentioned, 20, 30
Truth: KF writes "Intercepted Letters" for, 130, 134, 136, 138, 139, 153; mentioned, 131, 132, 133
Tuckerman, Henry Theodore, attends KF's lecture, 44
Twain, Mark. *See* Clemens, Samuel Langhorne

Uncle Tom's Cabin, KF on, 5

Vedder, Elihu: KF meets, 18; paints KF, 18n; invites KF to visit, 86n, 87, 93; KF invites to meet Wilde, 164; mentioned, 35
Vezin, Hermann: and SMT, xxvii, 144, 145, 146; on KF's English debut, 22; on KF's *Extremes Meet*, 132; and KF's Fechter biography, 160n, 165; mentioned, 119, 120, 123n, 141n, 170

Victoria, Queen: and KF, xxi, 139n; holds service for son's recovery, 98; knights Stanley, 124n; mentioned, 84n, 128

Wales, John, mismanages LDA, 163, 171
Walter, John: KF arranges to meet, 127, 128; mentioned, 85, 86n, 138. *See also Times* (London)
Ward, Genèvieve: KF's friend, 117; acts with KF, 121–22; and SMT, 145, 147; mentioned, 141n, 170
Watterson, Henry: KF freelances for, 116; dilatory in paying KF, 119, 128
Whipple, Edwin Percy: attends KF's lectures, 40, 61n; mentioned, xxx
Whiting, Lilian: KF's friend and biographer, 167; reports communicating with KF's spirit, 233n; letters to, 167–69, 173, 176, 186–87, 192–93, 195–96, 215, 229–34
Wilde, Oscar: on SMT, xxviii; lunches with KF, 164; KF on, 165; acts in *Patience*, 165n; mentioned, 82n
Willard, Frances, E.: president of WCTU, xxv; includes KF in *Woman of the Century*, 215n
Willcox, Kate (KF's cousin), KF and her mother support, 89, 92n, 100, 101, 141
Williams, George F., letter to, 207
Winter, William: *Tribune*'s drama critic, 53; publishes poems, 140; letters to, 109, 145, 148
Woman's Christian Temperance Union: Frances Willard president of, xxv; KF on, 200
Women's Suffrage, KF on, 90
Woodhull, Victoria: KF detests, 75n, 139; nominated for presidency, 94n; as lecturer, 140n
Worth, Charles Frederick: KF visits, 137, 139n; mentioned, 158

Yates, Edmund: KF on, 102; and SMT, 144; and KF's Fechter biography, 160n, 165; mentioned, 169, 170
Yosemite National Park, KF and Muir promote, 210
Young, John Russell, and *Tribune*, 43, 45

Carolyn J. Moss, formerly an associate professor and head of the English Department at the University of Kentucky-Paducah Community College, is now an emerita of Southern Illinois University at Carbondale. Her wide-ranging publications include articles on Jefferson, Lincoln, John Brown, Wordsworth, Dickens, George Eliot, Trollope, and of course, Kate Field. She has also published the *Bibliographical Guide to Self-Disclosure Literature* and has co-authored two books with Sidney P. Moss, *Charles Dickens and His Chicago Relatives* and *The Charles Dickens-Thomas Powell Vendetta*.